ISSUES IN BIOMEDICAL ETHICS

HIV and AIDS, Testing, Screening, and Confidentiality

ISSUES IN BIOMEDICAL ETHICS

General Editors
John Harris and Søren Holm

Consulting Editors
Ranaan Gillon and Bonnie Steinbock

The late twentieth century has witnessed dramatic technological developments in biomedical science and in the delivery of health care, and these developments have brought with them important social changes. All too often ethical analysis has lagged behind these changes. The purpose of this series is to provide lively, up-to-date, and authoritative studies for the increasingly large and diverse readership concerned with issues in biomedical ethics—not just health care trainees and professionals, but also philosophers, social scientists, lawyers, social workers, and legislators. The series will feature both single-author and multi-author books, short and accessible enough to be widely read, each of them focused on an issue of outstanding current importance and interest. Philosophers, doctors, and lawyers from a number of countries feature among the authors lined up for the series.

HIV and AIDS

Testing, Screening, and Confidentiality

Edited by

REBECCA BENNETT
and
CHARLES A. ERIN

OXFORD

UNIVERSITY PRESS

Great Clarendon Street, Oxford OX2 6DP

Oxford University Press is a department of the University of Oxford
It furthers the University's objective of excellence in research, scholarship,
and education by publishing worldwide in

Oxford New York
Athens Auckland Bangkok Bogotá Buenos Aires Calcutta
Cape Town Chennai Dar es Salaam Delhi Florence Hong Kong Istanbul
Karachi Kuala Lumpur Madrid Melbourne Mexico City Mumbai
Nairobi Paris São Paulo Singapore Taipei Tokyo Toronto Warsaw

with associated companies in Berlin Ibadan

Oxford is a registered trade mark of Oxford University Press
in the UK and in certain other countries

Published in the United States
by Oxford University Press Inc., New York

British Library Cataloguing in Publication Data

Data available

Library of Congress Cataloging in Publication Data

HIV and AIDS, testing, screening, and confidentiality / edited by
Rebecca Bennett and Charles A. Erin.
(Issues in biomedical ethics)
Includes bibliographical references and index.
1. HIV infections—Diagnosis—Moral and ethical aspects. 2. HIV
infections—Diagnosis—Law and legislation. 3. HIV infections—
Diagnosis—Social aspects. 4. Confidential communications—
Physicians. I. Bennett, Rebecca. II. Erin, Charles A. III. Series.
[DNLM: 1. HIV Infections—diagnosis. 2. AIDS Serodiagnosis.
3. Mass Screening. 4. Ethics, Medical. 5. Confidentiality.
WC 503.1 H676 1999]
RA644.A25H57855 1999 362.1'969792075—dc21 98–46291
DNLM/DLC
for Library of Congress
ISBN 0–19–823801–0

10 9 8 7 6 5 4 3 2 1

Typeset by Hope Services (Abingdon) Ltd.
Printed in Great Britain
on acid-free paper by
Biddles Ltd.,
Guildford and King's Lynn

Preface

The impetus for this volume was provided by the research project 'AIDS: Ethics, Justice and European Policy'. This Concerted Action was supported by Directorate General XII of the European Commission under its Biomedicine and Health Research Programme (BIOMED 1) and ran for three years from January 1993. The coordinating group for this project was centred within the Centre for Social Ethics and Policy at the University of Manchester, with John Harris, Sir David Alliance Professor of Bioethics at the University and Research Director of the Centre, as Project Coordinator. The research group comprised more than thirty leading experts in diverse fields—applied philosophy and ethics, law, theology, social policy, virology, epidemiology and medicine, psychology, education, and sexology—from several countries in Western, and (under DGXII's Cooperation in Science and Technology with Central and Eastern Europe (PECO) Programme) Central and Eastern Europe.

The chief aim of this Concerted Action was to identify basic principles of, and sketch an ethical framework for, European social and legislative policy on HIV and AIDS. We started with an informing hypothesis, *reciprocity of obligations*,[1] which was extensively refined and clarified during the course of the Project and which, we now believe, can form a guiding principle in the development of European social and legislative policy on HIV and AIDS. Our formulation of this hypothesis involves a conception of reciprocity of obligations holding between the State and the HIV-positive individual, that is, of a reciprocity between obligations *to* the HIV-positive individual and obligations *of* the HIV-positive individual. The obligation incumbent on the State is to act in a manner which enables the HIV-positive individual to fulfil his or her obligation to protect others. In

---

[1] For a more detailed discussion of this conception of reciprocity of obligations, as it was originally formulated, see Charles A. Erin and John Harris, 'AIDS: Ethics, Justice and Social Policy', *Journal of Applied Philosophy* **10** (1993): 165–73. The concept of reciprocity is, of course, nothing startlingly new. Consider e.g. the following passage from Hume's 'Of Suicide': 'All our obligations to do good to society seem to imply something reciprocal. I receive the benefits of society, and therefore ought to promote its interests' (David Hume, *Writings on Religion*, edited by Anthony Flew (La Salle, Ill.: Open Court, 1992)).

the context of HIV, this requires that the State create a social environment in which HIV-positive persons can practically and psychologically exercise responsibility to themselves and others. With this reciprocal relationship as the guiding principle for social policy on HIV and AIDS, our aim was to construct a policy framework which minimizes the usual tension between the rights of individuals on the one hand, and the public health perspective, with its emphasis on social protection, on the other. Policy based on these reciprocal obligations would aim to reduce the rate of HIV transmission while protecting the rights of those already infected.

Over the three years, we addressed a great many AIDS-related issues, but, from the first, some of the most complex and troubling were raised by testing and screening for HIV, especially in regard of the confidentiality of the results of such testing and screening. We returned to these themes at several points during the course of the project, but the chapters collected here were specifically commissioned for this volume. They have, however, proved instrumental in the development of the thinking on these issues of the Group as a whole.

It would have been naïve to hope for consensus among such a wide-ranging group of researchers, but consensus was not ever a specific aim of the Project. Such consensus as has emerged can be gauged from the summary of recommendations taken from the Project's Final Report to the European Commission and reproduced in the Annexe. These recommendations are, we believe, more likely to have authority and be endorsed in the community at large than if we had adopted a self-consciously homogeneous style of approach.

Similarly, no conscious effort was made to achieve uniformity of approach in the selection of authors for this volume. We hope to reflect not only the diversity of relevant disciplines, but also the rich plurality of cultures, religions, and other influences that (co-)exist within the European Union.

Clearly, the number of participants and consultants brought together for the Project was substantially greater than the number of authors whose essays are collected here. However, the valuable contributions of all those involved in the project to the testing and screening debate should not be underestimated, and, to this extent at least, all have played a significant part in the engendrure of this collection of essays.

The list of participants in the project is a long one, but it is only right and just that each be acknowledged here: Inez de Beaufort, Bela

Blasszauer, Margaret Brazier, Gerald Corbitt, Anthony Dyson, Calliope C. S. Farsides, Eugenijus Gefenas, Dieter Giesen, John Harris, Heta Häyry, Matti Häyry, Medard T. Hilhorst, Søren Holm, Elena Kabakchieva, Ewa Kujawa, Mary Lobjoit, Sandor Magyarodi, Catherine Manuel, Constantin Maximilian, Mike Moran, Maurizio Mori, Ivo Procházka, Richard Prusa, Alicja Przyluska-Fiszer, Lorraine Sherr, Ladislav Soltes, Andrzej J. Szwarc, Anton Vedder, Sanda Viorel, and Tzecomir Vodenitcharov. We owe an incalculable debt of gratitude to all these people for their unstinting commitment to the project, and their readiness to give freely of their time and expertise.

Our sincere thanks are due also to the many other people who have very generously contributed to the Project, either as consultants or as guest speakers at the several conferences and workshops we convened. These include: Bert van Alphen, Miriam Aziz, Valerie Brasse, Hilary Curtis, H. van Deutekom, Ralph DiClemente, Heather Draper, Dolores Dooley, Richard Freeman, Marie Fox, H. F. L. Garretsen, Alex Gromiko, the Honourable Mrs Justice Hale, John Harrington, Steffan Jonhcke, Sakari Karjalainen, Aantje Kharagjitsingh, Diana Kloss, Jørgen Haahr Kristensen, Mary Haour-Knipe, H. M. Laane, Oliver Leaman, P. J. van der Maas, Hope Massiah, Jean McHale, Maureen Mulholland, Sue Newman, Nicola Pasini, Catherine Peckham, Edward P. Richards III, Peter Rossell, Jane Rowley, Sue Scott, Theo Smit, Tom Sorell, E. Ph. R. Sutorius, Wim van't Veer, and M. Vos.

A special debt is owed to Valérie-Lina Bernard, our Project Administrator, who is also responsible for the translation from the original French of Catherine Manuel's chapter in this edition.

Finally, and most importantly, we are grateful to Directorate General XII of the European Commission for their support of 'AIDS: Ethics, Justice and European Policy', without which this volume would not have been produced. In particular, it is a great pleasure to thank Dr Christiane Bardoux, our Scientific Officer at DGXII, for her constant support and guidance.

Rebecca Bennett and Charles A. Erin

Manchester
1997

Contents

Notes on Contributors

Inez de Beaufort is Professor of Medical Ethics at the Medical Faculty of the Erasmus University, Rotterdam. She is a member of the Dutch Health Council, the Medical Ethics Committee of the Royal Dutch Medical Association, and a member of several other committees. Her publications include 'Between the Scylla of too much paternalism and the Charybdis of too much freedom: Some ethical questions regarding MSAFP screening', in A. Mantingh *et al.* (eds.), *Screening in Prenatal Diagnosis* (Groningen: Ac. Press, 1991), 'The right to perfect parents? The right to perfect children? Perspectives of the unborn', in I. de Beaufort and M. Hilhorst, *Kind, ziekte en ethiek* (Ambo, 1993).

Rebecca Bennett is Lecturer in Bioethics at the Centre for Social Ethics and Policy, University of Manchester. She was formerly Research Fellow on the Commission of the European Communities' Biomedicine and Health Research Programme Projects 'AIDS: Ethics, Justice, and European Policy', and 'Communicable Diseases, Lifestyles, and Personal Responsibility—Ethics and Rights'. Her publications on HIV/AIDS include 'Mandatory Testing of Pregnant Women and Newborns: A Necessary Evil?', *AIDS/STD Health Promotion Exchange*, No. 4, 1997, 7–8, (with John Harris) 'Testing and Screening for HIV' in Lord Kennett (ed.) *Parliaments and Screening* (John Libbey, 1995) and (with Manuel *et al.*), 'Législations adopteés pour faire face à l'épidemie de sida', *Santé Publique* **8**/1 (1996): 41–52.

Margaret Brazier LLB, of the Middle Temple, Barrister, is Professor of Law and a Director of the Institute of Medicine, Law and Bioethics at the University of Manchester. She is a member of the Nuffield Council of Bioethics. She publishes widely on both medico-legal problems and the law of torts, and is the current editor of *Street on Torts* and *Clerk and Lindsell on Torts*. Professor Brazier's publications include 'Embryos' Rights: Abortion and Research', in Freeman (ed.), *Medicine, Ethics and Law* (MDA Stevens, 1988); 'The Challenge to Parliament: A Critique of the White Paper on Human Fertilisation and Embryology', in Anthony Dyson and John Harris (eds.), *Experiments on Embryos* (London: Routledge, 1989);

Medicine, Patients and the Law, 2nd edn. (Harmondsworth: Penguin Books, 1992), and (with Nina Fletcher, Janet Holt, and John Harris), *Ethics, Law and Nursing* (Manchester: Manchester University Press, 1994).

Gerald Corbitt is Consultant Clinical Scientist and Deputy Clinical Manager in Microbiology and Virology at Manchester Royal Infirmary, and Honorary Lecturer in Virology at the University of Manchester. He has been involved in HIV diagnosis since 1985 and has lectured extensively on the subject. His publications include 'Early confirmation of HIV p24 antigenaemia in infants born of HIV-positive mothers', *Journal of Infection* **26** (1993): 349–51; (with P. Tilston), 'Detection of hepatitis C virus RNA in serum, by combining reverse transcription and polymerase chain reaction in one tube', *Journal of Virological Methods* **44** (1993): 57–66, and (with D. J. Morris and E. Crosdale), 'Same-day testing for human immunodeficiency virus antibodies', *Journal of Virological Methods* **49** (1994): 367–70.

Heather Draper is Lecturer in the Centre for Biomedical Ethics at Birmingham Medical School. She is co-editor of *Ethical Issues in Anaesthesia* (1994). Her primary research interest is the ethical implications of reproductive technology but she also writes on the ethics of health care management and the interface of business and health care ethics. She is a Committee Member of the United Kingdom Forum for Health Care Ethics and Law.

Charles A. Erin is Senior Lecturer in Applied Philosophy, and Head of Centre, the Centre for Social Ethics and Policy, and a Fellow of the Institute of Medicine, Law and Bioethics at the University of Manchester. He is Associate Project Coordinator of the Commission of the European Communities' Biomedicine and Health Research Programme (BIOMED 2) Projects 'Communicable Diseases, Lifestyles, and Personal Responsibility—Ethics and Rights' and 'Reproductive Choice and Control of Fertility'. He was formerly Associate Project Coordinator of the BIOMED 1 Project 'AIDS: Ethics, Justice, and European Policy'. He has written on diverse subjects in the fields of Biomedical Ethics and Applied Philosophy and his publications related to HIV/AIDS include (with John Harris), 'AIDS: Ethics, justice, and social policy', *Journal of Applied Philosophy* **10** (1993): 165–73; (with John Harris) ' "Living wills": Anticipatory decisions and advance directives', *Reviews in Clinical*

Gerontology **4** (1994): 269–75; and (with Manuel *et al.*), 'Législations adopteés pour faire face à l'épidemie de sida', *Santé Publique* **8**/1 (1996): 41–52.

Calliope C. S. Farsides is Lecturer in Medical Ethics at the Centre of Medical Law and Ethics, King's College, University of London. Dr Farsides is a member of the Steering Committee of the UK Forum in Health Care Ethics and Law, and a member of the Editorial Advisory Board for the *Journal of Medical Ethics*. She has published in a number of areas of health care ethics, but is currently concentrating her attention on ethical issues arising in the care of the dying on which subject her publications include 'Active and passive euthanasia', *Care of the Critically Ill* **8** (1992); 'Law, morality and euthanasia', *Care of the Critically Ill* **9** (1993); and 'Allowing someone to die', in L. Sherr (ed.), *Grief and AIDS* (London: Wiley, 1995).

Dieter Giesen was Professor of Law and Head of the Working Centre for German and International Medical Malpractice Law, at the Free University of Berlin, Berlin. He was Visiting Fellow of Pembroke College, Oxford University, Visiting Professor at Melbourne University Law School, and Fulbright Visiting Professor at the University of Illinois, and was a member of the German Federal Parliament's Commission on the Rights of Women in Society, the Society of Comparative Law, and the Society of Public Teachers of Law (UK). He was a member of the Editorial Boards of *American Journal of Law and Medicine* (Boston*)*, *Journal of Contemporary Health Law and Policy* (Washington), *Medical Law International* (London), *Medical Law Review* (Oxford), *Professional Negligence* (London), and *Medicine and Law* (Mmabatho, South Africa), among others. His many articles to professional journals (in German, English, French, and Spanish) and books include *Medical Malpractice Law* (1981) [also in German], *Arzthaftungsrecht* (1983), 4th edn. 1995; *International Medical Malpractice Law—A Comparative Law Study of Civil Liability arising from Medical Care* (1988), and *Familienrecht* (1994). Tragically, Dieter Giesen died before he could see this contribution in print. The editors are honoured to have had this opportunity of working with him and to be able to include this chapter in the volume.

Heta Häyry is Docent and Head of the Department of Practical Philosophy at the University of Helsinki, Docent of the Philosophy of Law at the University of Lapland, and Senior Research Fellow at the Academy of Finland. She is an adviser to the Finnish National Board of Health and Social Security on social ethics and health care ethics, and in 1992–4 she was a member of the Research Council for the Humanities in the Academy of Finland. She is also a Board Member of the International Society for Value Inquiry. Her publications in English include *The Limits of Medical Paternalism* (London: Routledge, 1991) and many articles on health care ethics and general philosophy, among them 'AIDS now' in *Bioethics* **1** (1987) and 'AIDS, society and morality—A philosophical survey' in *Philosophia* **19** (1989).

Medard T. Hilhorst is an Associate Professor in Health Care Ethics in the Department of Medicine and Health Care and in the Department of Philosophy at the Erasmus University of Rotterdam. He has published in the field of future generations, environmental ethics, and animal ethics. Currently his main research interests are in medical technology and ethics, and in (medical) professional responsibility. He is a participant in a BIOMED 2 project 'Communicable Diseases, Lifestyles, and Personal Responsibility', and is Associate Coordinator of the BIOMED 2 project 'Beauty and the Doctor—The Ethics of Appearance'. Recent publications include (edited with Inez de Beaufort and Søren Holm) *In the Eye of the Beholder: Ethics and Medical Change of Appearance* (Scandinavian University Publishers, 1996), and 'The ethical assessment of new technologies—the case of ECMO', in R. I. Misbin and B. Jennings (eds.), *Health Care Crisis: The Search for Answers* (Frederick, Md.: University Publishing Group, 1995). He has been a member of the Dutch National Committee on AIDS Prevention, and the Committee on Tuberculosis of the Dutch Health Council, and is currently on the Council's Committee on New HIV Medication and the Threat of Resistance. He is also a member of the board of both the Dutch Society of Ethicists and the Dutch Association for Bioethics.

Søren Holm is a Danish doctor with qualifications in medicine, in health care ethics, and in health economics. He is Reader in Bioethics at the Institute of Medicine, Law and Bioethics at the University of Manchester. He was formerly Senior Research Fellow in the Department of Medical Philosophy and Clinical Theory, University of Copenhagen, and Visiting Research Fellow at the Institute of Pharmacology, Unit of Neuro-Psychiatry, University of Copenhagen. He is a member of the Danish Council of Ethics. He is the author of many papers on Health Care Ethics, including 'A common ethics for a common market?', *British Medical Journal* **304** (1992): 434–6; 'The spare embryo—a red herring in the embryo experimentation debate', *Health Care Analysis* **1** (1993): 63–6; 'Genetic engineering and the North-South Divide', in Anthony Dyson and John Harris (eds.) *Ethics and Biotechnology* (London: Routledge & Kegan Paul, 1993): 47–63, and 'American Bioethics at the crossroads—a critical appraisal', *European Philosophy of Medicine and Health Care* **2** (1994): 6–23.

Mary Lobjoit is a medical doctor and an Honorary Lecturer at the Centre for Social Ethics and Policy, University of Manchester. Formerly a Student Health Physician in the University of Manchester, she has a special interest in psychotherapy. Her publications include (with Margaret Brazier, eds.), *Protecting the Vulnerable: Autonomy and Consent in Health Care* (London: Routledge, 1991).

Catherine Manuel is Maître de Conférence in the Laboratoire de Santé Publique, Faculté de Médecine, Université Aix Marseille II, Assistance Publique Marseille, France. Since 1989, she has been in charge of a research group on the ethical implications of the AIDS pandemic within the Public Health Laboratory and her publications with that group include (with others), 'Ethics and AIDS: the protection of society versus the protection of individual rights', *AIDS and Public Policy* **6** (1991): 31–6; (with others), 'AIDS—a social dilemma: detection of seropositives', *European Journal of Epidemiology* **7** (1991): 139–46; and (with others), 'The ethical approach to AIDS: a bibliographical review', *Journal of Medical Ethics* **16** (1990): 14–27. Dr Manuel's other publications include (with J. L. San Marco), *SIDA—Les Enjeux Éthiques* (Éditions Doin, 1994), and (with others) 'Vertical transmission of HIV: rediscussion of screening', *AIDS Care* **7** (1995): 657–62.

Edward P. Richards III is Professor of Law at the University of Missouri at Kansas City. He has an extensive background in the medical sciences and has acted as Special Counsel to Health Directors at both the state and local level. His many publications include (with Katharine C. Rathbun), *Law and the Physician: A Practical Guide* (Little, Brown & Co., 1993); 'The jurisprudence of prevention: society's right of self-defence against dangerous individuals', *Hastings Constitutional Law Quarterly* **16** (1989): 329; and

'Colorado public health laws: a rational approach to AIDS', *University of Denver Law Review* **65** (1988): 127, and he co-authors the law and engineering section of *IEEE Engineering in Medicine and Biology*.

Peter Rossell is Senior Lecturer and Director of the Dept. of Medical Philosophy and Clinical Theory, University of Copenhagen. He has been involved in research in research ethics and informed consent issues since the late 1970s.

Lorraine Sherr is a Consultant Clinical Psychologist and Senior Lecturer in Health Psychology at the Royal Free Hospital School of Medicine, London. She has been the Chair of the British Psychological Society Special Group on AIDS. Dr Sherr edits the international journal *AIDS Care*, and is the founding editor of the new journal *Psychology, Health and Medicine*. She has written numerous texts and chapters on AIDS and HIV infection including *HIV and AIDS in Mothers and Babies* (Oxford: Blackwell Scientific, 1991); *AIDS and the Heterosexual Population* (Switzerland: Harwood Academic, 1993); *Grief and AIDS* (London: Wiley, 1995); and *AIDS as a Gender Issue* (London: Taylor & Francis, 1996).

Tom Sorell is Professor of Philosophy at the University of Essex. He is the author of a number of books including *Moral Theory and Capital Punishment* (Blackwells, 1987) and (with John Henry) *Business Ethics* (Butterworth/Heinemann) and is working on a book on the limitations of moral theory.

Anton Vedder is post-doctoral researcher at the Schoordijk Institute for Jurisprudence and Comparative Law of the Faculty of Law of Tilburg University. He has published several articles and two books on ethical aspects of HIV/AIDS and ethics, on the values of personal autonomy and privacy, and on ethical questions relating to life and health insurance, including *The Values of Freedom* (Utrecht: Aurelio Domus Artium, 1995).

1

Introduction

REBECCA BENNETT AND CHARLES A. ERIN

It would be difficult to justify a claim that the HIV pandemic presents us with novel philosophical challenges. Nevertheless, HIV and AIDS can be said to have attached a new urgency to the practice of Bioethics, and to the role of moral theory in the formulation of public policy. Over the past decade and a half, we have witnessed waves of complacency among those who (believe they) are not HIV positive, and vicious social discrimination against those who are (thought to be) HIV positive. Even though one of the lessons of the history of epidemics is that coercive measures rarely, if ever, work, some say we should view HIV/AIDS as 'just another epidemic' and demand similarly draconian public health interventions as have been employed in the past for other epidemics. However, there are at least two ways in which we may view HIV/AIDS as different. First, there is the often intimate and private nature of the transmission routes, several of which lean crucially on what may broadly be termed an individual's 'lifestyle'. Second, there is the age in which we live, and upon which AIDS has impacted, to take into account: it is not an overstatement of the truth to say that we live in an age of human and civil rights, and, thus, that we must be far more cautious now than we have been in the past, when it comes to the implementation of policies which infringe upon the liberties of individual citizens. It is against this background that the practical issues of testing and screening for HIV and questions over the confidentiality of the results of such testing and screening must be examined and understood.

In order to successfully negotiate our way through this complex moral terrain, it is important to be clear about precisely what is involved, technically, in testing and screening for HIV. In 'HIV Testing and Screening—Current Practicalities and Future Possibilities', Gerald Corbitt profiles the various stages which can be identified during the progression of HIV infection and draws the distinctions between the currently recognized variants of HIV: whilst combination tests which are reactive to both HIV-1 and HIV-2 have been available since the beginning of this decade, the emergence of new variants, such as subtype 'O', points up the need for the continued development of testing procedures. Corbitt takes us through the current range of testing procedures and protocols, explaining the respective advantages and limitations of these tests. He describes the problem of false negative and false positive results, and the difficulties inherent in the identification of neonatal HIV infection and of the early stages of infection. Finally, he explores the expected future developments in testing procedures raising the possibility of the testing of 'non-invasive samples' such as urine and saliva, the simplification of testing to allow the test to be performed outside the laboratory, and development of more sensitive tests which would allow earlier diagnosis of infection.

Counselling, both prior to and following a test for HIV antibody, is now widely recognized as an important part of the testing process and, as Gerald Corbitt is careful to make clear, such counselling is not only aimed at providing technical information regarding HIV and the test, but is essential if the person undergoing a test is to be optimally psychologically prepared to deal with the implications of the test result, whether positive or negative. In 'Counselling and HIV Testing: Ethical Dilemmas', Lorraine Sherr gives a thorough examination of the variety of reasons why it may be claimed that counselling around the HIV antibody test plays a crucial role. Sherr goes on to highlight the complex ethical dilemmas that must be dealt with in different testing situations, antenatal and infant testing for example. Of particular interest to the ethicist is Sherr's contention that 'Counselling was put forward as a panacea but in reality it may have been the cloak behind which many ethical issues were conveniently brushed.' Sherr is concerned that, although there is consensus that counselling is desirable, in many cases the quality of the counselling provided is not given a high enough priority—there is little consistency, regulation or evaluation of counselling and counsellors in this area. Ultimately, Sherr argues that HIV testing should not be seen as an end in itself, but rather as one of the many tools in the fight against HIV and AIDS.

In the context of AIDS, some of the most basic tenets of the 'liberal' tradition dominant in Europe have been severely challenged.

One of the chief effects of this challenge has been a renewed focus on the relationship between the State and the citizen. Indeed, there is growing trend of opinion which sees testing and screening for HIV as a paradigm case of the tension between the rights of individual citizens and society's interest in the protection and promotion of public health. This balance between the need to protect the public against infection and the need to protect HIV-positive individuals against unethical treatment can be approached from a variety of viewpoints. There are those who claim that coercive public health measures such as routine, or even mandatory screening and regular breaches of confidentiality in order to warn others are necessary evils to prevent widespread harm. Others insist that, both on grounds of efficacy and ethics, HIV testing must be offered on a voluntary and strictly confidential basis.

In 'HIV Testing and Screening: Benefits and Harms for the Individual and the Community', Catherine Manuel adopts a pragmatic approach and evaluates the real benefits and costs of testing and screening, at both the individual and community levels. We should not forget, Manuel warns, that since screening is an act of preventative medicine, and as such does not stem from the individual, we are justified in demanding conclusive evidence that screening will be beneficial to a significant proportion of those screened before it is imposed.

She examines the benefits and drawbacks for three groups of individuals: 'no-risks' individuals; individuals who take risks and test HIV negative; and individuals found to be HIV positive. For those people who know that they have not been exposed to any risk of infection, testing will provide no benefit whatsoever. Whilst there are several benefits of screening for those in the second category, the relief of a negative result for HIV might lead them to revert to risk-taking. Manuel examines the third category under four heads: therapeutic benefits; benefits linked to prevention; negative psychological effects; and negative social effects.

Manuel's cost-benefit analysis leads her to conclude that the interests of the community and the individual can be viewed as one and the same, and that public health considerations actually require the respect of individual rights. Indeed, Manuel argues, those coercive measures such as mandatory testing which at first blush might appear aimed at protecting the interests of the community may well jeopardize prevention opportunities and so produce the opposite of the desired effect. To prevent this, we must favour voluntary testing, confidentiality, and anti-discrimination.

A rather different view is provided by Edward P. Richards III in his 'HIV/AIDS: Testing, Screening and Confidentiality—An American Perspective'. Whilst this volume aims to provide a European perspective, it would be inappropriate in a work of this scale to ignore the American experience. As Richards rightly points out, 'HIV policy in the United States is important not only because it has dominated public health discourse in the United States for nearly fifteen years, but because the United States has a disproportionate impact on disease control programs throughout the world.' Richards sets his arguments against a historical account of the evolution of public health measures for the control of infectious diseases in America. While Manuel argues for an emphasis on individual rights and a greater reliance of public health efforts on the responsible behaviour of HIV-positive individuals, Richards' avowed bias is towards disease-control measures to protect the uninfected. He asserts that, in the USA, HIV/AIDS has been dealt with as a political issue, rather than as a problem for public health. If we are to understand how this attitude came about and just what its implications are for American citizens, it needs to be put into historical perspective: 'For good or ill, our response to HIV/AIDS was predetermined by forces in place long before the first AIDS cases were diagnosed.' Richards identifies a change in the 'mission' of US health departments since the Second World War. With the development of antibiotics and effective immunization programmes, support for disease control, and the often draconian measures which accompanied it, waned, and has been replaced by a primary concern with individual health care and its attendant emphasis on patient autonomy, privacy, and the use of high technology medicine. This Richards views as the antithesis of public health which conceives of *society* as the 'patient'.

Strong political pressure which ensures that disease-control policies are unable to impinge on HIV-positive individual's rights, he believes, has weakened public health codes. With the emergence of viruses such as Hanta and Ebola, and, in particular, with the re-emergence of bacterial conditions in forms resistant to antibiotics, Richards foresees a serious threat, especially among those states which have witnessed the enervation of their general disease-control measures in direct response to HIV/AIDS. This, he feels, may signal a reappraisal of public health policy in the USA, and a move back to dependence on disease control rather than medical technology.

Is there a lesson for Europe here? This is debatable. Admittedly, the last two decades have witnessed the gradual evolution of a doctrine of patient autonomy, fully endorsed in the writings of most ethicists and at least partially now recognized and enforced by the law and in medical practice. Patient autonomy is increasingly perceived as a manifestation of the individual's rights of self-determination and privacy, universally regarded as pillars of the civil liberties enjoyed by citizens of the European Union. And emerging European policies on public health do reflect a characteristic concern for conceptions of individual liberty and dignity: it is acknowledged that the State should refrain from intervention in private lives save where the individual's health state or lifestyle endangers others.

What, however, is the responsibility of the State when failure to screen or treat blood products endangers the individual? How far should knowledge of the risk of contaminated blood products be shared with the unwitting patient? Can States argue that the rights of individuals infected by blood supplies must be subordinated to the greater good of preserving the blood supply for all? The comparative legal analysis of liability for HIV-infected blood provided by Dieter Giesen in 'Compensation and Consent: A Brief Comparative Examination of Liability for HIV-Infected Blood' highlights the different approaches to this problem of the American, German, and English jurisdictions respectively. In the context of American Common Law, Giesen shows that the perceived need to maintain an adequate blood supply has prompted American lawmakers to limit the right of the HIV-infected plaintiff to compensation on the 'highly questionable premise that blood is not a product'. Working on the assumption (unproven) that imposing civil liability on hospitals and blood banks would jeopardize the supply of blood, American courts have adopted the view that blood transfusion is a *service*. Giesen is critical of this approach and maintains that even if it were valid there remains a strong case against the manufacturers of *blood products* based on strict liability or warranty and he finds no reason why these manufacturers should benefit from a special exemption. It remains possible for a plaintiff to make out a case in negligence against the hospital or blood bank, but in doing so he faces considerable difficulties in trying to prove negligence on the part of the supplier of the blood, and causation of the HIV infection.

Unlike the USA, the German courts have concentrated on providing general rules of 'procedural fairness and just compensation'. The German approach rests on the view that once the risk of infection through blood transfusion was identified, this fact should have been disclosed to potential recipients of transfusions. Giesen further explores these duties of disclosure in his analysis of the law relating to informed consent of patients to the transfusion of blood. The standard of disclosure which the law imposes on doctors and others in order for consent to be valid, and which will determine to what extent the right to self-determination is respected, varies considerably. In England, a doctor will not be held liable if, in his conduct of treatment or diagnosis, he conforms to the practice of a responsible body of medical practitioners. Giesen finds it regrettable that the English courts have seen fit to sanction the application of a doctor-centred and, thus, he believes, paternalistic approach in the context of blood transfusions.

Giesen contrasts this English approach with that of most other Common Law jurisdictions which have developed standards of disclosure based on the informational needs of the 'reasonable patient'. German-speaking jurisdictions have taken this one step further adopting a 'subjective patient' test which requires medical professionals to meet the informational needs of the *actual* patient. Guided by this patient-centred approach the German Federal Supreme Court has required hospitals to inform patients of the risk of HIV infection via blood transfusion and of the possibility of autologous transfusion or donation by family members. Giesen argues that, due to its basis in the concept of reasonableness, an objective test of causation, falls short of respecting the right of self-determination: adequate protection is only provided by a subjective test of causation.

Another way of addressing the apparent dilemma thrown up by the conflict-of-rights view is to look to the question of who is responsible for an individual's health state. Is an individual responsible for her own health state? Is the State responsible for an individual's health state? If the individual is responsible for his own health state, then the State can justifiably relinquish all obligations in relation to health care, or so some might wish to argue. And one does hear such arguments raised in relation to the AIDS pandemic when, currently, treatments for HIV infection can be very expensive. In 'Individual Responsibility for Health', Inez de Beaufort takes on this kind of argument in the two chief forms in which it has been put forward in the Dutch context. In its strongest guise, as defended by H. M. Dupuis, the argument claims that in certain circumstances—scarcity of resources—those who are responsible for their ill-health should be excluded from health-care provision. De Beaufort's critique involves, on the one hand, an appeal to solidarity as, in some sense, a trump of justice based on past actions, and, on the other, a 'complex' analysis of scarcity which, in many situations at least, is more realistic than Dupuis' 'absolute' notion.

A more moderate view has been defended in the Netherlands by G. M. van Asperen. While accepting that it is a good that people be free to choose their own lifestyles, van Asperen argues that it is unreasonable for society to foot the bill for ill-health which results from an unhealthy lifestyle, and that those whose need for health care provision comes of their self-chosen and avoidable preferences should pay themselves for that health care through additional insurance cover. De Beaufort debunks the notion that unhealthy lifestyles are always *freely chosen*, and does so without jeopardizing a firm commitment to individual autonomy. She asserts that we ought simply to accept the Orwellian observation that people 'want to be good, but not too good and not quite all the time', and this should be factored into health care insurance. Whilst de Beaufort does not impugn a moral duty to live healthily, she would nevertheless prefer to live in a Good Samaritan type of society than a Pharisaic one, and surely she is not alone in this.

Soren Holm takes a different tack in his approach to this issue. In 'Is Society Responsible for My Health?' he questions the usual assumption that if the individual *is* responsible for his own health state then society is thereby relieved of such responsibility. Holm argues that it is misguided to assign this priority to individual responsibility, and that even if individuals do have a responsibility for their own health, some societies have extensive responsibilities for their citizens' health. He adopts a political philosophical analysis based on the Hobbesian notion that 'the legitimation of the sovereignty of the state must lie in its ability to protect its citizens from harm'. To bring this account up to date, we must recognize that in many modern societies the threats from which citizens now need protection are not the 'enemies' which Hobbes originally envisioned, but come of poverty, pollution, and ill-health, for example. If such salient protections of individual citizens are not forthcoming from the State, then such citizens are thereby put outside the law, and whilst these 'outlaws' are deprived of the protection of the law, neither are they bound by it. Thus, says Holm, if a society deserts HIV-positive persons it thereby relinquishes any claim that HIV-positive citizens should behave responsibly. He produces a compelling argument for viewing a state of good health as a basic need. And this is foundational to society's duty of protection of its citizens' health. Moreover, just because society *can* not (fully) discharge this duty does not relieve society of it. Holm does contemplate situations in which this obligation might be voided, but these involve situations, wars for example, where the survival of the State, or the lives or social functioning of many of its citizens, are under threat.

Holm identifies a particular problem which may arise in societies with public health care systems of the British or Scandinavian type, systems which Hobbes did not envisage, and where the health care that a citizen may need is unavailable—either through the system or, because of the distortions the system makes on the market in health care, through private means. In such a situation, the citizen is afforded a prima-facie right to attempt to meet his need in any way possible, even those that are illegal. Holm suggests two possible solutions: first, the State could augment the public system to account for all legitimate needs of its citizens; or, second, the system could be reorganized so as to provide these citizens with the opportunity to obtain privately the health care they need.

Clearly, where we place responsibility for health state will have a substantial effect on the health care professional–patient relationship. Responsibility for health state, however, is only one of several factors that can distort this relationship which in the context of testing and screening for HIV plays such a crucial role. Four of the essays collected here focus on aspects of the relationship between the health care professional and her patient, in particular the various obligations of the former. Two of them address medical confidentiality as it relates to the warning of third parties. Anton Vedder, in 'HIV/AIDS and the Point and Scope of Medical Confidentiality', examines why medical confidentiality is so highly prized and whether breaches of confidentiality are ever justified, even in cases where not to do so may lead to the harming of third parties. He analyses the view that a health care worker's duty to respect confidences derives from the foundational principle of respect for individual autonomy which is standardly taken to justify attenuation of a strict duty of confidentiality in cases where others will be put at risk of harm. The problem Vedder sees in this line of argument lies with the *specification* of harms taken as justification for infringements of autonomy and medical confidentiality. The undoubted vulnerability of third parties 'does not yield determinate criteria as to the assessment of the kinds of harm . . . *qua* character'. There is, of course, great difficulty in predicting the probability of harm to third parties, *except*, perhaps, where we have good reason to suppose that HIV-positive people will neither inform third parties nor take measures to minimize the chances of HIV transmission. In these cases, infringement of confidentiality *might* be justified, but this does not entail a *policy* of mandatory partner notification.

To understand why this is so, says Vedder, we need to explore the basis of medical confidentiality, and in particular the relation between individual autonomy and medical information. Allowing a person discretionary control over who should have access to her medical information affirms, emphatically, respect for individual autonomy. Vedder's analysis of the 'special character' of personal medical information reveals that breaches of medical confidentiality which are not sanctioned by the individual concerned may cause her emotional and material harm, and it is the individual who is best positioned to judge the harm that may be done. Generally, control over personal information facilitates, to a degree, control over the kinds of interpersonal relationships one has, and, to this extent at least, is an important aspect of agent's life. But do the implications of such deliberations, as weighty as they are, really constitute a watertight argument for the maintenance of medical confidentiality, even where third parties are thereby put at risk? The presumed probability that third parties *will* be put at risk is key to the success of arguments for strict adherence to the duty of medical confidentiality, but, Vedder contends, we have no ground to suppose that *all* persons who test positively for HIV will refuse to notify partners and not behave responsibly. This line of argument, derived from the principle of respect for autonomy, leads Vedder to conclude that where a person who tests positively for HIV makes it expressly clear that he is not prepared to take any action to protect others from the risk of infection by him, here, *perhaps*, we have a reason for thinking of him as residing outside the moral community and thus not deserving of the moral privileges associated with membership of it.

At a much more pragmatic level, removing the guarantee of absolute medical confidentiality could lead to an erosion of trust in health care professionals and so jeopardize public health. Discrimination against those who are HIV positive is a fact, and is likely to disincline those who consider themselves to be 'at risk' from voluntarily seeking an HIV test if confidentiality is not to be maintained. Such reasoning, says Vedder, provides a strong argument against legitimation of occasional or systematic breaches of confidentiality. Vedder's analysis provides no easy way out of the health care professional's dilemma, but, he suggests, some relief might be gained from redoubling efforts to persuade HIV-positive persons, through counselling, to do what is morally right.

But should such 'moralizing' lie within a health care professional's remit? Whilst addressing similar terrain as Vedder, Medard Hilhorst focuses squarely on the obligations of health care workers. In 'Can Health Care Workers Care for their Patients and Be Advocates of Third-Party Interests?' Hilhorst asserts that the duties of health care workers are best viewed as 'derived duties', that is, they are derived from the duties of HIV-positive persons. And just as HIV-positive individuals have moral duties to protect others from infection, he argues, so health care workers have a moral obligation towards these 'third parties'.

Hilhorst describes how the health care worker has a 'manifold obligation' when dealing with a patient who is found to be HIV positive: he will have a 'role-based' duty to the patient; a general duty (of an *'in rem'* nature) to promote sound public health policy; and possibly a specific duty to warn named third parties. The interests of third parties may not coincide with those of the HIV-positive person, and thus, says Hilhorst, the health care worker is under a different duty. A health care worker's professional (role-based) duties are additional to the 'human' and 'civic' duties which he shares with HIV-positive people. And, though it may not be easy for the HIV-positive person to bear in mind her duties toward third parties, the health care worker has a role-based duty to remind her of these duties during the pre-test dialogue.

The duty of the health care worker towards third parties is, however, reliant upon the HIV-positive person's ability, or willingness, to identify them. Where third parties cannot be identified, the duty of the health care worker to third parties is limited to an attempt to persuade the HIV-positive person to change her behaviour so as to minimize the risk of her transmitting HIV to third parties. This helps us understand that the health care worker can only discharge his duties to third parties through (his influence with) the HIV-positive person. And this raises the question of whether the health care worker should 'teach her a lesson in medicine or morality'. Whilst the health care worker may be no more of a moral expert than any other person, his professional role puts him in a position not only to give technical information but also to bring to the HIV-positive person's attention the moral repercussions of her actions. By helping the HIV-positive person take moral hold of her life, the health care worker, albeit indirectly, promotes the interests of third parties, but thus the health care worker is, and, Hilhorst asserts, should be a 'moralizer'.

It can be argued that health care workers are relieved of *any* responsibility towards third parties since they are obligated by the 'SNH norm'—have safe sex (S), use clean needles (N), and act hygienically (H)—to take responsibility for themselves. However, Hilhorst's analysis reveals that, as a norm, SNH is neither sufficient nor necessary, not least because it is overly idealistic in a world of complex human relationships. Rather, he advocates adherence to a 'CSA norm'—consciousness of risks associated with certain behaviour (C), speaking about it (S), and acting accordingly (A)—which encompasses the interests of third parties. The health care worker has a significant role to play in helping the HIV-positive person to apply the CSA norm in her particular context.

Hilhorst ends with a discussion of exceptional cases in which a person who discovers herself to be HIV positive refuses to act morally and is clearly prepared to put third parties at risk. Whilst Hilhorst sees such cases as calling for clear regulation, he is careful to delimit the domain of regulation to such cases only. Beyond these bounds, society should maintain a liberal approach and so optimize the chances that the health care worker will successfully persuade an HIV-positive person to behave morally.

But what if it is the health care professional who knows or suspects herself to be HIV positive? In contrast to Vedder and Hilhorst, Calliope C. S. Farsides considers the problem of confidentiality from the other side of the health professional–patient relationship. In 'HIV Infection and the Health Care Worker: The Case for Limited Disclosure', Farsides considers the duties of health care workers who have reason to believe that they are HIV positive and examines whether these duties include a duty to disclose HIV status to patients and colleagues. She makes a case for the limited disclosure of HIV status by a health care professional in a context of reciprocal duties between employee and employer. The claim is that health care professionals have a prima-facie duty to disclose their HIV status where it can be shown that disclosure of this information will facilitate the protection of others from infection. A health care professional who is aware of his HIV-positive status but is not motivated to disclose this information by a sense of duty alone, should, Farsides suggests, be shown that he will not lose out by being open about his HIV status, or, even better, that he may benefit.

Farsides envisages that if reciprocal duties are developed between the health care professional and his employer then we may begin to move towards a situation where workers willingly disclose status to an occupational health practitioner, receive support and guidance, and are protected from discrimination and unfair treatment. Moreover, infected health care workers should be allowed to stay in jobs as long as they are able to perform the requisite tasks associated with them, while patients and colleagues remain protected from infection by good standards of practice without necessarily needing to know the individual's HIV status.

Farsides goes on to address the question of whether a patient needs to know the HIV status of his carer for us to be able to claim that his autonomy has been respected and he has fully consented to treatment. Some might argue that in the same way as the possible side effects of various treatments must be made clear in order that a genuine consent to that treatment can be obtained, so the disclosure of the HIV-positive status of carers involved in a patient's care should be made a condition of consent. Farsides offers a solution to this problem of consent which pre-empts the need for disclosure of a health care worker's HIV status. She suggests that where a health care worker who knows or suspects she is HIV positive withdraws from procedures involving a real risk of infection, however small, or from practice altogether, his consent could not be said to be invalid on account of inadequate disclosure. Thus, if a patient refuses to be treated by the carer on the grounds that he believes her to be HIV positive, he would simply be discriminating against that person and a 'duty to respect someone's autonomy should not require us to pander to views that can be shown to be bigoted or prejudicial'. Farsides' approach provides a solution to the dilemma posed by the concatenation of the principle of confidentiality as it relates to the HIV status of health care workers and the duty of care health care workers have to their patients. She demonstrates how, by taking their duty to protect others from harm seriously, health care workers may obviate the need to make full disclosure of their HIV-positive status.

These issues of disclosure and confidentiality as discussed by Vedder, Hilhorst, and Farsides emphasize the need for clarity in regard to just what should be the nature of the relationship between a health care professional and her patient. HIV disease, raising as it does so many questions about individual privacy and patient confidentiality, particularly as they relate to testing and screening, throws this issue into high relief. In 'Fiduciary Relationship: An Ethical Approach and a Legal Concept?' Margaret Brazier and Mary Lobjoit contend that our best chances of securing productive resolutions of the ethical and legal dilemmas raised by screening for HIV will follow from recognition that the relationship between patients and health care professionals constitutes a partnership, 'a true therapeutic alliance'. To this end, they develop the concept of fiduciary relationship between patient and health care professional.

Brazier and Lobjoit's analysis of the legal experience regarding screening for HIV in England leads them to charge 'common law chaos'. Their examination of the practice of screening, inconsistencies in consent procedure, and the legal ramifications thereof (possibly extending to the criminal law), reveals a distinction between patient and professional standards, and the common law persists in viewing the relation between patient and health care professional as adversarial. They are led to conclude that '[t]he law is asking the wrong questions in the wrong language'. The right questions, in the right language, they contend, are to be found with a fiduciary principle which reflects the special position of trust in which health care professionals are held by patients. The fiduciary relationship takes trust as a causal antecedent of effective treatment, and calls for frankness by both parties in the partnership. '*Real* consent' is only possible where patient confidentiality is respected, but this is not to imply that the patient has only rights against the health care professional and is free of obligations. Rather, Brazier and Lobjoit view the collaboration as involving a reciprocity of obligations: each partner must seek to ensure that the other is apprised of the information she requires to enable her to fulfil her role in the partnership. The extent of the disclosure will vary according to the respective needs of the particular individuals concerned, and the fiduciary relationship is also dynamic in the way it allows for the evolution of such needs over time.

As a legal concept, fiduciary relationship has its roots in property law, and the real challenge for Brazier and Lobjoit is to demonstrate that the ethical approach 'can . . . be clothed with legal reality'. Using the Canadian experience as a basis, they show up the artificiality of the problems envisaged in the English jurisdiction and, in so doing, successfully demonstrate the compatibility of the ethical approach with the legal concept.

Clearly, issues surrounding HIV/AIDS and confidentiality are complex. On the one hand, the stigmatizing nature of the condition suggests that access to information generated by testing for HIV should be controlled; on the other, this information can be seen to be of great value to epidemiologists, insurance companies, and others, and thus, in certain situations, some might argue for the legitimacy of breaches of confidentiality. Manifestly, in view of the pronounced sensitivity of information like an individual's HIV status, and in view of the vast potential for the misuse of such information at the expense of the individual's interests and, perhaps, *contra* their rights, such an argument must not be allowed to proceed too quickly.

In 'Ethical Aspects of the Use of "Sensitive Information" in Health Care Research', Søren Holm and Peter Rossel investigate what 'sensitive information' is and what an individual's relationship is to information about him. There are many different items of information which may be labelled 'sensitive', but a person's HIV status is clearly one of the most sensitive. Holm and Rossel's analysis of 'sensitive information' within the general setting of medical and epidemiological research helps put the various strands of debates over confidentiality and privacy into a philosophical context.

Information about citizens has always been stored, but it is the rapid advance of so-called 'information technology', bringing with it an unprecedented facility for storage, transmission, retrieval, and linkage of vast amounts of data, which is responsible for considerable public unease as to the potential for misuse of information pertaining to citizens. Medical research and, in particular, modern epidemiology rely in no small way on access to such data, and health care researchers and epidemiologists are thus understandably concerned about the possibility of future regulation of data registers and the form it may take.

Whilst much has been written on the possibility of *un*authorized access to, and misuse of stored information, Holm and Rossel focus on *authorized* access and thus a very different type of potential misuse. Via an iterative process of (re-)definition of 'sensitive information' as it relates to persons, they conclude that 'sensitive' turns out to be 'just a technical term for "potentially harmful"'. Despite the context sensitivity of 'potentially harmful information', particularly to societal norms and/or prejudices, it remains a useful concept if accompanied by clear specification of the context in which the information is produced, stored, used, and so on.

From the viewpoint of the individual to whom potentially harmful information relates, it seems that it is the element of control over that information which is key, even where an individual's behaviour does not transgress the norms and prejudices prevalent in a given society. In an attempt to conceptualize the relationship between a person and information about him, Holm and Rossel analyse a cluster of moral rights which afford a person protection from unsanctioned interference by others: the right to personal integrity, the right to autonomy, and the right to privacy. Taking a psychological view of integrity, the right to personal integrity may be understood as a person's right to be the person he is, but, Holm and Rossel show, this right will only be infringed by unauthorized disclosure of personal information in unusual cases. Similarly, the right to autonomy fails, on their analysis, to provide the required control over personal information. They conclude that an extensive right to the control of personal information can only be founded on the right to privacy which, according to their account, is the 'weakest' of the three rights. To this, they add a duty not to harm others (as opposed to a right not to be harmed), which, in the context of medical research, falls on the researcher.

Holm and Rossel are thus moved to assert that the 'use of information in public and private registers must be controlled to prevent infringements of privacy and possible harm to others'. However, their consideration of how best to devise an effective system of regulation, and their examination of the specific problems thrown up by the application of new diagnostic technology, particularly genetic technology, to old, stored biological samples, lead them to conclude that the introduction of rigorous, general rules for the regulation of personal information within the health care setting constitutes an imperfect approach to the control of information. Rather, they advocate a policy of determining the possible harm that might be caused to individuals, their relations (and descendants), and the group(s) to which they belong, by the dissemination of items information on a case-by-case basis.

Attempts to gain information about the HIV status of an individual are motivated by the considerable value this information is perceived to have. Information of this kind may be valuable not only to the subject of the test, but may allow others to avoid risk or take a more calculated risk, and here 'risk' may be interpreted in a wide sense, encompassing physical risk, to, for example, sexual partners, and financial risk, for example to insurance brokers.

It is easy to see the value of information about HIV status to insurance companies, but does this interest justify insistence on disclosure? Tom Sorell and Heather Draper address this question in 'AIDS and Insurance'. They ask whether it is morally supportable for insurers to charge higher premiums, or even refuse cover to individuals who are perceived to be at 'high risk' of HIV infection? They argue that where refusals to insure or increased premiums do not deprive applicants of health insurance (where public health care insurance is paid for through taxes), the moral case for restricting insurers' ability to refuse or set high premiums may not be very strong. In this situation, it may also be that the limited amount of uptake in these types of market justify insurers being careful about the risks they take on. Where commercial health insurance is dominant, Sorell and Draper claim, the morality of the situation is different. Where there is a relatively small state health insurance scheme, they suggest that premiums be fixed for those thought to be at higher risk of HIV infection at levels which reflect the profits generated by the far greater number of low-risk policies taken.

In the same way that it is morally important to ensure access to commercial health insurance where refusal would prohibit individuals from obtaining adequate health care, Sorell and Draper argue, it may also be morally important to ensure access to commercial insurance—in countries like the UK where refusal can prohibit, for example, access to adequate housing, and to secure income in periods of illness for the self-employed, and provide for loss of income when an income earner in a household dies.

We may, of course, think of several reasons, which do not rely on a financial incentive, why an individual may wish to know his own HIV status or that of another person, and reasons why some bodies—medical researchers, for example—may be interested in knowing the HIV status of individuals or groups of individuals within society. But 'being interested in knowing' and 'having a legitimate interest in knowing' are, philosophically speaking, not the same. What are supportable grounds for overriding the principle of respect for the personal autonomy of an individual or group of individuals? Can we ever be morally justified in obtaining information about a person's HIV status irrespective of her wishes in the matter? Such questions are addressed by Rebecca Bennett within the context of HIV testing of pregnant women.

In 'Should We Routinely Test Pregnant Women for HIV?' Bennett seeks to establish whether this particular group of people constitute a special case. The kind of routine testing which has been called for for pregnant women is not something society would so readily countenance for other groups—homosexual men, for example. Are there sound moral arguments to be adduced in support of such calls? Or may it be that pregnant women are being singled out simply, but cynically, because they do not constitute a 'community' *per se*, and lack an effective lobby in support of their interests?

Recognizing the problems, both practical and moral, inherent in routine testing, Bennett attempts to discover if there exist benefits to the individual or to society which may be viewed as so overwhelming that they justify overriding the negative aspects. One by one, she constructs and analyses five of the most plausible arguments which may be postulated in favour of routine testing of pregnant women: (i) to allow women to make fully informed decisions about their futures; (ii) to give health care professionals the information they need to protect themselves from possible infection; (iii) to produce epidemiological data; (iv) to allow women to protect their own health; and (v) to benefit the resulting child.

Bennett shows that if (i) holds water, it is a justification of the routine testing, not of all pregnant women, but of all persons. Similarly, (iii) does not provide a reason for the routine testing of pregnant women, but rather for including pregnant women in an unlinked screening programme. Even if (ii) was to be taken as a serious concern, Bennett asserts, the practical difficulties associated with testing for HIV (the so-called 'window period', and so on) imply that health care professionals should treat those pregnant women who initially test negatively for HIV *as if they were HIV positive* and take all appropriate precautions, and, this being so, there is no need to test in the first place. There is, as yet, no convincing evidence to justify taking (iv) as a realistic concern, and until evidence can be produced that pregnancy has a detrimental effect on the health of an HIV-positive woman, says Bennett, it cannot stand as a justification of routine testing.

Only (v) seems to merit serious consideration. There is a sense in which pregnant women *do* constitute a special case: generally, it is possible for HIV-positive people to protect others from risk of the infection by them without knowing their HIV status, but the same does not appear to be true of a pregnant woman's protection of the child she will bear. If women become aware of their HIV-positive status early in pregnancy, so the argument goes, they will thus be in a position to avail themselves of those measures currently available to minimize the risk of vertical transmission. However, whilst there is some evidence that such measures could reduce vertical transmission rates, it is currently inconclusive and incomplete. And even if conclusive evidence was discovered, Bennett would still prefer a policy of routinely *offering* testing for HIV to pregnant women rather than routine testing.

The general questions which lie behind Bennett's discussion of the particular case of testing of pregnant women (and Sorell and Draper's discussion of insurance) are taken up by Heta Häyry in 'Who Should Know about My HIV Positivity and Why?' Häyry identifies five groups who *might* have an interest in knowing about a person's HIV-positive status: the person herself; people with whom she comes into close physical contact—a group which may extend beyond sex partners, needle sharers, and those to whom she sells or donates organs, cells or other body tissues, to those who deal with her health care needs, family and friends, business colleagues and clients, and so on; those with whom she has made compacts which engender legal rights or obligations—employers/employees, insurance companies, business associates; those (state officials of one kind or another) who are charged with ensuring citizens do not inflict harm to themselves or others; and, finally, there are those who feel they should be entitled to know about this person's HIV-positive status just in case they come upon her in their everyday lives.

Arguments in justification of disclosure will vary substantially according to, and within, each of these categories, but they will fall into three types: prudential arguments, which focus on the continuing self-interest of individuals; moral arguments, which enjoin us to do what is right and shun what is wrong—of the several moral theories which provide a particular view of the right and the wrong, Häyry concentrates on negative utilitarianism, pure deontology, and virtue ethics; and, finally, the type of argument which relies on legality and socio-political expediency. Häyry applies each of these three types of argument to each of the first four of the categories of interested parties in turn. As for the fifth category, she shows, with short shrift, that 'the moralistic zeal is founded on irrational fears and aversions rather than on any genuine regard for the good of society'.

Häyry's analysis yields the following results. All those in a position to be harmed, physically or financially, by a person's HIV-positive status have a prudential reason to attempt to ascertain that information—the person herself is exempted as the knowledge may not improve her quality of life. Ethically, a person's prima-facie moral duty to protect others from harm appears to entail that she should discover her HIV status. Furthermore, the moral theories Häyry deploys suggest that a person who knows she is HIV positive is under a prima-facie obligation to disclose her status to those she might infect, to economic associates she might otherwise wrong, and to public authorities which can use the information to curtail the spread of HIV disease. Generally, however, against a background which involves the constant threat of discrimination, these prima-facie moral duties cannot be used as grounds for the imposition of legal sanctions.

Heta Häyry's consideration of the major ethical theories reveals that they will all support a prima-facie moral obligation to know about one's HIV status. Erin takes this as the most promising jumping off point from which to address the vexing question of whether an individual can ever be said to have a right to remain in ignorance of her HIV status. Several of the authors in this volume, either explicitly or by implication, touch upon the notion of a person holding a right to remain in ignorance, and this reflects the recurrence of this theme in the extant literature on testing and screening. Many take it for granted that such a right exists. And some even imply that it is a 'general' right, held by all those who can hold rights—although some deny its existence altogether.

In 'Is There a Right to Remain in Ignorance of HIV Status?', Erin sets himself a relatively modest task: if he can show that a person has a moral obligation to know his HIV status in certain circumstances, then he will have shown that, *in those circumstances*, the person cannot possess a right to remain in ignorance and, thus, that the right to remain in ignorance cannot exist as a 'general' right, if it exists at all.

Adopting a consequentialist approach, Erin examines possible motivations for wishing to remain in ignorance of HIV status, and pits these against considerations of harm and wrong to others which would ground a moral obligation to discover one's HIV status. He shows that the obligation to protect others from harm or wrong which may come of our autonomous choices and consequent acts is an overarching moral imperative. However, as applied to knowledge of one's HIV status, it will engender an obligation to know *only* in contexts where we are not prepared to behave as if we are HIV positive. Where I can reasonably ensure that no wrong or harm to others will follow from my choice to remain in ignorance of my HIV status, I may be free to remain in ignorance thereof. Insofar as an obligation to discover HIV status can be adduced in certain circumstances, the right to remain in ignorance, if it can exist as a right cannot exist as a general right.

Overall, the general impression this volume gives is that we will not readily tolerate great inroads into the moral and legal protection of individuals on account of the perceived interests of a conflated view of society and the State. If the authors gathered here can be considered to be in any way fairly representative of a cross-section of academic opinion within the European Union, it seems that the liberal tradition, for all its alleged shortcomings, remains healthy in Europe. However, what consensus comes out of this collection of essays seems to indicate a need to delimit the notion of individual rights, or at least to reinterpret this notion to broaden the strict focus on the right to privacy, the right to remain in ignorance, and, generally the (wide view of the) right to act autonomously. This hardly amounts to an undermining of such considerations. Rather, there seems to be a call for more reliance on the moral sensitivities of individuals to the interests of other individuals who may be put at risk by the enactment of fully autonomous choices. Interestingly, nobody here makes specific calls for legislation to enforce what they conceive to be the moral obligations which fall to individuals. Instead, the call is for more serious and careful examination of the moral basis of our relationships with other individuals, particularly health care professionals, and our relationship with the State.

We hope and trust that the essays collected here will further debate over the issues raised by testing and screening for HIV.

2

HIV Testing and Screening: Current Practicalities and Future Possibilities

GERALD CORBITT

Introduction

The human immunodeficiency virus (HIV) was first recovered in 1983 by researchers in Paris, France.[1] The virus initially carried a variety of names—human T-lymphotropic virus type III (HTLV III), lymphadenopathy-associated virus (LAV), and AIDS retrovirus (ARV) but by consensus the term HIV is now universally applied to the agent.[2]

During the course of infection with the virus a number of stages can be documented and these are accompanied by changes in various markers of the virus infection which are detectable in the serum (serological markers) (Fig. 2.1).

Primary infection

Following exposure and infection by HIV there is an initial period during which specific antibodies to the various virus proteins (antigens) have not yet been produced. This is known as the window period and in the case of HIV may last for eight to ten weeks. During this time it may be possible to detect another marker of virus infection, the p24 (core) antigen, which is a structural component in the

[1] F. Barre-Sinoussi, J. C. Cherman, F. Rey, M. T. Nugeyre, S. Chamaret, J. Gruest, et al., 'Isolation of a T-lymphocyte retrovirus from a patient at risk for acquired immune deficiency syndrome (AIDS)', Science 220 (1983): 868–71.
[2] Human Retrovirus Subcommittee of the International Committee on the Taxonomy of Viruses, 'What to call the AIDS virus?' Nature 321 (1986): 10.

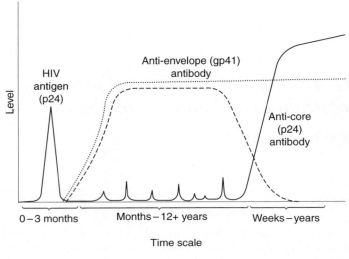

FIG. 2.1

central part of the virus particle.[3] However, this antigen usually only appears transiently for a few days or weeks and may be missed if a serum sample is not collected at the appropriate time.

Asymptomatic period

A range of antiviral antibodies generally appear as the infected person mounts a full serological response (seroconversion) and these will then persist for long periods (months to years). During this time the person will continue to release p24 antigen into the bloodstream as the virus replicates and the quantities will vary with time. This is frequently not detectable since antibody directed against it (anti-p24 antibody) will combine with, or coat, the antigen and mask its presence.

[3] J. Goudsmit, D. A. Paul, J. Lange, H. Speelman, J. Noordaa, H. Van der Helm, *et al.*, 'Expression of human immunodeficiency virus antigen (HIV-Ag) in serum and cerebrospinal fluid during acute and chronic infection', *Lancet* ii (1986): 177–80; B. Soto, C. Rey, J. Peneda, I. Aguado, M. Leal, and E. Lissen, 'HIV-1 antigen as the one marker in the early stage of HIV-1 infection', *Vox Sanguinis* 60 (1991): 241.

HIV disease (AIDS)

Eventually, as the infected individual progresses to HIV disease, the immune capabilities begin to decline and some of the circulating antibodies to HIV are no longer detectable in the serum (e.g. anti-p24 antibody). This is accompanied by the reappearance of high levels of p24 antigen, coinciding with massive viral replication and the death of large numbers of white blood cells known as T4 lymphocytes whose function is central to the maintenance of an effective immune response.

The development of a serological test for HIV, which was quickly accepted as the aetiological agent of AIDS, required the successful laboratory culture of very large quantities of the virus which could then be used as an antigen in the tests. The first such tests became widely available for evaluation during early 1985,[4] and testing was introduced on a large scale in the UK in September of that year through the Blood Transfusion Service, the Public Health Laboratory Service, and Regional NHS virology laboratories.[5]

It was initially believed that the human immunodeficiency viruses comprised a single antigenic type, i.e. they were all very similar in structure, but in 1986 a second HIV was discovered in healthy Senegalese prostitutes and later found to be associated with an AIDS-like illness in the West African mainland and some of the off-shore islands.[6] The initial virus described in 1983 became known as HIV-1 and the West African virus as HIV-2. For some years, until 1989, assays were produced carrying specific reactivity only to HIV-1. Some of the viral proteins of HIV1/2 are common, i.e. shared, and therefore there is an element of cross-reactivity for HIV-2 in assays for HIV-1. However, the degree of cross-reactivity is very variable and in some assay formats may be absent. Combination tests carrying true dual reactivity to both HIV-1 and HIV-2 became available during 1989–90.

---

[4] P. N. Lelie, H. W. Reesink, and H. Huisman, 'Evaluation of six enzyme immunoassays for antibody against human immunodeficiency virus', *Lancet* ii (1986): 483–6.

[5] DHSS, 'Information for doctors concerning the introduction of the LAV/HTLV III antibody test', *DHSS* (Oct. 1985) CMO (85) 12.

[6] F. Clavel, D. Guetard, F. Brun-Vezinet, S. Chamaret, M. Rey, M. O. Santos-Ferreira, *et al.*, 'Isolation of a new human retrovirus from West African patients with AIDS', *Science* **233** (1986): 343–6.

Screening and Testing

The development of test systems for the detection of antibody to HIV led to their application in a series of approaches which can be broadly divided into screening and testing.

Screening is the wide-scale application of a single antibody test for HIV to selected populations and may be on a named or anonymous basis. In the UK, the former would include screening of blood donors and voluntary antenatal screening, and the latter would include unlinked anonymous screening of genitourinary medicine clinic attendees, intravenous drug users, antenatal clinic attendees, and neonates.

Testing is the process whereby individual patients are investigated for the presence or absence of HIV antibody either because they present with a clinical illness which may be indicative of HIV infection or because they have been identified as being at risk of HIV infection and have requested a test for HIV antibody (through general practitioners, genitourinary medicine clinics, HIV clinics, same-day testing centres, etc.). Such approaches each generate their own particular dilemmas, many of which are discussed elsewhere in this volume.

The Tests

It is not the intention, nor is it within the scope, of this brief account to give an exhaustive description of all assay types. Tests for detection of HIV infection can have a range of formats and can be based on:

Detection of antibody

(i) *Enzyme immunoassays (EIA)*
     Whole virus lysates
     Recombinant protein antigens
     Synthetic antigens (peptides)
(ii) *Other screening assays*
     Particle agglutination assays
     Haemagglutination assays
     Latex agglutination assays
     Solid phase immunoassays

(iii) *Confirmatory tests*
      Immunoblotting (Western blotting, line immunoassays)
      Immunofluorescence assays (IFA)
      Radioimmuno precipitation assays (RIPA)
      Virus neutralization

Detection of virus or viral antigens

  (i) Virus culture
 (ii) Enzyme immunoassays (antigen capture)
(iii) Radioimmunoassay
(iv) Polymerase chain reaction (PCR)

The majority of laboratories testing for antibody to HIV utilize some form(s) of EIA since these are readily available, fit into the testing routine of most virus laboratories, and results can be quantified and records retained.

In its simplest form the EIA would take the form shown in Fig. 2.2. There is some sort of solid phase (plastic well, plastic bead) coated with HIV antigen(s) to which is added the test serum which may or may not contain antibodies to the virus. After a period of time, during which any HIV antibodies should combine with the antigen on the solid phase, the serum is removed and unreacted antibodies are washed off. Following this an anti-human immunoglobulin (antibody to human antibodies) raised in some other animal (often goat) and labelled with an enzyme (horseradish peroxidase or alkaline phosphatase) is added to the system. Again, after a period of incubation, the unreacted antibodies are washed away and a colourless chemical substrate for the enzyme is added. If all layers of the reaction mix have remained adherent, the enzyme will react with the

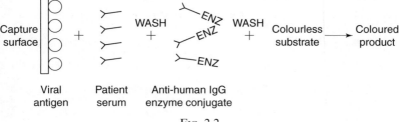

FIG. 2.2

substrate to produce a coloured product which can be detected by eye and whose level may be quantitated using a special reader.

The initial tests to become available were, of course, prepared from HIV-1 and utilized whole virus recovered from lysed, infected, cultured lymphocytes as an antigen. Unfortunately there are a number of problems which have subsequently become apparent in the use of such lysates. They are extremely variable from one batch to another with respect to the range and quantity of the viral antigens they contain. They also contain proteins (mitochondria, histocompatibility antigens) from the cells used to grow the virus and from constituents (sera) of the cell culture medium. Such assays generally lacked specificity and were prone to show false reactivity (false-'positive' results) due, amongst other reasons, to reaction of patient antibodies (e.g. antimitochondrial, anti-HLA) with these non-HIV antigens in the test systems. In the early days of HIV testing a number of salutary lessons, both from the patient aspect and from the laboratory side, were learned about the importance of ensuring specific, true positive results. The occurrence of even a small number of false positive results can have profound implications when testing a population who might be at low risk of infection (e.g. blood donors). Similarly, of course, false negative results arising from inadequately sensitive assays can have serious consequences for recipients of infectious blood or tissues. Such concerns led to the adoption of a multiple-test approach for reactive sera together with the derivation and publication of suggested test algorithms. Such a test approach is still used in those countries whose health care systems can support the cost even though the specificity of present test systems is very high.[7]

Reactivity against HIV-1 and HIV-2 together with considerably increased specificity and sensitivity, has been achieved by the replacement of crude viral lysate with either recombinant antigens[8] or synthetic peptides.[9] Recombinant antigens became available when the genome of HIV was sequenced and its genes identified. The genes could then be excised, inserted into an expression vector which could

[7] PHLS AIDS Diagnosis Working Group, 'Towards error free HIV diagnosis: notes on laboratory practice', *PHLS Microbiology Digest* **9** (1992): 61–4.

[8] P. N. Lelie, C. L. van der Poel, H. W. Reesink, H. G. Huisman, C. A. B. Boucher, and J. Goudsmit, 'Efficacy of the latest generation of antibody assays for (early) detection of HIV 1 and HIV 2 infection', *Vox Sanguinis* **56** (1989): 59–61.

[9] L. McAlpine, J. V. Parry, P. P. Mortimer, and C. MacDonald, 'Sixteen combined anti-HIV 1/2 screening assays', *Medical Devices Directorate Evaluation Report* (1993) MDD/93/17.

then be transfected into a bacterial or yeast system and the HIV antigen could be recovered in high quantity from the culture fluid. Sequencing the genome also permitted the synthesis of completely synthetic peptides (15–40 amino-acids long) which mimicked the antigenic sites (epitopes) on the native HIV proteins. There are several advantages to such approaches. No infectious virus is handled, false test reactions due to spurious proteins are minimized or eliminated, and since the antigenic material is physically small compared with whole virus a high density of antigen can be packed onto the solid phase which leads to a high level of test sensitivity.

The current range of EIAs for HIV-1 and HIV-2 represent some of, if not the, most sensitive serological tests currently available for the diagnosis of infectious disease.

New HIV Variants

HIV is a virus which is capable of exhibiting considerable genetic, and hence phenotypic, change both within a single, infected individual and within the world population as a whole. Two highly divergent isolates of HIV-1, provisionally named subtype 'O' to designate that they are genetic 'Outliers' of the currently accepted HIV-1 family, have recently been described and characterized.[10] They appear to be largely associated with patients of Cameroon origin but a few infections have also been reported in Gabon and France. It has become apparent that some commonly used anti-HIV screening kits fail to identify patients infected with the viruses.[11]

It is perhaps not surprising that such strains appear from time to time but it highlights the need both for kit manufacturers and laboratories using screening kits to be aware of such possibilities, however remote, and respond to such situations rapidly. Serum panels from persons infected with HIV-O have been collected together and these

[10] L. G. Gurtler, P. H. Hauser, J. Eberle, A. von Brunne, S. Knapp, and L. Zekeng, 'A new subtype of human immunodeficiency virus type 1 (MVP-5180) from Cameroon', *Jounal of Virology* **68** (1994): 1581–5; M. V. Haesevelde, J.-L. Decourt, R. J. de Leys, B. Vanderborgt, G. van der Groen, H. van Heuverswijn, *et al.*, 'Genomic cloning and complete sequence analysis of a highly divergent African human immunodeficiency virus isolate', *Journal of Virology* **68** (1994): 1586–96.

[11] I. Loussert-Ajaka, T. D. Ly, M. L. Chaix, D. Ingrand, S. Saragosti, A. M. Courouce, *et al.*, 'HIV-1/HIV-2 seronegativity in HIV-1 subtype O infected patients', *Lancet* **343** (1994): 1393–4.

have been used to determine which commercial kits are likely to fail to detect individuals infected with such variants.

Laboratory Test Approaches

In view of the range of assays available a test approach generally adopted is for the patient serum to be assayed for HIV-1 and HIV-2 antibodies by EIA and if there is no reaction in the initial screen a negative report is issued. If the initial screen is 'reactive', a second test approach of a mechanistically different nature is employed to retest the serum. The rationale behind this is the argument that a false-positive reaction generated in the first type of test is unlikely to be generated in the second type of test if the mechanism by which it can be generated is absent (see below).

Should the second test produce a 'reactive' result it is not unusual for a laboratory to use a third (confirmatory or supplemental) assay such as Western blot or line immunoassay (LIA) before issuing a positive report. These latter tests employ solid phases such as white nitrocellulose on which a range of antigens of the virus are present and an EIA is performed which localizes a colour reaction at each point on the nitrocellulose where patient antibody reacts with HIV antigen. It is possible with the LIA to incorporate both HIV-1 and HIV-2 antigens in the same strip since these are striped on using a machine and as the antigens are recombinant or peptide they can be quantified ensuring excellent batch uniformity leading to highly reproducible results. It is only after completion of three reactive tests that laboratories in the UK would normally report a patient positive for HIV antibody.

Such a test result indicates previous exposure to HIV, persistent infection with the virus (since the virus integrates a DNA copy of its genome into the chromosome of infected human cells), and infectiousness (which will vary in degree during the remainder of the infected person's lifetime). Contrary to the preaching of the popular press this is not an AIDS test since AIDS is a clinical, not a laboratory, diagnosis.

Sensitivity, Specificity, and Predictive Value of Serological Tests

The determination of a test result as positive or negative can be a complex procedure and relies on choosing a test with a high positive predictive value. This was defined by Galen and Gambino as 'how accurately a test predicts the presence or absence of disease'.[12]

The answer can be derived from an analysis of three variables—sensitivity, specificity, and prevalence.

For an antibody screening assay, sensitivity can be defined as the ability of an assay to score samples from infected individuals as positive for specific antibodies and samples should include those taken in the early stages of seroconversion (e.g. IgM response, low antibody levels) as well as those taken in the later stages of the disease (e.g. IgG response).

Specificity can be defined as the ability of an assay to score samples from non-infected individuals as negative for specific antibodies and samples should include those from normal healthy donors together with those from individuals affected by other diseases including pathological conditions which might give rise to false-positive reactions.

Prevalence can be defined as the incidence (cases per 100,000) of the disease of interest in the population being tested within a given time period.

The positive predictive value (PPV) of a serological assay is the percentage of positive results that are true positives when the test is used to screen a mixed population of both uninfected and infected individuals. Likewise the negative predictive value (NPV) is the percentage of negative results that are true negatives. The values obtained will depend on the number of false positives and false negatives produced by the test under evaluation in relation to the number of true positives and true negatives and the prevalence of infection in the population.

$$\text{Sensitivity} = \frac{\text{True positives}}{\text{True positives} + \text{False negatives}} \times 100$$

$$\text{Specificity} = \frac{\text{True negatives}}{\text{True negatives} + \text{False positives}} \times 100$$

[12] R. S. Galen, and S. R. Gambino, *Beyond Normality: The Predictive Value and Efficiency of Medical Diagnosis* (New York: Wiley, 1975).

$$\text{Positive predictive value} = \frac{\text{True positives}}{\text{True positives} + \text{False positives}} \times 100$$

$$\text{Negative predictive value} = \frac{\text{True negatives}}{\text{True negatives} + \text{False negatives}} \times 100$$

An ideal serological test would establish the presence or absence of infection in every individual screened, i.e. there would never be any false-positive or false-negative results.

In practice, the perfect test does not exist. This becomes particularly evident when screening populations who might be expected to have a low prevalence of antibody under test. In the case of HIV antibody such a population would be UK blood donors. The currently available tests for HIV antibody are extremely sensitive (>99.8 per cent) and specific (>99.8 per cent) but the prevalence of HIV infection in many of the populations screened is often <0.1 per cent.

The PPV of EIA tests for screening blood donations (assumed prevalence 0.02 per cent) using such tests would be 9.0 per cent which means that for every true positive detected, nine other sera will be incorrectly identified as positive in an initial screening.

As the prevalence of infection in the population increases the incidence of false positives decreases. At a prevalence of 1.0 per cent the same EIA test will have a PPV of 83.4 per cent and at a prevalence of 10 per cent the PPV will have risen to 98.2 per cent.

Thus in test populations with a high prevalence of HIV infection a single test for antibody will detect a large proportion of true positives and yield relatively few false positives. Use of a single screening assay on a population with a low prevalence of HIV infection is simply not acceptable since many of the 'reactive' results obtained will be false positives. The way round this problem is to use additional EIAs or other supplementary tests (Western blot, LIA) to retest initially reactive sera.

Other Test Approaches

Any brief outline of HIV testing would be incomplete without a mention of the value of detection of the core (p24) antigen of the virus and of the polymerase chain reaction. Detection of the p24 antigen (so called because the protein has a molecular weight of 24 kilodaltons) can be achieved by using an EIA based on the technology previously outlined. In this type of test the plate carries an antibody to the p24 antigen which will capture any free p24 antigen in the patient serum. Such captured antigen is then detected by way of an enzyme-labelled anti-p24 antibody and a suitable substrate.

The test may be positive in a serum taken from an infected patient in the period prior to the development of antibodies, may become positive during the asymptomatic phase of the infection, and is generally positive when patients move into overt HIV disease. It is not a test which has been applied in screening programmes, but is of diagnostic value only.

The HIV polymerase chain reaction (PCR)[13] is an elegant molecular diagnostic technique which employs small pieces of single-stranded nucleic acid, chosen to be specific for the virus, to prime a reaction in which large quantities of a section of the pro-viral DNA genome can be replicated in the laboratory. In an optimized reaction the amplification can be one millionfold and the net result is that readily detectable quantities of a piece of HIV genome can be rapidly produced in the laboratory from patient material such as infected white blood cells.

The most useful application of this technique in the diagnostic laboratory has been in the examination of neonatal blood.

Laboratory Diagnosis of HIV Infection in Children

AIDS was first reported in children in 1982 in the USA and in 1984 in Europe. The World Health Organization (WHO) has estimated that over one million children have been infected with HIV worldwide.[14] The most common route of HIV infection in children is vertically from the mother. Such infection can occur during development in the womb (*in utero*),[15] during birth (intra-partum),[16] or after

---

[13] C. Y. Ou, S. Kwok, S. W. Mitchell, D. H. Mack, J. J. Sninsky, J. W. Krebs, *et al.*, 'DNA amplification for direct detection of HIV-1 in DNA of peripheral blood mononuclear cells', *Science* **239** (1988): 295–7.

[14] WHO, 'Current and future dimensions of the HIV/AIDS pandemic: a capsule summary', WHO/GPA/RES/SF1/92.1 (1992).

[15] E. Jovaisas, M. A. Koch, A. Schafer, M. Stauber, and D. Lowenthal, 'LAV/HTLV III in 20-week fetus', *Lancet* **ii** (1985): 1129.

[16] A. Ehrnst, S. Lindgren, M. Dictor, B. Johansson, A. Sonnerborg, J. Czajkowski, *et al.*, 'HIV in pregnant women and their offspring: evidence for late transmission', *Lancet* **338** (1991): 1007–12.

birth via breastmilk (post-partum)[17] and at present it is not possible to reliably determine the proportion of infections falling into each category.

Definitive determination of infection in the neonate can be problematic. Tests for HIV antibody are currently of no value since an HIV-positive, pregnant woman will pass large amounts of antibody to her developing child transplacentally (the natural process whereby a mother transfers a broad spectrum of immunity to her newborn thus offering protection to a wide range of common pathogens during the first 6–9 months of life).

In theory it might be possible to detect HIV-specific IgM in the neonate since this antibody class is too big to cross the placenta and hence, if present, must have been formed *de novo* by the child. In practice, tests for the detection of HIV IgM have not proved to be of value.

For many years after the development of HIV antibody tests a diagnosis of infection in the child, in the absence of clinical illness, was assumed if a positive HIV antibody test persisted beyond fifteen months.

In the last two to three years improved technologies have permitted refinement of both the p24 antigen test[18] and the polymerase chain reaction (Roche Diagnostic Systems, Herts) to allow reliable diagnosis of HIV infection in the neonate during the first 1–3 months of life.

Quality Assurance, Quality Control, and Quality Assessment

Quality assurance is the total process whereby the quality of laboratory services can be guaranteed and represents a continuing process of monitoring test systems for reproducibility and reliability thus facilitating corrective action when problems are detected.

Quality control covers the laboratory procedures which are designed to achieve this end and should cover all aspects of the laboratory from receipt of the specimen to issue of the report.

[17] P. Van de Perre, A. Simonon, P. Msellati, D.-G. Hitimana, D. Vaira, A. Bazubagira, *et al.*, 'Postnatal transmission of human immunodeficiency virus type 1 from mother to infant', *New England Journal of Medicine* 325 (1991): 593–8.

[18] L. Kestens, G. Hoofd, P. L. Gigase, R. Deleys, and G. van der Groen, 'HIVag detection in circulating immune complexes', *Journal of Virological Methods* 31 (1991): 67–76.

Quality assessment is the process whereby quality control procedures are challenged by submission of specimens of known, but
undisclosed, content (proficiency testing).

It is essential that any laboratory undertaking serological testing
of patient material adopts appropriate systems to monitor the accuracy and reproducibility of results. At HIV-test level these should
include the examination of appropriate positive and negative serum
controls and ideally the examination of appropriate internal positive
control sera[19] and/or seroconversion panels together with regular
participation in external quality assessment schemes.

Counselling, Consent, and Confidentiality

In the UK a test for HIV antibody has been available on request
through general practitioners, genitourinary medicine clinics, and
special HIV clinics since the test was introduced in 1985. It has been
Department of Health policy that the offer of a test be accompanied
by appropriate pre- and post-test counselling and that the issues of
informed consent and confidentiality are fully addressed. These
issues were also fully endorsed by the British Medical Association[20]
and the UK Central Council for Nursing, Midwifery and Health
Visiting.[21]

Counselling

The main purpose of the pre-test counselling is to make the person
fully aware of the nature of the test and of the fact that it is a test for
HIV infection and not AIDS. Points for discussion would normally
include reasons for requesting the test, possible risk activities, what
the test result will mean, the attitude to a positive result, the attitude
to a negative result, whether the result should be discussed with
others, and the social stigma of undergoing HIV testing.

Post-test counselling is absolutely essential in order to ensure that
the recipient of the test result can fully consider the implications

[19] D. Samuel, 'The preparation and use of hepatitis and HIV quality control sera
for internal quality control', in J. Hawkins (ed.), *Internal Quality Control for
Serodiagnosis: Principles and Practice* (London: PHLS, 1994): 4–5.

[20] British Medical Association, 'HIV antibody testing: summary of BMA guidance', *British Medical Journal* **295** (1987): 940.

[21] UKCC, *Confidentiality*, UKCC Advisory Paper, April 1987.

for himself of either a positive or, just as importantly, a negative result.

Pre- and post-test counselling should ideally be carried out by the same person.

Consent

The UK Central Council for Nursing, Midwifery and Health Visiting gives clear advice that practitioners expose themselves to the possibility of civil action or criminal charges if they personally take blood specimens without consent. If they knowingly collude with a doctor in obtaining such specimens, then charges of aiding and abetting an assault are liable.

The General Medical Council also makes it clear that HIV testing requires the explicit consent of the patient which should be preceded by appropriate counselling.

Confidentiality

Issues of consent and confidentiality are covered in detail elsewhere in this volume. However, these are both issues in which laboratories undertaking HIV-antibody tests frequently find themselves involved. Laboratory requests cards often give no indication that the patient has consented to the test and the onus for determining this then falls onto laboratory personnel. Also laboratories are frequently asked to fax results of HIV antibody tests to open facsimile machines in surgeries, wards, and offices.

Changing Approaches

In December 1992 in the UK, the Department of Health (DoH) issued guidance on the extension of HIV testing through additional sites.[22] The guidance was discussed at length during the early part of 1993 but there was a general feeling that a widespread extension of the service offered was not necessary and, more importantly, no additional funding was available for such service extension.

---

[22] Department of Health, 'Additional sites for HIV antibody testing', *DOH* PL/CO(92)5 (1992).

However, there was a general agreement that a more rapid turn-around of results was desirable since many clinics/laboratories were operating a seven-to-fourteen-day system leading to an agonizingly long wait for those persons pursuing an HIV test. There are now a large number of same-day or twenty-four-hour testing clinics operating in the UK although the laboratory test regimes offered through such clinics differ considerably and have not always yielded a fully confirmed result on the day that the blood sample was taken.

My own laboratory offers fully confirmed HIV antibody testing on a same-day/twenty-four-hour basis on four days of the week using an initial highly sensitive, peptide-based EIA for primary screening followed by concurrent tests using a gel-agglutination test and a solid phase immunoassay for sera which initially test reactive.[23]

New Developments in Testing Procedures

There have been a number of areas of test development in recent years. Of particular interest have been the development of rapid tests and of tests which permit antibody detection in body fluids such as urine and saliva.

Rapid tests permit the determination of a test result in about ten minutes. Such systems are based on sealed cartridge units carrying a membrane in which HIV-1 and HIV-2 specific antigens are immobilized and beneath which is an absorbent material to facilitate flow of reactants through the membrane. In effect an EIA is performed upon the membrane and any reactivity shows up in the generation of a coloured spot or symbol. These devices are extremely sensitive but display a lower specificity than conventional EIAs thus yielding more 'false-positive' reactions.[24]

Salivary and urine tests for anti-HIV antibody are in an early phase of evaluation.[25] It is important that the salivary samples examined should be rich in crevicular fluid (from the crevice between the

[23] D. J. Morris, G. Corbitt, and E. Crosdale, 'Same-day testing for human immunodeficiency virus antibodies', *Journal of Virological Methods* **49** (1994): 367–70.

[24] G. Leadbetter, J. F. Peutherer, S. Burns, J. M. Inglis, J. V. Parry, P. P. Mortimer, *et al.*, 'Ortho Diagnostics (DuPont) Hivchek 1 + 2 anti-HIV kit' *Medical Devices Directorate Evaluation Report*, MDD/91/05 (1991).

[25] P. P. Mortimer and J. V. Parry, 'Non-invasive virological diagnosis: Are saliva and urine samples adequate substitutes for blood?', *Reviews in Medical Virology* **1** (1991): 73–8.

gum margin and the teeth) since this fluid reflects the constituents of the plasma. Work is underway to determine the best devices for collecting such specimens. Since both saliva and urine have been shown to contain a range of immunoglobulin molecules the assays for anti-HIV antibody have been based on techniques whereby the test surface carries an antibody to human immunoglobulin which will capture human antibodies when the specimen is added to the system. The portion, if any, of these antibodies which are specific for HIV is then sought out by adding HIV antigen combined in some way with an enzyme which, after addition of a substrate, will generate a colour signal indicating a positive result.

The advantages of saliva/urine tests are that they are non-invasive, simple, rapid, inexpensive, and can be readily applied to children, intravenous drug users, and large survey populations.

One of the worries about all three of these test approaches is that they lend themselves to opportunities for 'self-testing' by individuals and there have been fears that they may become generally available over pharmacy counters in a similar way to pregnancy kits. There are clear dangers in this, particularly with respect to avoidance of access to appropriate counselling and in the higher level of 'false-positive' reactions generated. In the UK legislation has been passed which forbids companies producing and marketing such kits from retailing them to anyone other than bona fide testing laboratories.[26]

The Future

Development of HIV tests along four lines may be expected.

There will be continuing investigation of testing methods using non-invasive samples such as saliva and urine since there are distinct advantages for both patients and health care staff in eliminating the use of needles and venepuncture procedures.

There will be development of kits and test devices which permit the simultaneous detection of a range of reactivities to different infectious agents. For example in the UK it is presently mandatory to test organ donors for hepatitis B, hepatitis C, and HIV, and a number of companies are working to produce a test device which will perform all three assays at once.

[26] Public Health, England and Wales. Public Health, Scotland (1992). Statutory Instrument 460. The HIV Testing Kits and Services Regulations 1992. HMSO.

There is a move also to simplify test procedures to a point where tests can be performed outside the diagnostic laboratory, e.g. in the doctor's surgery or at the patient's bedside, but of course this would require the production of extremely reliable, as well as rapid, test systems.

Finally, there are moves to produce more sensitive tests, perhaps based on the detection of immunoglobulin M (the first antibody type to be produced during the course of an infection) and immunoglobulin A (secretory immunoglobulin produced at mucosal surfaces). Such kits should permit an earlier diagnosis and thus narrow the window period which precedes the development of antibodies.

The future will also see changes in the way in which tests are employed and there are continuing pressures for the adoption of wider application of the test procedures and easing of the informed consent rules from some quarters.

The balance between the advantages and disadvantages of having an HIV test is a contentious and constantly changing issue which necessarily parallels our changing knowledge about the infection.

In view of the adverse psychological and social consequences of a positive test result some health professionals and voluntary carers have actively discouraged HIV testing urging that the adoption of 'safer' sexual and drug-using behaviour will prevent transmission of HIV.

More recently there has been a shift to promote the clinical advantages of knowing HIV-antibody status as early as possible. The Chief Medical Officer for the DoH in 1990 voiced support for HIV-antibody testing for people who believe they may have been at risk from HIV. There have been several studies which suggest that some people who are HIV positive but free of symptoms could benefit from the early use of the anti-HIV drug Zidovudine and from prophylaxis (preventive treatment) against a very common lung infection of patients with HIV disease known as pneumocystis pneumonia.

The former belief has again generated numerous dilemmas. There is a lack of information about the effects of Zidovudine treatment in women and the drug is not recommended for women who are pregnant.

On a more controversial note the results of a large Anglo-French three-year study (Concorde) of the effects of Zidovudine indicate that there is no long-term benefit on either survival or progression to

AIDS when the drug is given early in the course of infection compared with being given at the onset of HIV disease.[27] However, this conclusion is not generally accepted and appears to be at variance with the findings of some other chemotherapeutic trials.[28]

Nonetheless there has been an overall trend towards change in our attitudes to HIV testing from initial discouragement to the active promotion by the DoH of greater availability of testing.

[27] Concorde Co-ordinating Committee, 'Concorde: MRC/ANRS randomised double-blind controlled trial of immediate and deferred zidovudine in symptom-free HIV infection', *Lancet* **343** (1994): 871–81.

[28] D. A. Cooper, J. M. Gatell, S. Kroon, N. Clumeck, J. Millard, F. D. Goebel, *et al.*, 'Zidovudine in persons with asymptomatic HIV infection and CD4+ cell counts greater than 400 per cubic millimeter', *New England Journal of Medicine* **329** (1993): 297–303.

3

Counselling and HIV Testing: Ethical Dilemmas

LORRAINE SHERR

Counselling has become a catchword associated with HIV infection and AIDS. It has entered the arena from the start of the epidemic as a direct result of the need for information transfer, behaviour change, and as a possible solution to action in the face of ignorance and uncertainty. Yet now, with the hindsight of over a decade of experience with HIV infection and AIDS, the nuances of counselling, psychological intervention, and client care need to be carefully scrutinized. A variety of ethical issues permeate the debate and cannot be overlooked.

Psychological issues ramify throughout the field of HIV and AIDS work, from prevention, to testing, to disease handling, and to carer interventions. The range of interventions under this umbrella is vast, often disparate, and rarely comprehensively evaluated. This chapter will attempt to examine some of the benefits and pitfalls of psychological care and approaches in HIV infection and to evaluate the efficacy of current strategies. This will be carried out with a particular focus on potentially sensitive ethical areas, especially in relation to HIV testing, confidentiality, and rights.

Psychological Care

Psychological care is not a new concept. Consumer demands in health care have resulted in a growing lobby to provide for emotional care in the presence of physical illness. This was often unsatisfactory because of insufficient training and skills of medical practitioners,[1]

---

[1] See G. P. Maguire and D. R. Rutter, 'History taking for medical students—deficiencies in performance', *Lancet* (Sept. 1976): 356–8; P. Maguire, S. Fairbarn, and

insufficient time in medical consultations,[2] a belief in the medical model for illness and health,[3] or for economic or social restraints. HIV and AIDS opened a new chapter. Not only was the medical cure elusive, but the disease was transmissible and stigma-bound. Behaviour and behaviour change were key elements for understanding, management, intervention, and scrutiny—thus placing the whole epidemic into the realms of behavioural science. It also provided a new opportunity and a new beginning which probably facilitated the incorporation of psychological care into HIV and AIDS care from the start of the epidemic in the West.

Input generally took the form of unmonitored 'counselling', and tended to focus on two key areas, namely HIV testing and care of the individual with HIV infection or AIDS.

HIV Testing

Early on in the epidemic an antibody test became available to examine the presence of antibodies to human immunodeficiency virus (HIV).[4] This antibody test had high specificity and sensitivity, and, when used in conjunction with confirmatory tests, was able to identify antibody in blood samples (and latterly in saliva samples). Although of enormous potential utility, such a test has inherent limitations. These surround the whole nature of testing, as well as some of the limitations of the test itself. The test could not identify source of infection, disease state or stage, or predict disease course or outcome. It was also limited in that, as an antibody test, it could only register positive when sufficient quantum of antibody had been produced. This could take up to twelve weeks and run the risk of missing true infection in this early 'window' period, when an individual may not only be HIV positive, but also viraemic and thus potentially

C. Fletcher, 'Consultation skills of young doctors: benefits of feedback training in interviewing as medical students persist', *British Medical Journal* **292** (1986): 1573–6; G. P. Maguire, 'Doctor patient skills', in M. Argyle (ed.), *Social Skills and Health* (London: Methuen, 1981); P. Ley, *Communicating with Patients—Improving Communication, Satisfaction and Compliance* (London: Croom Helm , 1988).

[2] See Ley, *Communicating with Patients*.

[3] See M. Stacey, *Changing Human Reproduction—Social Science Perspectives* (London: Sage, 1993).

[4] See P. Mortimer, 'ABC of AIDS: The virus and the tests', *British Medical Journal* **294** (1987): 1602–5.

more able to transmit infection to others. Ultimately, its limitation lies in its ability to detect a condition for which there is no cure.

Counselling around this particular test had a crucial role. Ideally counselling was put forward as the remedy to a number of problems, namely:

Informed consent

As with all tests, there is a need for an individual to consent, from a basis of full information, to a test with dramatic sequelae on their life. Guidelines for consent provide for prior consent, medical advice, and patient decisions.

Pre-test counselling was put forward as the solution to this issue. Yet McCann and Wadsworth noted that 59 per cent of a cohort of 252 HIV-positive gay men reported no information at the time their blood was taken. [5]

The question of informed consent where children is concerned is invariably ignored in study reports.

Risk assessment

As HIV is transmitted in specific ways (via body fluids, sexually, via organ transplants, and transplacentally), clear case histories could allow for informed risk assessment. This was relevant for both possible infection and future prevention. However, such assessment is obviously contingent on full disclosure and hence the establishment of trust is a key element for accurate appraisal. Although short interventions are possible to assess risk,[6] full trust and interaction may take longer.

Preparation for test outcome

The dramatic effects of HIV infection and AIDS on life expectancy, life course, sexuality,[7] procreation,[8] health,[9] and psychological

[5] K. McCann and E. Wadsworth, 'The experience of having positive HIV antibody test', *AIDS Care* **3**/1 (1991): 43–53.

[6] See R. Bor, R. Millar, and H. Salt, 'Uptake of HIV testing following counselling', *Sexual and Marital Therapy* **6**/1 (1991): 25–8; R. Bor, R. Millar, and M. Johnson, 'A testing time for doctors counselling patients before an HIV test', *British Medical Journal* **303** (1991): 905–6.

[7] See D. Ostrow, *Behavioural Aspects of AIDS* (New York: Plenum Press, 1990).

[8] See L. Sherr, S. Jefferies, and C. Victor, 'General Practice pregnancy care and the challenges of HIV', *AIDS Patient Care* **6**/2 (1991): 62–6.

[9] See A. M. Johnson and M. W. Adler, 'ABC of AIDS. Strategies for prevention', *British Medical Journal* (Clin Res ed.), **295**/6594 (1987): 373–6.

well-being[10] required sound preparation. This was (and still is) considered a specific remit which necessitated high-quality counselling to pre-empt and possibly prevent psychological trauma and to promote coping.

Behaviour change

Perhaps the most important factor associated with HIV testing was the role of behaviour and behaviour change. From the start of the epidemic specific behaviour has been associated with virus spread. It is the self-same behaviour adjustment which prevents spread, and protects against infection. Thus behaviour change needs to be addressed in those who test negative and those who test positive. Indeed, there are many who argue that the test itself is probably less relevant than the behaviour change associated with the testing process.

However, such behaviour change is not automatic.[11] Although pre- and perhaps post-test counselling was initially presumed to be the panacea against any at-risk behaviour, psychological models have always pointed out the complexity of human behaviour, and the great difficulties experienced in any attempts to change behaviour, yet alone sustain such changes in the longer term. In effect, the magic of counselling could possibly never, in one-off sessions, change people's sexual and drug-using behaviour.

There are others who question the link between counselling and directive behaviour change. This is especially problematic when the behaviour change is not one such as protection against transmission of HIV via sex (e.g. the adoption of condoms) but where there are less clear objectives such as the discouraging of HIV-infected women from becoming pregnant or bearing children.[12]

[10] See S. Perry, L. Jacobsberg, and B. Fishman, 'Suicidal ideation and HIV testing', *Journal of the American Medical Association* **263** (1990): 678–82.

[11] D. Higgins, C. O. Gallavotti, K. Reilly, D. Schnell, M. Moore, D. Rugg, D. and R. Johnson, 'Evidence of the effects of HIV antibody counselling and testing on risk behaviours', *Journal of the American Medical Association* **266**/17 (1991): 2419–29; British Psychological Society Special Interest Group on AIDS, *Consultative Document on Counselling HIV Testing and Behaviour Change* (UK Dept. of Health, 1993).

[12] See Working Group on HIV Testing of Pregnant Women and Newborns, 'HIV Infection: Pregnant Women and Newborns—A Policy Proposal for Information and Testing', *Journal of the American Medical Association* **264**/18 (1990): 2416–20.

Therapeutic care

Counselling, prior to testing as well as immediately upon receipt of results, could potentially provide the initial point for good therapeutic relationships. This may be an essential requirement in the event of future HIV infection which may tax the individual's coping to the limit as they navigate through the traumatic phases of HIV disease.

Information provision, decision-making, and a balanced consideration of costs and/or benefits, advantages and/or disadvantages are relevant in situations where testing is voluntary. True counselling cannot be undertaken in circumstances where the test is compulsory (i.e. where effective choice is not built into the counselling process), or where there is discrimination based on the test outcome.

Decision-making

The provision of counselling would facilitate, allow, and even promote individual decision-making. This is of particular importance when there is no cure to hand, when medical interventions are still subject to debate, and where prophylaxis has side effects which ought to be weighed clearly in terms of advantages and disadvantages. An interesting example of this is the recent promotion of antibiotic treatment of young babies to protect against AIDS-related respiratory infections. Given the difficulties in establishing true positivity in newborns, it would mean unnecessary drug treatment for children (up to 87 per cent according to the European Collaborative Study estimates) who would subsequently serorevert and be virus free.[13]

Decision-making about treatment to prevent vertical transmission of HIV may also be crucial. Currently there are a number of advances in interventions, all fraught with complex decision pathways. Trial ACTG 076 showed that the administration of Zidovudine to women during pregnancy, labour, and to the infant for six weeks reduced vertical transmission from 25 to 8.3 per cent.[14] However, it is unclear which element of the protocol was effective, whether the results generalize to all women with HIV, what the

---

[13] European Collaborative Study, 'Risk factors for mother-to-child transmission of HIV-1', *Lancet* **339** (1992): 1007–12.

[14] E. Connor, R. Sperlling, R. Gelber, *et al.*, 'Reduction of maternal infant transmission of HIV type 1 with Zidovudine treatment', *New England Journal of Medicine* **331** (1994): 1173–80.

long-term effect of AZT on the unborn child could be (especially for the three-quarters of the sample who would not have been HIV infected anyway),[15] and what the effect of monotherapy on the women's future drug resistance and combination therapy treatment would be.[16]

What are the Presumptions of Counselling?

Presumptions of counselling are rarely clarified. Yet it would seem that if the decision to test has already been taken, counselling takes on a different role from one of 'informed decision-making'. For example, St Louis *et al.* report on all USA applicants to Job Corps who 'began screening for HIV antibody on all residents' and 'all receive counselling before and after testing and are notified of test results'.[17]

Can there be counselling (and, indeed, informed consent) if the test is to be carried out routinely anyway? Van Lith reported that 5–25 per cent of pregnant women studied did not feel completely unrestrained in making up their mind whether to undergo a test.[18]

Why Test?

In most areas the use of any test needs careful consideration. This is fed by the accuracy of the test outcome, the test procedures themselves, the impact and ramification of the result, and finally the cures

---

[15] P. Rowe, 'US Expert panel reaffirms benefit of perinatal zidovudine', *Lancet* **349** (Jan. 1997): 258; P. Toltzis, C. Marx, N. Kleinman, E. Levine, and E. Schmidt, 'Zidovudine-associated embryonic toxicity in mice', *Journal of Infectious Diseases* **163**/6 (1991): 1212–18.

[16] For a full discussion, see H. Minkoff and M. Augenbraum, 'Antiretroviral therapy for pregnant women', *American Journal of Obstetrics and Gynecology* **176**/2 (1977): 478–89; as well as the *Lancet* report on the occurrence of vaginal cancers in the progeny of Zidovudine-treated mice (**349** (Jan. 1997)); and for the impact of a positive test on pregnant women see e.g. J. Laurence, 'Zidovudine in pregnancy—More questions than answers', *AIDS Reader* **4** (1994): 74–6.

[17] M. St Louis, G. Conway, C. Hayman, C. Millar, L. Petersen, and T. Donero, 'HIV infection in disadvantaged adolescents', *Journal of the American Medical Association* **266**/17 (1991): 2388.

[18] J. Van Lith, T. Tijmstra, and G. Visser, 'The attitudes of pregnant women towards HIV testing', *Nederlands Tijdschrift voor Geneeskunde* **133**/25 (1989): 1273–7.

and interventions available to ameliorate or eradicate the condition highlighted by the test. With HIV infection this is problematic.

Testing can be carried out for personal information, for hospital or research information, for epidemiological purposes, or for preventive measures. Test procedures can be informed or anonymous. People who are screened can either self-refer, be counselled, identified by a series of defined risks, or routinely offered testing. There are many variants of these procedures where centres offer 'opt-in' or 'opt-out' options.

Some centres test in the belief that options are taken up which in reality are not. For example, the issue of termination of pregnancy shows wide variation. In one study, Sherr *et al.* found that 60 per cent of doctors treating pregnant women strongly endorsed advising termination in the presence of HIV and believed that well over half of the women would actually terminate.[19] In reality, under 10 per cent opt for termination in the presence of HIV.[20] Furthermore, of those who do terminate, many proceed to a subsequent pregnancy. Indeed, Temmerman *et al.* note that HIV-positive women who give birth to a baby who is HIV positive are more likely to want a subsequent pregnancy.[21]

Problems with HIV Testing

There has been a universal rush to screen for HIV which is fraught with problems. For a start it is not an end in itself, and simply a tool in the ongoing saga of HIV disease. Some areas have provided particularly ethical dilemmas.

[19] L. Sherr, S. Jefferies, and C. Victor, 'General practice pregnancy care and the challenges of HIV', *AIDS Patient Care* 6/2 (1992): 63.

[20] P. Selwyn, R. Carter, E. Schoenbaum, V. Robertson, R. Klein, and M. Rogers, 'Knowledge of HIV antibody status and decisions to continue or terminate pregnancy among intravenous drug users', *Journal of the American Medical Association* 261 (1989): 3567–71; F. Johnstone, R. Brettle, L. MacCallum, J. Mok, J. Peutherer, and S. Burns, 'Women's knowledge of their HIV antibody state its effect on their decision whether to continue pregnancy', *British Medical Journal* 300 (1990): 23–34.

[21] M. Temmerman, S. Moses, D. Kiragu, S. Fusallah, I. Wamola, and P. Piot, 'Impact of single session post-partum counselling of HIV infected women on their subsequent reproductive behaviour', *AIDS Care* 2/3 (1990): 247–52.

Antenatal HIV testing

As HIV can be transmitted across the placenta, there is a vast amount of antenatal HIV testing. At times this is done on request, at times as a matter of routine. Some centres ensure full informed consent, whereas others may overlook the details of such procedures. Some women are unaware of their blood being tested. Some centres (e.g. in Sweden) test all antenatal women, whereas others select. In Sweden, the 'acceptance' rate is reported as high (97 per cent).[22] Similarly, a study in Rwanda reports 'all women were tested at the time of their first prenatal visit'.[23]

The issue is one of great difficulty raising numerous ethical and legal problems. There is clearly a need to provide guardianship for the rights of those who are not able to ensure their own rights and women may be particularly vulnerable when entering the unknown territory of antenatal clinics. They are often confronted with multiple tests, and consent (whether informed or implied) may well be overlooked. In such settings agreement is invariably high (e.g. Lindsay *et al.* cite 96 per cent agreement).[24] HIV testing should be viewed within this broader context. It carries with it specific difficulties in that it is invariably the mother who is tested (despite the fact that male infection also poses a risk to the mother and the unborn child). Many centres have unclear policies about whom to test, when to test, and what testing regimes should be offered. Testing at first booking clinic (prior to twelve weeks' gestation) runs the risk of missing women in the window of infection if the very act of conception was the act of HIV transmission. One-off testing may miss new infections in women who are sexually active during pregnancy and tend not to utilize condom protection when the risk of pregnancy becomes irrelevant. Indeed, van de Pere notes that newly infected women are more likely to transmit HIV transplacentally and hence any testing

---

[22] A. Blaxhult, C. Anagrius, M. Arneborn, K. Lidman, S. Lindgren, and M. Bottiger, 'Evaluation of HIV testing in Sweden 1985–1991', *AIDS* 7 (1993): 1625–31.

[23] M. Bulterys, A. Chao, A. Dushimimana, P. Habimana, P. Nawrocki, J. B. Kurawige, F. Musanganire, and A. Saah, 'Multiple sexual partners and mother to child transmission of HIV-1', *AIDS* 7 (1993): 1640.

[24] M. Lindsay, H. Peterson, T. Feng, B. Slade, S. Willis, and L. Klein, 'Routine antepartum HIV infection screening in a inner city population', *Obstetrics and Gynaecology* **74**/1 (1989): 289–94.

policy should be particularly concerned about identification during the course of pregnancy.[25]

No study has reported on any practice or routine where the male partner is tested during pregnancy, despite the fact that maternal infection may be directly linked to paternal risk behaviour and that sexual exposure during pregnancy can affect the vertical transmission rate.[26] When the decision to inform male partners and bring them in to clinics rests with the pregnant woman, uptake is low. For example Ryder *et al.* report that only 3 per cent of male partners attended the clinic after their female partners were diagnosed as HIV positive.[27]

Centres need to have a clear understanding about whose interest is being served by such testing. Many believe the unborn infant has rights of its own. Vertical transmission rates, when studied in longer-term prospective studies, are seen to vary from as low as 12.9 per cent to approximately 30 per cent in areas of greater endemic infection and wider-spread poverty and virus penetration.[28] The cause of such variation is unclear and can reflect a host of possible factors including virus strain, host factors, background medical health, or time of exposure. Infection during pregnancy poses potentially greater risk to the neonate, yet this is seldom addressed.

Some staff may feel ill-founded concerns about their own health if treating someone with HIV infection. Although this is no rationale for screening, it certainly can account for some screening. Such fears should not be dismissed, but should rather be addressed via adequate universal infection control and staff education.

Some centres report on exceedingly high test uptakes, yet note many women do not return for results. In such circumstances the centres need to examine the impact of social pressure and high status coercion which may, wittingly or unwittingly, persuade women to

[25] P. Van de Perre, A. Simonon, P. Msellati, D. G. Hitimana, D. Vaira, A. Bazubagira, C. Van Goethem, A. M. Stevens, E. Karita, and D. Sondag-Thull, 'Postnatal transmission of HIV type 1 from mother to infant. A prospective cohort study in Kigali Rwanda', *New England Journal of Medicine* **325**/9 (1991): 593–8.

[26] See Bulterys, *et al.*, 'Multiple sexual partners'.

[27] R. Ryder, V. Batter, M. Nsuami, N. Badi, L. Mundele, B. Matela, M. Utshudi, and W. Heyward, 'Fertility rates in 239 HIV-1 seropositive women in Zaire followed for 3 years post-partum', *AIDS* **5** (1991): 1521–7.

[28] European Collaborative Study, *Lancet* **339** (1992): 1007–12. L. Sherr, 'Women and power issues surrounding HIV/AIDS and pregnancy', in I. Schenker, G. Sabar-Friedman, and F. Sy (eds.), *AIDS Education Interventions in Multi-Cultural Societies* (New York: Plenum Press, 1996): 103–12.

accept any number of tests in the belief that her care may be jeopardized if she refuses. For example, Larsson *et al.* report that in Sweden HIV tests were offered to all women and 99.3 per cent accepted.[29]

In the early days of the epidemic, HIV testing in pregnancy offered no recourse to cure or treatment. However, by 1994 this situation had changed dramatically.[30] Yet the changes may have made the problems more difficult in terms of decision-making. A number of interventions now make it state of the art for a woman to have access to her HIV status if she so chooses. The interventions are all still under study and they are all contingent upon complete maternal compliance. They are all based on the prevention of infant infection and some pose potential hazards to the woman herself.[31] The interventions currently under debate are the administration of antiretroviral drugs (AZT).[32] The findings from these studies have resulted in an overwhelming call for antenatal testing (always of the woman and not the man) with some centres, such as New York, going to the extremes by mandating antenatal HIV testing.[33] A meta-analysis of seven longitudinal prospective studies was carried out to investigate the effects of caesarean section on vertical transmission.[34] The overall finding showed a slight protective factor (despite the fact that some studies showed a disadvantage of the procedure).[35] Clearly the only way the question can be addressed is by the provision of a randomized controlled trial. In order to establish an effect, the study would need to recruit over 1500 pregnant HIV-positive women. In addition the advent of trial 076 may confound any findings. Such a trial is under way, but experiencing difficulties in recruiting women

[29] G. Larsson, L. Spangberg, S. Lindgen, and A. B. Bohlin, 'Screening for HIV in pregnant women: A study of maternal opinion', *AIDS Care* 2/3 (1990): 223–8.

[30] Connor *et al.*, *New England Journal of Medicine* 331 (1994): 1173–80. Rowe, *Lancet* 349 (1997): 258. Toltzis *et al.*, *Journal of Infectious Diseases* 163/6 (1991).

[31] Rowe, *Lancet* 349 (1997): 258. Toltzis *et al.*, *Journal of Infectious Diseases* 163/6 (1991).

[32] Connor *et al.*, *New England Journal of Medicine* 331 (1994): 1173–80.

[33] E. Cooper, 'Mandatory HIV testing of pregnant delivering women and newborns—a legal, ethical and pragmatic assessment', Paper presented at XI International Conference on AIDS, Vancouver, 1996, Abstract WeD 491; J. Beder and N. Beckerman, 'Mandatory HIV screening in newborns: the issues and a programmatic response', XI International Conference on AIDS, Vancouver, 1996, Abstract ThC 4613.

[34] D. Dunn, M. Newell, M. Mayaux, *et al.*, 'Mode of delivery and vertical transmission of HIV-1—a review of prospective studies', *Journal of Acquired Immune Deficiency Syndromes* 7 (1994): 1064–6.

[35] European Collaborative Study (1994) 'Caesarean section and risk of vertical transmission of HIV-1 infection', *Lancet* 343 (1994): 1464–7.

who are willing to subject themselves to a random allocation to vaginal versus caesarean delivery. Hence the researchers have moved their recruitment sites to Soweto.[36] The ethical considerations of such research imperialism needs close questioning, particularly the extent to which it is ethical to carry out an operative delivery on women who may not have recourse to electricity and running water on their discharge home, nor a health welfare system to take care of their needs in the future. This is also an interesting study in terms of its ethics, given that there are well-documented hazards of caesarean section for HIV-positive women.[37] Breastfeeding has been shown as a route of HIV transmission and discussions about bottle-feeding are also seen as part of the counselling process.[38] A number of other interventions are in various stages of development.[39]

The call for HIV testing of pregnant women needs constant thought and update with advances in medical care.[40] This is especially so given the fact that the majority of women in antenatal clinics will test HIV negative. This raises the questions about the use of the intervention for prevention. It also challenges policy to provide a more comprehensive approach which should target resources at HIV-positive women (many of whom may well consider a pregnancy in the presence of the new interventions);[41] or at couples before conception (such as family planning clinics and termination of pregnancy clinics), which may allow for a different way of contemplating the issues.

Infant testing

HIV testing of infants needs careful scrutiny. For a start, there are a number of studies of children tested where no clear indication is

---

[36] L. Sherr, 'Pregnancy and childbirth', *AIDS Care* **9**/1 (1996): 69–77.

[37] A. Semprini, C. Castagna, M. Ravizza, S. Fiore, V. Savasi, M. Muggiasca, E. Grossi, B. Guerra, C. Tibaldi, G. Scaravelli, E. Prati, and G. Pardi, 'The incidence of complications after caesarean section in 156 HIV positive women', *AIDS* **9** (1995): 913–17.

[38] D. Dunn, M. L. Newell, A. Ades, and C. Peckham, 'Risk of HIV type-1 transmission through breastfeeding', *Lancet* **340** (1992): 585–8.

[39] L. Sherr, S. Jefferies, C. Victor, and J. Chase, 'Antenatal HIV testing: which way forward?' *Psychology Health and Medicine* **1**/1 (1996): 99–112.

[40] *Ibid.*

[41] L. Sherr, J. Barnes, J. Elford, R. Miller, and M. Johnson, 'HIV interventions in pregnancy—the views of HIV positive people', *British Journal of Health Psychology* in press.

given to the nature, form, or presence of counselling. Consent issues become problematic and interventions as a result of knowledge of status are also the subject of debate. The position was greatly compounded by the fact that in the early years HIV status of the infant was very difficult to establish as the standard HIV antibody tests gave only an indication of maternal status. Until maternal antibody was shed, which can take over two years of life, the presence of HIV antibody in infant blood could not categorically infer positivity in the infant. It could, however, give clear indication of maternal HIV status. As such infants can be used as a vehicle to examine maternal infection. The ethical issues this raises and safeguards which are needed in such circumstances are enormous.

More recently polymerase chain-reaction (PCR) methods are available which can establish status much earlier in life.

Infant testing should not be conducted without clear thought to a number of measures beyond the initial test. First, the issue of consent must be addressed. Who should give it, and what happens if there is a difference of opinion? Consider, for example, a case in which the doctors want to test and the parents do not, or, the unhappy circumstance in which one parent gives consent and the other withholds it. As there is no cure for the infant, there is the dilemma of the acceptability and advisability of various forms of intervention and management strategies. It is still unclear what are the benefits and risks of HIV interventions, and it is also unclear who should make decisions for the infant. Secondly, there is the question regarding knowledge of the infant's status. Who should be party to such knowledge, how should it be controlled, and how can that be guaranteed? If there is a breach in such control, is there compensation or redress? The child will obviously need to be informed at some appropriate time. As it is not possible to inform a newborn, there needs to be clear policy about telling the child. Prior to any testing, this must be addressed. It should include an examination of when to tell the child, how to tell, who should do the telling, and the necessity to anticipate the needs of the child in response to such information.

The situation can become extremely complex in a variety of circumstances. For example, cases of adoption may want to examine the issue of HIV infection, as may foster care.

Testing children

The literature often conflates all children, from infancy to early teens. This does not allow for the dramatically differing insight, abilities, and needs of the developing child. Somehow, different rules about consent and counselling are applied in studies of children. For example, Hersh *et al.* studied 101 Romanian children who were tested for HIV with no mention of any preparatory procedures. Indeed they report that the Ministry of Health tested 'all children less than 4 years of age living in (abandoned child) facilities'.[42] This was supplemented by 'sporadic testing of older institutionalized children'.[43]

Testing those with limited cognitive capacities

Counselling relies upon the ability of an individual to understand and debate the complex issues surrounding HIV. This becomes difficult or even impossible for those with limited cognitive capacities, those too young to comprehend, those who do not share the language of the institution, or those who are provided with written information but are reluctant to reveal illiteracy.

Blood banks

Obviously the greatest need has arisen in the blood banks where donor screening is imperative. Internationally, a few cases have come to light when identified at times of donations. This has complications in terms of tracing prior donations and recipients. Yet the very fact that blood donation is voluntary may change the way some of the problems associated with counselling and testing are viewed. Given that people can choose whether or not to donate blood places them in a somewhat different category from those who are pregnant who have less of a choice about associated care. The sheer volume of clients has often resulted in scant counselling. Some centres resort to written information which probably serves more as information imparting than any true form of counselling. There is always a

---

[42] B. Hersh, F. Popovici, Z. Jezek, G. Satten, R. Apetrei, N. Beldescu, R. George, C. Shapiro, H. Gayle, and D. Heymann, 'Risk factors for HIV infection among abandoned Romanian Children', *AIDS* 7 (1993): 1618.
[43] *Ibid.*

concern where status may be known to the blood bank service but not to the donor. Policy needs to be clearly worked out about how to protect the confidentiality of the donor while still ensuring a virus-free blood bank and protecting the health status of the recipients.

Testing in the developing world

An alarming trend has been monitored of Western nations collaborating in large-scale studies in developing countries where high numbers of individuals are subjected to testing. Often the protocols and ethics would not be transferable to their home country. This means that many epidemiological studies gather large samples of data from the underprivileged, the poor, and those with least resources to react or to refuse. Sometimes testing or research trial entry brings with it free medical care and attention—an option with little choice for some of the underprivileged.

Conflicting Needs

Antenatal testing brings with it the difficult issue of conflicting needs. Both the needs of the baby and the mother are often weighed up—usually at odds with each other. The needs of the father are rarely discussed, but fathers are rarely (if ever) included in screening. This conflict is not only permeated by staff but experienced by women. In a study by Larsson *et al.*, consent to testing was as a result of considerations for the baby in 63 per cent of cases (and concern for own health in 54 per cent of cases).[44] Many studies on women have been carried out in an attempt to understand paediatric infection. This has meant that early studies failed to follow through variables for the mother once the infant was born, thereby losing vital data and understanding on the natural history and course of disease in post-partum women.

Protection of the mother is rarely integrated into policy. For example 'semen washing' has been available as a procedure for many years now.[45] This procedure would allow a couple where the father is positive and the mother is negative to conceive a baby without

[44] Larsson, *et al.*, *AIDS Care* **2**/3 (1990): 223–8.
[45] A. E. Semprini, S. Fiore, and G. Pardi, 'Reproductive counselling for HIV discordant couples', *Lancet* **349**/9062 (1977): 1401–2.

exposing the mother to unnecessary levels of infected semen. To date, not one of the pregnancies via this method in the Semprini study has resulted in a positive baby or mother.[46] Yet few centres adopt the procedure and information is not generally available to discordant couples.

Counselling and Testing

While the debate has raged about the pros and cons of testing, few researchers have focused on the problems of counselling. Psychological interventions are often poorly evaluated. This is made difficult because of the problems with clear outcome measures as well as difficulties in observation, recording, and quantifying the processes of counselling which are time-consuming and vary according to the individual counsellor, client, and circumstance.

Yet a number of problems cannot be overlooked simply because there is a consensus that 'counselling is desirable'.

Who Does the Counselling?

The first problem which besets the area is one of competence and skill. Traditionally counselling has been undertaken by psychology and psychiatry professionals, with a growing input from social workers and other health care workers. Training is rarely standardized and minimum standards are rarely enforced. Given that the difference between good communication skills and therapeutic counselling is rarely elaborated, many workers are trained for the former but believe they are qualified for the latter.

Within the AIDS literature there are a wide range of counsellors, ranging from 'unqualified' workers, to self-help groups, to those with recognized qualifications. Counselling training has been fostered with gusto by most AIDS and HIV organizations, ranging from the World Health Organization to the National AIDS Counselling Training Units in the UK, to similar institutions the world over.

A whole host of professionals take on the role of counselling. Davison *et al.* reported on a UK survey with 98 per cent response

---

[46] A. E. Semprini, 'Insemination of HIV negative women with processed semen of HIV positive partners', *Lancet* **341**/8856 (1993): 1343–4.

rate from 299 obstetric units.[47] Counselling was given 'by the obstetrician alone at 47 per cent' and by others including midwives with training, microbiologists, and trained counsellors. Post-test counselling was given by obstetricians, haematologists, and paediatricians. Few units had access to a trained counsellor. Wenstrom and Zuidema describe counselling being performed 'by specially trained nurses who loosely followed a script'.[48] Kamenga reports their counselling team comprising of 'a male physician and one of two female nurses'.[49] Heyward reports that counselling was carried out by 'a trained Zairian health worker who could speak the participant's language'.[50] Midwives are most commonly cited as conducting HIV counselling in obstetrics.[51]

Bor *et al.* report on counselling in a specialized AIDS-counselling unit staffed by 'two full-time trained counsellors'.[52] Mason *et al.* report that initially counselling was carried out by 'a research assistant'.[53] Subsequently they saw the need to provide special training to medical, social work, and nursing staff. Bor *et al.* urge doctors to take on the challenge of HIV counselling,[54] yet many physicians feel ill-equipped to do counselling. Henry *et al.* report that physicians

[47] C. F. Davison, A. E. Ades, C. N. Hudson, and C. S. Peckham, 'Antenatal testing for Human Immunodeficiency Virus. Results from the Royal College of Obstetricians and Gynecologists National Study of HIV infection in pregnancy', *Lancet* ii/8677 (1989): 1443.

[48] K. Wenstrom and L. Zuidema, 'Determination of the seroprevalence of HIV infection in gravidas by non-anonymous versus anonymous testing', *Obstetrics and Gynecology* **74**/4 (1989): 559.

[49] M. Kamenga, R. Ryder, M. Jingu, N. Mbuyi, L. Mbu, F. Behets, C. Brown, and W. Heyward, 'Evidence of marked sexual behaviour change associated with low HIV-1 seroconversion in 149 married couples with discordant HIV-1 serostatus: experience at an HIV counselling centre in Zaire', *AIDS* **5**/1 (1991): 61–7.

[50] W. Heyward, V. Batter, M. Malulu, N. Mbuyi, L. Mbu, M. Louis, M. Kamenga, and R. Ryder, 'Impact of HIV counselling and testing among child-bearing women in Kinshasa, Zaire', *AIDS* **7** (1993): 1633.

[51] L. Howard, D. Hawkins, R Marwood, D. Shanson, and B. Gazzard, 'Transmission of HIV by heterosexual contact with reference to antenatal screening', *British Journal of Obstetrics and Gynecology* **96** (1989): 135–9; J. Medows, S. Jenkinson, J. Catalan, and B. Gazzard, 'Voluntary HIV testing in the antenatal clinic. Differing uptake rates for individual counselling midwives', *AIDS Care* **2**/3 (1990): 229–33; A. Foldspang and M. Hedegaard, 'Anxiety in voluntary HIV antibody testing in pregnancy and its implications for preventive strategies', *Danish Medical Bulletin* **38**/3 (1991): 285–8.

[52] Bor *et al.*, 'Uptake of HIV testing following counselling'.

[53] J. Mason, J. Preisinger, R. Sperling, V. Walthr, J. Berrier, and V. Evans, 'Incorporating HIV education and counselling into routine prenatal care: a program model', *AIDS Education and Prevention* **3**/2 (1991): 118.

[54] Bor *et al.*, 'A testing time for doctors counselling patients'.

dealing with AIDS are not adequately supported in efforts to provide counselling.[55] Sherr *et al.* report that 78 per cent of a sample of general practitioners thought pre- and post-test counselling was very important but only 10 per cent thought they were skilled to provide it.[56] Those who were low in counselling proficiency were more likely to refer their patients to hospital centres and less likely to discuss HIV with their patients.

When is the Counselling Done?

There is little consistency about the timing of counselling—especially pre-test counselling. Although this question is rarely raised for debate there may be a strong case that decision-making is more difficult if testing is done at the same time as counselling. People may have different views if they are allowed cooling-off periods or time to muse on information they are given. Some studies report counselling in non-optimal circumstances. For example, Ryder *et al.* record testing of 5916 women 'presenting at the hospital's labor room in active labor'.[57] Clearly, this may be a non-optimum time for counselling. Similarly Wenstrom and Zuidema report that on admission to Labour and Delivery suites women were 'queried with regard to . . . risk factors'.[58] The practice is widespread, and Heyward *et al.* also report that women were counselled and tested when first presenting immediately before childbirth.[59]

How Long Does it Take?

The time and resources devoted to the counselling process may directly affect the quality and efficacy of the process. There are no

[55] K. Henry, M. Maki, K. Willenbring, and S. Campbell, 'The impact of experience with AIDS on HIV testing and counselling practice', *AIDS Education and Prevention* 3/4 (1991): 313–21. See also A. Somogyi, J. Watson Abady, and F. Mandel, 'Attitudes toward the care of patients with Acquired Immunodeficiency Syndrome', *Archives of Surgery* **150** (1990): 50–3.

[56] Sherr *et al.*, 'General Practice pregnancy care'.

[57] Ryder *et al.*, 'Fertility rates in 239 HIV-1 seropositive women in Zaire'.

[58] Wenstrom and Zuidema, 'Determination of the seroprevalence of HIV infection'.

[59] Heyward *et al.*, 'Impact of HIV counselling and testing among child-bearing women in Kinshasa'.

clear guidelines as to this.[60] Various studies have reported vastly different time-scales for the procedure. Wenstrom and Zuidema report that scripted counselling sessions took about thirty minutes.[61] Bor *et al.* suggest that it can take ten to fifteen minutes.[62]

In antenatal clinics, counselling was seen as taking twenty-one minutes[63] in some studies, but as few as 2.8 minutes in a large clinic population.[64] This may well be as a result of the fact that the UK government ameliorated pre-test counselling in this group to pre-test discussion.[65]

Counselling Training

An entire industry has been created to train all manner of health care workers to carry out pre- and post-test counselling.[66] There is little evaluation of such short-term training. The evaluation that exists does show that information levels can alter,[67] but rarely examines direct practising skills.[68]

Prejudices of the Counsellor

Even when counselling is available, the content is often not regulated. This can result in the individual biases of the counsellor being the most important factor in test agreement—irrespective of risk

[60] British Psychological Society Special Interest Group on AIDS, *Counselling HIV Testing and Behaviour Change*.

[61] Wenstrom and Zuidema, 'Determination of the seroprevalence of HIV infection'.

[62] Bor *et al.*, 'A testing time for doctors counselling patients'.

[63] J. Banatvala and L. L. Chrystie, 'HIV screening in pregnancy—UK lags', *Lancet* **343** (1994): 1113.

[64] L. Sherr, C. Hudson, A. Bergenstrom, E. Bell, and E. McCann, 'Ante-natal HIV testing in four London hospitals', Paper presented at the European AIDS and Antenatal Testing Policy Meeting, Palermo, Sept. 1997.

[65] Dept. of Health, *Guidelines for Offering Voluntary Named HIV Antibody Testing to Women Receiving Antenatal Care* (London: HMSO, 1994).

[66] L. Sherr and A. McCreaner, ' Summary evaluation of the National AIDS Counselling Training Unit in the UK', *Counselling Psychology Quarterly* **2**/1 (1989): 21–31.

[67] L. Sherr, 'The impact of AIDS in obstetrics on obstetric staff', *Journal of Reproductive and Infant Psychology* **5** (1987): 87–96.

[68] C. Victor, S. Jefferies, and L. Sherr, 'Training in obstetric and paediatric HIV and AIDS', *Professional Care of Mother and Child* **4** (April 1993): 97–100.

level. This was certainly true in a study by Meadows *et al.* where all pregnant women booking for antenatal care over a twelve-month period were monitored. Counselling and routine offering of HIV tests was departmental policy. Uptake of test was analysed according to exposure to individual midwives. The variation was dramatic—ranging from 3.4 to 81.8 per cent.[69] Clearly, in this study the likelihood of being tested was a direct result of the individual variation in the midwives and not the risk factors of the women.

Although counselling is seen as 'non-directive', there are clear biases reported in the literature. For example, Temmerman *et al.* report 'we had hoped that our counselling sessions would encourage women to . . . limit their family size'.[70] Ryder *et al.* report on the 'disappointingly high fertility rates in seropositive women who had been provided with a comprehensive program of HIV counselling'.[71]

When pre-test counselling and post-test counselling become one

Some studies report HIV counselling but only on receipt of results. For example, Temmerman *et al.* provided counselling to all women who tested positive.[72]

Imposing Counselling

Scant attention is given to the client who may be able to choose whether to test or not, whether to take AZT or not, or whether to use condoms or not, and thus may equally want to choose whether they are counselled or not (and then by whom, for how long, and in what manner). Few studies report on counselling refusal. When this is documented, refusal is noted.[73]

Agreement

The literature and practice blurs agreement to testing with agreement to be given HIV test results. The latter is often presumed and rarely

---

[69] Medows *et al.*, 'Voluntary HIV testing in the antenatal clinic'.
[70] Temmerman *et al.*, *Aids Care* **2**/3 (1990): 250.
[71] Ryder *et al.*, 'Fertility rtes in 23g HIV-1 seropositive women in Zaire'.
[72] Temmerman *et al.*, *Aids Care* **2**/3 (1990): 247–52.
[73] e.g. Heyward *et al.*, 'Impact of HIV counselling and testing among child-bearing women in Kinshasa'. 20/431 women refused counselling in this study.

directly addressed. Although this distinction may not exist in the minds of the professionals, it is clearly made by test recipients. It would account for the often queried finding that large numbers of people consent to testing and never return for their results (Zenilman *et al.* found 39 per cent of positives and 37 per cent of negatives did not return).[74] The professionals comment on this quizzically, yet clearly the patients do not have a difficulty with this.

The obverse of this blurring may raise particular problems. A patient who consents to HIV testing but who has not explicitly consented to test-result provision may be unprepared for the results. Once a test result has been given the information cannot be rescinded and there are far-reaching ramifications for the individual and the wider family.

Test Results

On the whole the literature records that most people do not divulge their test results. Temmerman *et al.* reported that only 37 per cent of pregnant women testing HIV positive informed their partners.[75] Heyward *et al.* noted that 2.2 per cent of their sample brought their partners to the clinic,[76] and Ryder *et al.* reported that only 3 per cent did so.[77] Melvin and Sherr recorded that no families in their study had informed the school of a child's status (and indeed only one family had informed the child of their own status).[78]

When 'No' really Means 'Yes'

In the interest of science there has been a peculiar use of consent as a variable or risk indicator rather than as a concept of agreement. There are numerous studies which give detailed results of HIV

[74] J. Zenilman, B. Erickson, R. Fox, C. Rechart, and E. Hook, 'Effect of HIV post-test counselling on STD incidence', *Journal of the American Medical Association* **2617**/6 (1992): 843–5.

[75] Temmerman *et al.*, *Aids Care* **2**/3 (1990): 247–52.

[76] Heyward *et al.*, 'Impact of HIV counselling and testing among child-bearing women in Kinshasa'.

[77] Ryder *et al.*, 'Fertility rates in HIV-1 seropositive women in Zaire'.

[78] D. Melvin and L. Sherr, 'The child in the family responding to AIDS and HIV', *AIDS Care* **5**/1 (1993): 35–42.

testing for women who 'declined', 'refused', or 'withheld consent'. For example, Larsson *et al.* report that 'a blind analysis of the blood specimens from the fifty-eight women who declined the test was performed'.[79] Clearly there is an assumption in these studies that declining testing does not mean that the test will not be carried out. Furthermore, this study reports that it was approved by a University Ethical Committee. Hull *et al.* quoted a prevalence rate of 3.8 per cent among STD clinic attenders who declined HIV antibody testing.[80] Jenum, in Norway, also reports that 2 per cent of women who declined HIV testing were HIV positive.[81] Barbacci *et al.* set out to 'assess the prevalence of HIV infection in women who did not volunteer for testing'.[82]

Seeking Consent—Reality or a Dream?

Although there is common agreement that consent for HIV testing (or any testing for that matter) is preferred practice, this is not always reflected in reality. McDonald provided an interesting overview of the situation in Australia, where no pre-test counselling prior to HIV testing was conducted by 25 per cent of obstetricians, 9 per cent of family practitioners, and 5 per cent of hospitals.[83] Furthermore, no specific consent for HIV testing was sought by 18 per cent of obstetricians. In the USA, Henry *et al.* surveyed testing practices in 371 hospitals. They noted that consent was obtained for 70.1 per cent of tests, was obtained and documented for only one in two cases, and that counselling only occurred for 51 per cent of cases.[84] Denayer *et al.* report that 49 per cent of their sample of Belgian gynaecologists tested for HIV without informing the patient.[85]

[79] Larsson *et al.*, *AIDS Care* 2/3 (1990): 224.

[80] H. F. Hull, C. J. Bettinger, M. M. Gallaher, N. M. Keller, J. Wilson, and G. J. Mertz, 'Comparison of HIV-antibody prevalence in patients consenting to and declining HIV-antibody testing in an STD clinic', *Journal of the American Medicine Association* **260**/7 (1988): 935–8.

[81] P. Jenum, 'Anti HIV screening of pregnant women in south eastern Norway', *NIPH Annual* **11** (1988): 53–8.

[82] M. Barbacci, J. Repke, and R. Chaisson, 'Routine prenatal screening for HIV infection', *Lancet* **337** (March 1991): 709.

[83] M. McDonald, J. Elford, R. Gabb, M. Ryan, and J. Kaldor, 'Counselling and consent for HIV-antibody testing in Australia', paper presented at *IX International Conference on AIDS*, Berlin, 1993. Ref.: PO-D15–3883, p. 865.

[84] Henry *et al.*, 'Impact of experience with AIDS on HIV testing'.

[85] M. Denayer, T. Jonckheer, P. Pliot, and A. Stroobrant, 'Antenatal testing for HIV' [letter], *Lancet* **335** (Feb 1990): 292.

Conclusion

HIV testing should not be seen as an end in itself but rather as one of the many tools in the total fight against HIV and AIDS. Counselling was put forward as a panacea, but in reality may have been the cloak behind which many ethical issues were conveniently brushed. As the epidemic moves forward there can be no complacency about the need to provide a rigorous assessment of policy and procedure. Hindsight, as always, will be the judge.

4

HIV Screening: Benefits and Harms for the Individual and the Community

CATHERINE MANUEL

Introduction

From an ethical point of view HIV screening can be seen in terms of conflicting rights: society is entitled to protect itself from a serious danger, if need be by authoritarian measures; infected individuals are entitled to freedom, to 'non-discrimination', to the respect of their privacy, etc. Of course one may ponder on the validity and the possible limitations of these rights depending on the circumstances and the seriousness of the epidemic which concerns us. I will use in this chapter a more pragmatic approach, and will reflect on the benefits for the individual and for the community, on the real positive and negative effects of screening. Indeed, I see it as essential to adopt a perspective which reveals the true efficacy of such practices and to discuss the least ethically controversial methods.

According to Ruth Faden:

No screening program can be justified either legally or morally without first satisfying public health criteria. . . . At the core of a public health framework for evaluating screening programs is a single criterion—the program's harm-to-benefit ratio, where harms and benefits are understood in terms of impact on a community's morbidity and mortality.[1]

Let us not forget that screening is an act of preventative medicine; that screening programmes are launched by the medical authorities,

Translated by Valérie-Lina Bernard, Centre for Social Ethics and Policy, University of Manchester.

[1] R. R. Faden, N. E. Kass, and M. Powers, 'Warrants for screening programmes: Public health, legal and ethical frameworks', in R. R. Faden, G. Geller, and M. Powers (eds.), *AIDS, Women and the Next Generation* (New York: OUP, 1991): 3–26.

that they are either suggested to, or imposed on the population, and that the initial request does not emanate from the individual as is the case in curative medicine. Thus, one should promise and demand a clearly assessable efficiency. Cochrane and Holand write:

We believe there is an ethical difference between everyday medical practice and screening. If a patient asks a medical practitioner for help, the doctor does the best he can. He is not responsible for defects in medical knowledge. If, however, the practitioner initiates the screening procedures he is in a very different situation. He should, in my view, have conclusive evidence that screening can alter the natural history of disease in a significant proportion of those screened.[2]

HIV-infected individuals are particularly vulnerable because of the perceived connotations linked to the most widespread transmission modes (homosexuality, drug addiction, multiplicity of sexual partners). They are threatened with stigmatization, violation of their privacy, breach of confidentiality, and social exclusion. According to Bartlett: 'HIV screening differs from other medical screenings because its consequences are not purely medical.'[3] Levine and Bayer expand upon this point:

HIV infection is not like other clinical conditions, even those that are potentially lethal. It carries not only great psychological burdens but the possibility of severe stigma and discrimination, including rejection or avoidance by health care workers and poor-quality treatment.[4]

We are not sure, therefore, whether it is worth testing those individuals, but if they are tested, it must be their own choice (voluntary testing) and the information must remain strictly confidential (anonymous or confidential testing).

The community, for its part, has every interest in finding efficient means of fighting the expansion of the epidemic. Knowledge of the serological status of the population, or of a part of it, is the first among those means. Depending on countries and cultures, it will be possible to choose between more or less coercive approaches which will more or less clash with individual interests. It is this balance, between the aims and the procedures chosen by public health for

---

[2] A. L. Cochrane and W. W. Holland, 'Validation of screening procedures', *British Medical Bulletin* **27** (1971): 3–8.

[3] J. A. Bartlett, 'HIV testing in North Carolina', *North Carolina Medical Journal* **51** (1990): 150–1.

[4] C. Levine and R. Bayer, 'The ethics of screening for early intervention in HIV disease', *American Journal of Public Health* **79** (1989): 1661–7.

HIV screening programmes and the personal harms and/or benefits to the tested individuals, which will interest me here.

At the Individual Level

The individuals affected by HIV screening vary according to the programmes implemented: these programmes can affect a very widespread population if they aim to be generalized, or large sections of it (antenatal, premarital screening, for example), or groups targeted according to risk factors, and I will return to these when I come on to deal with collective interests. First, I will examine the benefits and drawbacks for three groups:

- 'no-risks' individuals;
- individuals who take risks and test seronegative;
- individuals found seropositive.

Individuals who face no risk of contracting HIV

Individuals who can be said to face no risk of contracting HIV are monogamists with a monogamous partner or those with no sexual activity whatsoever, nor with any experience of intravenous drug use and whose history shows no transfusion, nor acupuncture, nor tattoos, etc. All these individuals will reap *no benefit whatsoever* from testing. If screening is established on a voluntary basis, we may expect that they will not resort to it. If it is imposed, it will be a totally arbitrary measure for them, causing only harms: that (minimal) of submitting to a blood test against their will; that (much more serious) of running the non-negligible risk of being mistakenly classified among the positive tests—'false positive'—which represents a potentially serious prejudice (i.e. the wait for the result, anxiety, etc.), even if a new sample for serological confirmation will reassure them within a few days. Indeed, it is known that HIV tests favour sensitivity in order not to 'overlook' any patient—'false negative'. Thus, it is the specificity of the tests which is not optimal as it can produce falsely positive results. This defect is highly enhanced when the screening is of populations among whom the prevalence of infection with the virus is very low. This large number of false positives is one of the reasons which render generalized screening, or the screening of very wide sections of the population, open to great criticism.

64   *Catherine Manuel*

Individuals who, having faced a potential risk, are found seronegative

For those who, having faced a potential risk, are found seronegative, there are several benefits to this knowledge. They will be reassured; if they are aware of having taken serious risks, a great weight will be lifted from their minds; their future prospects and plans will be clarified. This will offer the opportunity, in the course of a medical interview, to motivate them into behavioural changes with a view to prevention. The danger is that relief can foster the opposite reaction: 'I have taken risks and I have caught nothing; these risks are not as serious as I have been told; I can therefore carry on as before.' It will be up to the doctor to give the necessary warnings so that the test does not induce a false sense of security.

In effect, all results—whether positive or negative—must be communicated by a doctor (or by a health professional trained for these interviews) who will take the time to give the required explanations and to answer all questions. We have here an idea of how to organize these consultations, which must be taken into account.

Asymptomatic individuals found seropositive

Obviously, asymptomatic individuals found to be seropositive are those for whom benefits/harms require the most attention.

Therapeutic benefits

Undoubtedly, if a treatment truly capable of halting the evolution of the disease were discovered, the personal benefit of knowing one's serological status would be such that it would impose the notion of testing and that any individual worried about a possible risk would resort to it. We know that such a treatment does not currently exist, and this is the main charge against HIV testing. Indeed, it might be claimed that testing is not worthwhile unless a treatment of proven efficiency is available.

There are, however, arguments of a therapeutic order in favour of knowing the status of affected individuals. It has been proven, it seems, that early treatment with AZT delays the appearance of clinical symptoms. Its use is capital, considering the number of life years to be saved, and since one always hopes a new drug is about to be discovered. Though there are still many unknown factors regarding the long-term toxicity of the antiviral substances used, we can estimate, however, that having the use of a therapy benefits the individual. Furthermore, there is a positive moral factor—the feeling of 'doing something' which will give the patient some hope for a cure. Moreover, the affected individuals can be followed up, lead a more regular and healthier life(style)—many are motivated to diminish their tobacco, alcohol and drug consumption—take advantage of a prophylactic for opportunistic infections, of medical supervision of some associated diseases, such as tuberculosis, and so on.

Benefits linked to prevention

There are also benefits related to prevention. The knowledge of one's seropositivity leads to personal protection (safe intercourse, personal injecting devices, etc., to avoid reinfection). Above all, it leads to a protection of contacts: spouses, sexual partners, co-drug users. And, of course, what matters at this point is whether the precautions needed to protect those contacts will effectively be adopted.

One particular case is that of pregnant women who can be offered a voluntary termination of pregnancy, and this choice is another argument in favour of testing. But this is a very difficult choice because if 15 to 20 per cent of infants are infected, all will become orphans—motherless in all cases and sometimes fatherless too. Recent studies, showing that a treatment with AZT during the last weeks of pregnancy and the first few weeks of the infant's life reduces this figure to 8 per cent, are a powerful argument in favour of systematic testing. Many are thus in favour of instituting the compulsory testing of pregnant women for this reason.

Thus, the benefit of testing for the individual must be considered at different levels: for the individual who is tested, for his contacts, and for the prospective child when the individual is a pregnant woman.

I have shown that for the individual found seropositive there are several benefits to knowing his condition. Being able to protect his contacts is also a personal advantage. We can imagine the tragic remorse experienced by a person who has contaminated a close relation, say, and who deems himself responsible. We must insist on the fact that all these benefits are closely dependent on a serious and careful medical counselling which, as an imperative, comes with the test.

But what are the drawbacks, the negative effects of this knowledge?

Negative psychological effects

Essentially, the test may suddenly 'transform' a healthy individual into a diseased individual, and the emotional burden of such a discovery breeds anguish, depression, despair. We also know of many cases of suicide following the announcement of HIV seropositivity. Undoubtedly, being aware of such hopeless prospects, of a sinking future, shortens a normal life by a few years and we can argue in favour of people's right to ignore some serious aspects of their health and their becoming. This right to ignorance is one of the arguments against mandatory screening.

Negative social effects

It means a different look, even if not hostile, from close relations and the family circle. It very often means withdrawal from society, a break from the work environment and sometimes from family. Frequently, this announcement exposes secret behaviours, the use of drugs, a double life, a closet homosexuality, unknown liaisons of the spouse. All those facts, suddenly exposed, challenge the usual social life. Most of all, there is a potential stigmatization if the situation becomes known, which can lead to extremely serious consequences. We know the most violent reactions have been observed in the USA where haemophiliac children have been expelled from their schools, professionals have refused to treat infected patients, seropositive individuals have been physically threatened, have lost their jobs, their homes, their access to insurance and to social services. We know that even though these problems have proved less acute in Europe, any individual known to be seropositive will experience difficulties in being hired or in keeping his job, in taking out an insurance policy, and so on.

These are, therefore, very serious problems which, insofar as they are directly linked to the knowledge of serological status, must be considered when evaluating any screening programme. These non-negligible negative consequences represent an argument in favour of voluntary testing and call for an emphasis on a serious, medical, psychological, and social follow-up of the disturbed and vulnerable individual who has just been informed of his status.

At the Community Level

The discovery of HIV-detection tests and their usage since 1985 has been a very important tool in the understanding of the infection.

First, to discover the *evolution of the disease*—studies have been launched to find out whether all those presenting antibodies would develop the clinical symptoms (unfortunately, it has been proven to be so); we were able to determine the duration of the *silent* phase before the appearance of clinical symptoms (between eight and ten years), to determine also the latency phase between contamination and seroconversion (three months on average). These data are now established.[5]

Secondly, to know the infection's epidemiology in the community—evaluation of the contamination modes, of the threatened groups, of the affected sections (age, sex), of the geographical distribution of cases, etc. These data are very inaccurate and incomplete and would require an extension of screening programmes in order to become more complete. Indeed, such data are essential to evaluate public health actions, to work out the sharing of resources between campaigns of education and prevention, social and health care follow-up, etc.

Finally, we must ask the following question: can screening campaigns *limit the expansion of the epidemic* within the community? In other words, will the disclosure of the seropositive status be followed by a noticeable preventive action on dangerous behaviours? This is obviously a fundamental question with regard to the efficiency of HIV screening.

We can reasonably assume that many persons armed with the knowledge of their infected status will adopt a responsible attitude, will warn their partners, and take precautions against infecting them. We must, however, remain circumspect in this declaration as it is very difficult to 'dissociate the effect of measures taken by the whole of the population exposed to risks from behavioural changes of individuals having discovered their seropositivity following testing'.[6]

An article issued by the CDC[7] seeking to show the impact of testing on individual behaviours lists sixty-six studies (from 1986 to 1990) and demonstrates that the reduction in risk behaviours is significant, especially among homosexuals. But the psychological and

---

[5] See e.g. Gerald Corbitt, 'HIV Testing and Screening: Current Practicalities and Future Possibilities', Ch. 2 in this volume.

[6] Haut Comité de la Santé Publique, 'Avis sur le depistage de l'infection par le VIH' (Paris: Haut Comité de la Santé Publique, 1992): 1–40.

[7] D. Higgins, C. Galavotti, K. R. O'Reilly, D. J. Schnell, M. Moore, D. L. Rugg, and R. Johnson, 'Evidence for the effects of HIV antibody counselling and testing on risk behaviors', *Journal of the American Medical Association* **266** (1991): 2419–29.

environmental factors are such that we cannot conclusively prove the influence of testing and counselling on preventative behaviours.

A French study by the Haut Comité de Santé Publique (High Committee of Public Health)[8] reaches a similar conclusion. Indicators such as the increase in the sale of condoms or the decline in rates of sexually transmitted diseases provide evidence of behavioural changes towards increased prevention, but nothing enables us to link this to testing/screening. This acknowledgement of the uncertainty as to the influence of testing on behavioural changes, leads to a questioning of the main benefit of the campaigns one would like to see in the community, namely, can these programmes limit the expansion of the epidemic?

I will now specify some points about the modes of the screening programmes. What are the benefits and drawbacks of mandatory testing as opposed to voluntary testing, of named studies in relation to anonymous or blinded studies, and of campaigns involving large numbers or targeted at particular groups?

Mandatory/voluntary testing

The question raised here is the right of society to implement authoritarian measures on grounds of effectiveness. We cannot rule out completely any mandatory system under the pretext of ethics or the defence of human rights. We need only mention mandatory vaccination and the ensuing decline of contagious diseases to rest assured of the legitimacy of imposing certain measures.

In France, the Haut Comité de Santé Publique maintains:

There exists no general ethical objection to the practice of mandatory screening of a disease. Such *obligations* are already included in our legislation. Only the seriousness of the screened disease, the therapeutic possibilities, the objective demonstration of the service rendered to individuals or society enable us to consider an obligation as acceptable or not from an ethical point of view.[9]

As I have already said, mandatory HIV screening is questionable because of individual rights, i.e. the right to undergo a test or not; the right to know the result or ignore it; the risk of infringement of privacy for a condition primarily linked to personal and intimate habits; the fear that confidential data—all the more sensitive in the climate

[8] Haut Comité, 'Avis sur le depistage de l'infection par le VIH'.   [9] Ibid.

of suspicion surrounding AIDS—might be disclosed. All these reasons lead me to question the usefulness at the community level of such an obligation and whether such mandatory programmes are efficient.

My first point is of an epidemiological nature. Some support the view that it is necessary to know the evolution of the epidemic, that the notifications of AIDS cases represent very partial data, that we need accurate information on the prevalence of seropositives, and that we must avail ourselves of the means of gaining such knowledge. We know that the studies on voluntary groups are always biased. It is logical, therefore, to try to obtain accurate figures by imposing the test on particular sections of the population or at certain times of life which remain to be determined. This reasoning is coherent from a public health point of view, although some authors[10] believe it possible to obtain results just as useful through blinded studies on all available blood samples, drawn for other purposes, and thus the latter avoids implementing authoritarian measures, which is always better. I shall return later to these 'blinded' studies.

My second point is linked to what follows after the discovery of seropositivity. If a test is mandatory, we must think about what can be imposed thereafter should the test be positive: A ban on marriage? A mandatory abortion? An incursion into people's private lives and control over their sexual intercourse? All such suggestions are naturally absurd in our liberal societies. Besides, depending on the jurisdiction, one may not even have the legal right to warn the spouse or the sexual partner(s) if the infected person refuses to do so. For such a private and intimate area, one may consider that any coercion is improper, that a voluntary system is imperative, and that it is up to the individual herself to take the necessary decisions and modify her behaviour if it is dangerous.

In France, the Haut Comité de Santé Publique has stated, in a report of March 1992 in which it takes a clear stance against mandatory HIV screening:

A public health policy, when it comes to fighting AIDS, must incorporate the screening actions in the wider context of prevention and the taking of responsibility for the disease. Such a policy requires a trusting collaboration of the tested individuals, which is hardly compatible with the restricting

---

[10] R. Bayer, 'Screening and AIDS: The limits of coercive intervention', *Ann. NY Academy of Science* **530** (1988): 159–62; C. Levine, 'Has AIDS changed the ethics of human individuals research?', *Law, Medicine and Health Care* **16** (1988): 167–73.

character of mandatory screening. The individuals considering themselves 'at risk' are inclined to evade screening as soon as it is made mandatory, which diminishes its efficiency since it is precisely this sort of individuals who must be reached. When faced with a negative result, the health care staff can use this opportunity to make the individual adopt prevention measures. These will be facilitated by the voluntary nature of the procedure. When faced with a confirmed positive result, the individuals thus informed are all the more inclined to adopt a responsible behaviour—particularly with regards to not contaminating other persons—if the testing took place in an atmosphere of trust and psychological support, and this requires free consent.[11]

If our sole aim is epidemiological knowledge, mandatory screening might then be countenanced in order to gain more precise information. However, if we are attempting to modify the dissemination of the disease—which is still the final aim of the community—the process of making the individual in question responsible must begin as soon as he suspects that he may have taken risks and continue until a rational prevention is attained. The resort to testing should then be a logical part of this procedure; it should intervene on a voluntary, well-thought-out basis, with full knowledge of the facts, and should be followed by sensible changes in behaviours deemed dangerous.

To conclude this discussion of mandatory or voluntary HIV screening, we should make sure, before introducing a mandatory system, that it offers assured benefits from an efficiency point of view. For HIV infection it is more likely that a voluntary test, agreed to by the individual, will have real effects at a preventative level—the prevention being in the private domain.

Named or anonymous screening, or blinded studies?

Any named health datum risks a breach of medical confidentiality and, of course, this danger increases with a condition such as HIV infection which presents such highly sensitive connotations. If this information is known only to the medical body responsible for health care, follow-up, prevention, etc., then this knowledge is necessary. It is ethical if this knowledge is shared only by doctors—or carers—and if the confidential nature of these data is absolute. Currently, this is the case in France, unlike other countries which

[11] Haut Comité, 'Avis sur le depistage de l'infection par le VIH'.

have lifted secrecy in the case of AIDS. The basis of this breach of confidentiality in the view of these latter countries is the necessity to warn the partners of a seropositive individual and to trace them via programmes of named partner-notification and contact-tracing. The opposite reasoning—that of France and Italy, who have maintained strict confidentiality—says there exists a danger that the individuals who perceive themselves 'at risk' might avoid the medical structures if they are not absolutely certain about the secrecy. In fact, the estrangement of precisely those individuals who must be reached, would be disastrous at a collective prevention level.

I have said the danger at the individual level is that these data could become known to an employer, a school, an insurance company, the police, etc., which would engender serious consequences for the individual in question. At the community level, the fear is that such a disclosure would lead the individuals, for whom the importance of the test is essential, to avoid the screening centres and the medical structures. We have here a foreseeable and completely negative effect of screening organized on a named basis.

On the other hand, interesting epidemiological studies can be conducted with anonymous data, which enable us to gain a more or less accurate knowledge of the prevalence of the infection within the population, by, for example, gathering all HIV tests done, with each assigned an anonymous number to solve the problem of duplication. You can thus gain information on prevalence according to sex, age group, place of residence. However, there are difficulties in obtaining information regarding transmission modes as one needs to ask the individual precise questions about the risk factors. Generally, such studies allow only superficial epidemiological research and lack precise information. As no follow-up is possible, there are no means of monitoring the delay of appearence of the clinical disease, the effect of treatments on this delay, etc., all these notions being essential to improve our knowledge of the disease and its treatment.

Moreover, as the tests are currently done on a voluntary basis, such a collection is biased. To avoid bias caused by the voluntary system, we could resort to blinded studies as suggested by some authors,[12] i.e. perform an anonymous HIV test on all available samples from health care and prevention centres, blood banks, laboratories, and so on. Here again, you would obtain an interesting

[12] Bayer, 'Screening and AIDS'; Levine and Bayer, 'The ethics of screening for early intervention in HIV disease'.

estimate of the infection's prevalence, though it would not reflect the whole of the population but only that part of it which resorts to blood tests.

Thus sentinel hospital studies were organized under the direction of the CDC, whose aim was to determine the level of HIV prevalence among a large nationwide sample of hospital patients, and users of family planning centres, sexually transmitted diseases and tuberculosis services, drug users' clinics, etc. Random polls were done and analyses conducted on a selection of leftover blood drawn for other purposes. The only information available was age, sex, race, place, and month of sample.[13] The criticism that springs to mind is that those tests are done without the knowledge of patients. This goes against all fundamental rules of medical ethics which always require informed consent. However, Levine writes:

> The ethical justification for this type of research rests on the importance of the knowledge to society, the difficulty of obtaining unbiased population samples if consent were to be required, the lack of physical risk to the individuals since no extra blood is drawn, the lack of social risk since they cannot be identified in any way, and the availability of HIV-antibody testing in other anonymous or confidential settings for those who want to know their HIV status for clinical or public health reasons. Here is one instance in which the benefits to society have appeared, in the widely held American view, to outweigh the general requirement for informed consent.[14]

Levine notes that this opinion does not prevail in the UK or in the Netherlands, where similar proposals have been vigorously opposed. The objections there were that consent is ethically preferable to anonymity and can be obtained without biasing the results; and, secondly, that the lack of identifiers makes it impossible to inform those who test positive.

If blinded studies can be objected to at the level of consent, anonymity, on the other hand, answers the ever-present need for confidentiality. However, the various collections or investigations planned offer partial, biased, and therefore probably disappointing results. Named studies have indeed been conducted on a voluntary basis, such as the first investigations when the disease appeared which were conducted on cohorts of American homosexuals who, having agreed to participate in the research, were followed up for many years.

---

[13] Levine and Bayer, ibid.   [14] Ibid.

Systematic or targeted programmes?

It has already been mentioned that the screening of very wide sections of the population, where HIV prevalence is very low, would produce a very high number of false positives. Moreover, this low prevalence means the cost-effectiveness of such programmes would be derisory as compared with their expense and the small number of individuals detected. And as resources allocated to AIDS are obviously not inexhaustible, it would mean the massive use of these resources for a small benefit, whereas they could be used more profitably elsewhere. This is why, by targeting the campaigns on certain risk factors, we could reach a higher prevalence population—i.e. population groups among which the disease is more widespread: homosexuals, intravenous drug users, male and female prostitutes, prisoners, sexual multi-partners, haemophiliacs, polytransfused, etc. Among these groups, the prevalence of the infection could be compatible with a good use of screening.

However, we can see straightaway the ethical objections to such a selection, when the latter is based on private behaviours deemed, moreover, highly reprehensible by a large part of public opinion. Initiated campaigns, targeted at such groups, are clearly discriminatory and ethically unacceptable especially if those tests are mandatory and carried out without the knowledge of the individuals (in prisons, hospitals, etc.). Of course, if the test is suggested, i.e. voluntary and organized on an anonymous or confidential basis, there are then no ethical objections to 'targeting' such operations. You can, for example, choose STD clinics where the infection rate is high or drug users' centres, or even choose geographical areas where the prevalence is significant.

Individual GPs can also encourage their patients to undergo a test if they believe their history reveals behavioural risks. However, in the field of AIDS, we must be especially vigilant when implying the notion of 'risk factor' or 'risk behaviour'. Indeed, apart from the cases linked to transfusions, those behaviours have a marginal and reprobate connotation in our society, leading to discrimination and exclusion. If programmes are targeted at these groups, efficient measures of legal protection against any potential disclosure or stigmatization must then be devised. Otherwise, we will run the risk of intruding on privacy and breaching confidentiality. We will then risk ending up with the opposite to the sought-after goal—the individuals whose behaviour creates a greater risk will avoid the screening centres and medical consultations. Doctors will no longer have access to these threatened individuals, nor opportunities of counselling, the only possible means of prevention. We must avoid at all costs driving the disease 'underground', as the educational work of practitioners during medical consultations is essential.

Thus, the measures which at first sight seem 'worthwhile' for the community (mandatory testing, named data, targeted populations) risk in effect having very serious opposite effects by jeopardizing prevention opportunities. To avoid this, we must favour voluntary testing, followed by well-thought-out protection measures, decided by the individual; safeguard the secrecy of private data in order to keep the trust of individuals at risk; direct the efforts of public health towards making infected individuals act responsibly, since behavioural changes derive from this 'responsible awareness'.

Thus, we can say that the interest of the community and that of the individual are one and the same. Indeed, efficiency at the community level requires the respect of the affected individuals' rights and from an ethical viewpoint this is, of course, a positive conclusion for the coherence of our decisions.

5

HIV Testing, Screening, and Confidentiality: An American Perspective

EDWARD P. RICHARDS III

Introduction

The story of HIV[1] testing, screening, and confidentially in the USA is like the blind men and the elephant: what one sees depends on one's perspective and prior experience. A civil liberties lawyer concerned with the privacy of infected individuals would find the US approach a great success. A medical care provider concerned with the spread of HIV and the prompt treatment of infected individuals would see many lost opportunities. A public health specialist concerned with global communicable disease surveillance and control would see a disaster.

In this chapter I describe HIV testing, screening, and confidentiality in the USA. In keeping to this book's overall focus on testing, screening, and confidentiality, I have not dealt with health care services for persons with AIDS, AIDS education programmes, drug development and clinical trials, or basic science research. This narrow focus ignores much that is commendable, while, for better or worse, highlighting the issues which the USA has handled most poorly.

HIV policy in the USA is important not only because it has dominated public health discourse in the USA for nearly fifteen years, but because the USA has a disproportionate impact on disease-control programmes throughout the world. Many of the gains in world communicable disease control made in the 1960s and 1970s are being

[1] Since the underlying disease is HIV infection, with AIDS only representing one of many potential manifestations, I will refer to the disease as HIV infection, unless making a specific point about the subclass of symptoms defined as AIDS.

lost.[2] How much of this is because HIV policy in the USA has focused on individual cure and molecular medicine, thus discrediting disease control and surveillance? If these policies are wrong, if we do not draw the proper lessons from the HIV epidemic, then we will not be prepared for emerging infectious diseases.[3]

The Demographics of HIV in the USA

The first cases of what would be named AIDS were identified in the USA in 1981. The story of AIDS and confidentiality usually begins at this point, and the story of testing and screening begins in 1985, with the development of the first tests for antibodies to HIV. In most key ways, the story was over quickly: the core policies of the Federal government have shifted little since the mid-1980s, and the divisions between states that were evident in 1987 mostly persist. More critically, what were to become our HIV policies, and their epidemiological consequences, were already determined before the first case of AIDS was identified.

Demographics drove both the epidemiology of the HIV epidemic, and the political responses to it. While the USA has a strong Federal government, the individual states are surprisingly heterogeneous, both politically and demographically. The pattern of emergence of the HIV epidemic reflected the differences between large cities and towns, and the difference between social norms on the east and west coasts and the rest of the USA. HIV was originally concentrated in several metropolitan areas on the coasts: San Francisco, Los Angeles, Houston, Miami, and in the East Coast Metroplex from Baltimore through Washington, DC, New Jersey, New York City to Boston.

HIV was clustered in these cities because they had large IDU (intravenous drug-user) and gay communities in the late 1970s when HIV entered the USA. While all communities in the USA have gay men, it was these cities that provided the bath houses that made possible the high-frequency, anonymous sexual contacts necessary to rapidly spread HIV.[4] These cities also had the critical mass of IDUs

---

[2] Robert S. Desowitz, *The Malaria Capers* (New York: Norton & Co., 1991): 16.
[3] See the new journal from the CDC, *Emerging Infectious Diseases*. This is available on the World Wide Web at: http://www.cdc.gov/ncidod/EID/eid. htm. See also Richard Preston, *The Hot Zone* (New York: Random House, 1994).
[4] See generally, Randy Shilts, *And the Band Played On* (New York: St Martin's Press, 1987).

to support 'shooting galleries' and other practices that increased the sharing of needles and thus the transmission of HIV. HIV has spread widely since 1981, but it remains concentrated in the original cities of origin.

These demographics are important because public health policy in the USA is driven by the cities and states, not the Federal government. Rather than uniting the country in a common public health strategy, HIV further splintered decision-making, giving the USA separate policies for each of the fifty states, plus independent policies in several major cities. For example, some states require HIV reporting to public health authorities, many do not. Many states test and identify prisoners with HIV, but some do not. Some states carry out traditional contact-tracing to identify and warn persons who have been exposed to HIV, most do not. All states have laws governing the confidentiality of HIV-related information, consent for testing, involuntary testing, and screening for HIV. No two states have the same laws on these matters.

There are some general patterns. None of the states with large numbers of HIV cases requires named reporting, screens or identifies HIV-infected prisoners, or does contact-tracing. These states also tend to have the most intrusive privacy laws limiting the disclosure of HIV-related information, and among the best individual treatment and support programmes for persons with AIDS. From one perspective, these states, because of the large number of HIV cases, and thus the strength of their political advocates, are more sensitive to the rights and needs of the infected. From another, 'we failed to use the proven tools possessed by the field of public health to fulfil what should be the first responsibility in an epidemic: the protection of the uninfected.'[5]

HIV Testing

Public health policy in the USA explicitly encourages individuals who believe that they are at risk of HIV infection to be tested. Implicitly, however, we discourage testing by making it burdensome to be tested and to do testing. The most pervasive burden is that most

[5] Stephen C. Joseph, *Dragon within the Gates* (New York: Carroll & Graf Publishers, Inc., 1992): 27. Dr Joseph was commissioner of health for New York City during the 1980s.

states impose a special informed consent requirement before a person can be tested. This deviates from the general informed consent to medical treatment doctrine, which has been uniformly restricted to situations where patients suffer a physical injury which they were not warned about.[6] The courts have required informed consent for medical tests such as angiography that have substantial medical risks, and there is strong precedent for telling the patient the risks of not having a diagnostic test.[7] There was no requirement for specific informed consent to diagnostic tests that did not pose medical risks.

When HIV testing first became available, there was great fear that it would be used to identify and discriminate against infected persons. As a result of intense lobbying by gay and civil liberties groups, joined by public health personnel for reasons that are discussed later in this chapter, many states passed laws requiring a special informed consent for HIV testing. Most states also require that the person receive counselling before the testing, and after receiving a positive test result. Even in states that did not have specific statutory requirements, fear of litigation caused hospitals to adopt guidelines mandating special consents for HIV testing. These requirements burden testing in two ways.

First, as discussed later, specific consent laws make it impossible to do screening for HIV. Second, since there are no special consent requirements for other diagnostic tests that do not pose physiological risks,[8] the patient is implicitly told that this test is special, that it is not just a medical test. The consent forms often bias individuals against testing by stressing risks that are implicit in HIV infection, rather than in testing. These include possible discrimination by employers and landlords, and the effect of HIV status on the availability of insurance. Until the advent of 'triple-drug' treatment in late 1996 began to change perceptions about 'treatability' of HIV, few consent forms mentioned any of the benefits of testing, such as

[6] For a classic statement of the cause of action for informed consent, see *Canterbury* v. *Spence*, 464 F.2d 772, 790–91 (D.C. Cir.), cert. denied, 409 US 1064 (1972).

[7] *Truman* v. *Thomas*, 27 Cal.3d 285, 165 Cal.Rptr. 308, 611 P.2d 902 (1980).

[8] The California Supreme Court recently spoke directly to this issue in a case involving a claim that a physician should have disclosed certain information because it would have affected the patient's business and investment interests. The Court rejected this, holding that health care providers have no duty to warn patients about non-medical matters. *Arato* v. *Avedon*, 5 Cal.4th 1172, at 1189, 858 P.2d 598, at 609, 23 Cal.Rptr.2d 131, at 142 (Cal., Sept. 30, 1993).

prophylactic treatment of secondary infections and other precautions that can greatly reduce the morbidity of the disease and prolong life in some circumstances.

The most troubling aspect of special consent for HIV testing is that it presumes that it is proper to refuse testing. While this may be the case when an asymptomatic person is considering testing, it wreaks havoc when a potentially infected person is seeking medical care. HIV status is critical diagnostic information, certainly no less valuable than blood sugar or urinary protein. For HIV, however, Federal and state laws prevent physicians from refusing to treat a patient because of the patient's HIV status. Physicians are often forced to treat individuals without being able to determine their HIV status, even if this status is fundamental to their choice of therapy. This has been catastrophic in the case of pregnant women with HIV, for whom treatment dramatically reduces the chance of transmission to the fetus.[9]

Confidentiality

Keeping medical information confidentiality is a difficult problem. People the world over, and through history, like to talk about their ailments. Unauthorized disclosures by health care providers are not the source of most unwanted disclosures of HIV status, the infected individuals are.[10] The problem is that most of the health care in the USA is paid for by employers. Most of the claims under these employer-controlled health plans are reviewed, directly or indirectly, by the employers. To get one's care paid for, one must give up one's right to keep the information from one's employer. The employer might then gossip about the information, or, worse, fire the employee.

As states adopted special rules for consent to HIV testing, they also imposed special restrictions on how health care providers must handle information about a patient's HIV status. The goal was

---

[9] E. M. Connor, R. S. Sperling, R. Gelber, *et al.*, 'Reduction of maternal-infant transmission of human immunodeficiency virus type 1 with zidovudine treatment', *New England Journal of Medicine* **331** (1994): 1173.

[10] See generally ASTHO (Association of State and Territorial Health Officers), *Guide to Public Heath Practice: Principles to Protect HIV-Related Confidentiality and Prevent Discrimination* (Washington: ASTHO Publication, 1988). This report found no documented breaches of confidentiality by public health authorities.

primarily to prevent employers and landlords from getting information about the patient's HIV status. These restrictions ranged from just restating the general duty to keep medical information confidential, to restrictions on transferring the information to persons who would otherwise have access to the patient's medical records. In the most extreme cases, physicians were prevented from putting the patient's HIV status in the medical records, or sharing it with other health care providers who needed the information to best care for the patient.

Health care providers complained that it was impossible to maintain medical records such as hospital charts without mentioning information about a patient's HIV status. The patients found that the restrictions made it harder to get medical care because their physicians' could not share information with other health care providers. The restrictions also made it difficult for their insurers to obtain the necessary information to pay health insurance claims. As anti-discrimination in employment laws was strengthened, attacking the root cause for concern, the most Draconian of these restrictions on medical records were modified.[11] Confidentiality concerns have now shifted to whether there are situations, usually involving susceptibility to secondary infections such as tuberculosis, when the employee's HIV status poses a risk to others in the workplace.

The most contentious battle on confidentiality was whether the names of persons with a positive HIV test would be reported to the public health department, and, if the health department knew that a person was infected, whether it would investigate the case to determine source of the infection and to identify others at risk. HIV reporting and contact-tracing were rejected by most states, and by all those with a significant number of HIV-infected persons. While, as discussed later, our public health system was already greatly weakened before AIDS was discovered, the decision to not report HIV was the pivotal break with traditional disease control.

Reporting and Contact-Tracing before AIDS

In 1981, at the time AIDS was identified, all states required physicians, hospitals, and laboratories to report the names of persons with

---

[11] For a good review of confidentiality laws in 1990, see Harold Edgar and Hazel Sandomire, 'Medical privacy issues in the age of AIDS: legislative options', *American Journal of Law and Medicine* **16** (1990): 155.

serious communicable diseases, or diseases such as food poisoning which have particular public health significance. These infected persons are then contacted to assure that they receive any necessary treatment, and to investigate the spread of the disease. Most disease investigations are simple and unintrusive, delving into where you work, where you go to school, whether you have been to any parties, with whom your children play, or what you ate yesterday. Cooperation was seldom an issue, and was never coerced.

Sexually transmitted disease (STD) investigations are much more intrusive. The infected person will be asked to identify their sexual contacts, by name and address if possible. These contacts will then be interviewed and warned that they are at risk for a sexually transmitted disease. At no time is the infected person originating the report named. The contact is told no more than that he or she has been exposed to a STD and that the health department would like to help them get tested and any necessary treatment. This can be a very confrontational situation, especially when the contact has been monogamous and thought that his or her partner has been as well. These investigations are carried out by skilled investigators, and the health departments have effective systems to protect the infected person's privacy.

Since few people want others to suffer needlessly from disease, there was general cooperation with these investigations. People did not fear that the health department would divulge their confidences, and the health department clinics generally treated them with more respect than the private physician community. (After the sexual revolution, it is hard to remember that all STDs once carried a profound stigma.) There were always some people who did not want to name their contacts, or withheld some of the names. They were not coerced to divulge their contacts because a few holdouts do not affect the overall disease control programme.[12] Because of the communal nature of STDs, the contacts that patient A does not name will usually be named by patient B or C.[13] If the person is married, then the spouse's name is already known.

In the 1970s gay men in the cities with bathhouses generally looked to the health department clinic for STD treatment, rather than

[12] D. E. Woodhouse, J. B. Muth, J. J. Potterat, and L. D. Riffe, 'Restricting personal behavior: case studies on legal measures to prevent the spread of HIV', *International Journal of STDs and AIDS* 4/2 (1993): 114.

[13] Hebert W. Hethcote and James A. Yorke, *Gonorrhea Transmission Dynamics and Control* (New York: Springer-Verlag, 1984): 42.

private physicians. There was no opposition to testing, reporting, and contact-tracing for STDs. Nearly every gay man frequenting a bathhouse participated in the epidemiological investigations of hepatitis B. It was our knowledge of the spread of hepatitis B in the bathhouses, and from there into the blood supply, that allowed us to characterize the epidemiology of HIV so quickly. A higher percentage of infectious (primary) syphilis cases were gay men than heterosexuals, to the point that infection with syphilis was as good a predictor of homosexuality as was later infection with AIDS.

The First AIDS Cases

The traditional reporting and investigation system was critical to identifying and characterizing AIDS. When the first cases of unusual diseases among gay men were identified, no one realized their significance. The CDC reported the first cases as a syndrome, i.e. a clinical entity, defined by its symptoms, for which no etiologic agent is known. Following standard procedure, the CDC solicited reports of other patients who suffered from the same symptoms. As more cases were reported, the clinical picture was refined and the initial case definition was modified. As this continued, it became clear that the common element in the cases was suppression of the immune system, and that it was a disease of gay men. At this point the case definition used to solicit reports of cases became the definition of AIDS.

During the initial years of the epidemic, when it was not known how the disease spread or who was at risk, there was no opposition to the reporting of AIDS. As more cases of AIDS were investigated, disease control investigators tried to discover its epidemiology. It was soon obvious that this new disease had the same epidemiology as hepatitis B, and the rate of infection with both diseases was very high. Through compiling lists of persons with hepatitis B, the health departments had unwittingly compiled lists of the first men who would die of AIDS. While it would have been politically impossible, some public health physicians believed that we should have closed the bathhouses in the 1970s to prevent the hepatitis B epidemic. Their worst fears were now realized: the bathhouses had become the vector for a far worse infection.

As the toll from AIDS increased, the government was pressed to make disability payments available to persons with AIDS. A person diagnosed with AIDS was entitled to various government benefits, most important of which was Supplemental Security Income (SSI) payments, a Federal disability insurance programme funded by the Social Security Administration. Most of these benefits were available only to persons who filed a claim disclosing that one had been diagnosed with AIDS. This defused fears of reporting AIDS to health departments since there the government would get the information anyway.

The problem was persons who appeared to have AIDS, but who did not manifest the correct symptoms to come under the CDC definition. These people were said to have AIDS-related complex (ARC). While they were often sick and dying, they were invisible to epidemiologists because they were not systematically reported to public health departments. We later learned that IDUs were dying of HIV-related illnesses during the initial phase of the epidemic, but that we did not notice these deaths. The largest numbers of hidden cases were in Africa. HIV was not noticed in IDUs or Africans because these were populations that already had high death rates from communicable diseases.[14] IDUs and the Africans both died of the same diseases as before AIDS; they just died at a higher rate. Since we took these deaths for granted, we did not take notice of the increase in the fatality rate of their routine infections. In contrast, the gay men tended to develop unusual infections and rare tumours, which brought their cases to the attention of the reporting physicians.

The Discovery of HIV

When the human immunodeficiency virus was isolated, and the HIV-antibody test became available, AIDS should have ceased to exist. Once the etiologic agent is discovered, diseases are usually defined by that agent. AIDS should have been supplanted by HIV infection and HIV-related illness. While we might have retained a clinical definition to indicate the stage of the disease, there was no longer any justification for distinctions such as AIDS and ARC. At this point the politics of HIV overwhelmed the science.[15]

[14] Joseph, *Dragon within the Gates*: 114–15.
[15] See the discussion of 'AIDS speak' in ibid. 99–100 for an example of how politics even distorted the medical terminology used to discuss the disease.

Gay and civil rights groups resisted shifting from reporting AIDS to reporting HIV. Unlike AIDS patients, whose symptoms trigger government benefits, many persons with HIV are asymptomatic. Since there are no benefits attached to a diagnosis of HIV infection without the symptoms that define AIDS, they reasoned that the government did not have any need for information about HIV-infected persons. In the states with the great majority of the AIDS cases, AIDS advocacy groups and civil liberties lobbies such as the American Civil Liberties Union (ACLU) organized against HIV reporting and contact-tracing.

Colorado became a focal point of the national debate when Dr Thomas Vernon, the state health director, asked the legislature to pass the nation's first HIV-control law that was based on reporting, contact-tracing, and measures to assure that physicians would properly treat HIV-infected individuals.[16] While the proposed law provided the strongest protections ever proposed for public health information, it was vehemently opposed by all the national gay groups. Despite heavy lobbying, the Colorado legislature passed the proposed bill with only minor changes.[17] Most importantly, the law did not affect the health department's right to conduct other disease control activities.

Texas is an example of what happened in the states where the anti-reporting lobbies were more effective. In the late 1970s and early 1980s, Texas had systematically rewritten its antiquated public health code.[18] The revised Texas law allowed health officers to act decisively when necessary, while providing better review of public health orders and greater protection for individual liberties. After a debacle involving the mishandling of an HIV-infected prostitute by a city health director who was not familiar with the revised disease-control laws,[19] the legislature was lobbied to revise the disease-control laws to protect the rights of HIV carriers.[20]

[16] Thomas M. Vernon, George Thomasson, and Edward Richards, 'A preventive law plan for the Colorado AIDS control law', *Colorado Medicine Magazine* **86**/5 (1989): 78.

[17] Edward P. Richards, 'Colorado Public Health Laws: A Rational Approach to AIDS', *University of Denver Law Review* **65** (1988): 127.

[18] See Senate Bill No. 1064, Texas Session Laws, 68th Legislature, Regular Session, ch. 255, pp. 1116, 1124 (1983).

[19] For a discussion of this case, see Edward P. Richards and Katharine C. Rathbun, 'A Review of *Private Acts, Social Consequences* by Ronald Bayer', *Family Law Quarterly* **23** (1989): 137.

[20] Tex. Rev. Civ. Stat. Ann. Art. 4419b–1 (1987), recodified at Texas Health and Safety Code, ch. 81—Communicable Diseases 81.151 *et seq.* (1989).

The Texas legislature added sweeping procedural safeguards to all the disease-control laws, not just those governing HIV control. These included the right to appointed counsel, multiple court hearings, and the presumption that the disease carrier would remain at liberty during the proceedings. Under the old law, the health officer initiated restriction proceedings. This was revised to require that the health officer's request be channelled through the city, county, or district attorney, adding a layer of political review. Most difficultly, the disease carrier gets the right to a jury trial, with all the attendant delays and costs.[21]

Had these protections been restricted to HIV-infected persons, they would have had little impact on disease-control programmes. Irrespective of one's views about the advisability of using restrictions, including public health segregation, in the control of HIV, it has proven politically impossible in all but the most unusual circumstances. This is not the case, however, for other communicable diseases, especially tuberculosis. The practical effect of time-consuming and expensive protections for disease carriers is to make it impossible for the health departments to carry out effective disease-control programmes.[22] The impact on tuberculosis was seen a few years later when the rates of new infections began to increase. This prompted many states to return to more traditional disease-control laws for tuberculosis.

By 1988 the states had divided along lines defined by HIV reporting. No state with a high rate of HIV infection reports the names of HIV-infected persons. While the CDC has continued to refine its antiquated case definition for AIDS, this does little to encourage HIV reporting and partner notification. Federal funding grants for HIV require states with mandatory HIV reporting to establish sites where persons could be tested without being reported. Despite evidence that HIV reporting and contact-tracing is cost-effective, there has been little reconsideration of these polices in the states that have the vast majority of HIV-infected individuals.[23]

---

[21] 'The jury shall determine if the person is infected with or is reasonably suspected of being infected with a communicable disease that presents a threat to the public health and has refused or failed to follow the orders of the health authority.' Texas Health and Safety Code, ch. 81.170 (1989).

[22] For a case of documented spread of multidrug resistant tuberculosis because of inadequate health department restrictions, see Centers for Disease Control, 'Outbreak of multidrug-resistant tuberculosis—Texas, California, and Pennsylvania', *Morbidity Mortality Weekly Report* **39** (1990): 369.

[23] J. J. Potterat, N. E. Spencer, D. E. Woodhouse, and J. B. Muth, 'Partner notification in the control of human immunodeficiency virus infection', *American Journal of Public Health* **79** (1989): 874.

One of the great ironies of this failure to require reporting and investigation of HIV is that most states that do not require named reporting of HIV-infected persons have created exceptions to deal with public demands that people at risk be warned. California, for example, which has some of the strongest privacy laws on HIV-related information, allows physicians to notify spouses, sex partners, and fellow IDUs of their patient's HIV status.[24] Thus one of the most difficult and delicate public health duties, that of finding and notifying exposed persons while protecting the patient's confidentiality, is taken from the public department and left to physicians with no training or experience in disease control.

Screening

Since all states have specific consent requirements for HIV testing, it is impossible to do named screening for HIV. This does not mean that screening is not done: there were hundreds of thousands of screening tests done each year in the USA. The screenings were done blind, and the infected persons that were detected were not informed of their disease. The most common blind screening was of newborns. New York State, for example, screened all babies born in the state for HIV, but collected the data so that it could not identify the specific infected infants. While this complied with the laws banning testing without consent, it became controversial and was eventually stopped because it denied mothers and children the benefit of early diagnosis.[25]

There has been named screening of two subpopulations: military personnel and prisoners. The military, as a unit of the Federal government, with its own legal system, is not bound by state laws on civil matters such as HIV-testing requirements. The screening of the military provided the largest population samples to study the incidence of HIV at various points in time. Unfortunately these data are not of general applicability because the military has significantly different demographics from the general population, not the least because it

[24] Cal Health and Saf Code at 199.25 (1994). While this statute allows the health department to notify exposed persons if the patient's physician asks it to, it can choose to decline the request. Even if the health department acts on the request, it must then destroy all records pertaining to the infected person and his/her contacts, making it impossible to identify persons who pose a continuing risk to others.
[25] Linda Farber Post, 'Unblinded mandatory HIV screening of newborns: Care or coercion?', *Cardozo Law Review* 16 (1994): 169.

excludes gay soldiers and IDUs. These differences are thought to give the military a lower incidence of HIV than the general population.

Prisons have a higher rate of HIV infection than the general population, ranging up to 17 per cent of new inmates in prisons that are fed by cities with high rates of HIV infection.[26] These rates reflect the high proportion of new inmates that have been convicted for crimes related to drug use. Many were infected by sharing needles, but there are growing numbers of women who are infected in drugs-for-sex trades, or drug-related prostitution.

Several factors make HIV a very difficult problem in US prisons. First, the prison population in the USA is expanding much faster than the physical space necessary for housing the prisoners. This has led to severe overcrowding and the spread of communicable diseases such as tuberculosis.[27] Second, prisons must pay for medical care, including care for HIV-infected prisoners, from the general prison budgets. They cannot draw on health care funds provided for treatment of HIV-infected persons in the general population. Third, the legal standards for quality of prison life, medical care for prisoners, and even protection from violence are very low.

These factors combine to make most prisons in the USA frightening places. Violence is the norm, drug use is common, and homosexual rape is used both for sexual gratification and to enforce power hierarchies among prisoners.[28] A recent study has documented substantial transmission of HIV in prisons by looking at inmates who had been behind bars since 1977 or earlier, eliminating all those that had been outside the prison walls during this time, or had any opportunity to acquire the infection other than from a fellow prisoner. Of the 556 inmates that satisfied the study criteria, eighty-seven had undergone identified HIV screening, and of these, 18 (21 per cent) were HIV positive.[29]

[26] Peter S. Dixon, *et al.*, 'Infection with the human immunodeficiency virus in prisoners: meeting the health care challenge', *American Journal of Medicine* **95** (1993): 629.

[27] M. Miles Braun, *et al.*, 'Increasing Incidence of Tuberculosis in a Prison Inmate Population; Association With HIV Infection', *Journal of the American Medical Association* **261** (1989): 393.

[28] Jim Hogshire, 'So you're going to prison . . .' excerpt from book, 'You Are Going to Prison', *Esquire Magazine* **123** (1995): 91; see also David M. Siegal, 'Rape in prison and AIDS: a challenge for the Eighth Amendment framework of Wilson V. Seiter', *Stanford Law Review* **44** (1992): 1541.

[29] Randal C. Mutter, Richard M. Grimes, and Darwin Labarth, 'Evidence of intraprison spread of HIV infection', *Archives of Internal Medicine* **154** (1994): 793.

This study illustrates the problem of HIV-screening policies in prisons: do you do named screening and identify the infected prisoners? The state where the study was done, Florida, is one of the states with a high incidence of HIV in its prisons. As with the other states with high HIV incidence, Florida does not do named HIV screening.[30] The only prisoners whose HIV status were known were those that had previously asked to be tested for HIV, leaving a substantial number of cases undetected.

Those who oppose named screening see it as violating the prisoner's right to privacy, and potentially subjecting the prisoner to abuse by other prisoners and discrimination by the prison authorities.[31] Most courts have rejected this view,[32] and in other situations these same prison systems have cared little for their prisoners' privacy rights.[33] The failure to do named screening is probably best understood by looking at prison financial and medical resources. When a prisoner is identified as infected with HIV, or suffering from HIV-related illness, that prisoner is entitled to medical care and some accommodation to his or her impaired immune status. Named screening will only trigger more demands on already limited prison resources. If the prisoner's HIV status is unknown, the prisoner will not receive prophylactic treatment for secondary infections, resulting in a shortened life-span.[34]

Epilogue

The fragmented response to the HIV epidemic in the USA has two roots. First is the historical allocation of the police power (the power to protect the public heath and safety) to the states. Communicable diseases were inextricably intertwined with the colonization of the new world. Their catastrophic effects on unexposed populations were as important as military technology in displacing the indige-

[30] Albert R. Jonsen and Jeff Stryker (eds.), *The Social Impact of AIDS in the United States* (Washington, DC: National Academy Press, 1993): 180.

[31] For a legal case advocating this point of view, see *In re* Connecticut Prison Overcrowding and Aids Cases, 1990 WL 261348 (D. Conn., Dec 06, 1990) (NO. H–80–506(JAC), CIV. H–88–562.

[32] See *Dunn* v. *White* 880 F.2d 1188 (CA10 Okla 1989).

[33] See *Bell* v. *Wolfish et al.*, 441 US 520 (1979). While this case is several years old, prison conditions have deteriorated and prison authorities have only become more harsh in response.

[34] Jonsen and Stryker, *Social Impact of AIDS in the United States*: 182.

nous peoples.[35] Once the colonies were established, they were ravaged by epidemic diseases.[36] The abatement of nuisance and the quarantine of disease carriers demanded prompt action. In a time of slow communications and limited governmental infrastructure, that meant that the police power had to be vested in the officials of the towns, not the colonial government, or the English Parliament.

When the Constitution was drafted in 1787, the central issue was balancing the power of the central government against that of the states.[37] The police power was among the powers left to the states. While the Federal government has reclaimed the police power in many areas, especially environmental law, it has left public health to the states.[38] As a result, there is no US Health Department, no US Public Health code, no US Health Officer, and the Surgeon-General has become a figurehead.[39]

The second root of this fragmented policy is that health departments since the 1960s have shifted their emphasis from communicable disease control to providing indigent health care. Health officers are no longer chosen for their expertise in disease control. Health departments have adopted the clinical physician's focus on individual care and rights. This is the antithesis of public health: society is the 'patient' in public health, the rights of the individual are subsumed by the need to protect society. By the mid-1970s, disease control had become such a low priority in the USA that we allowed hepatitis B to spread with little effort at control, setting the stage for the explosive spread of HIV.

The USA must re-evaluate its policies on testing, screening, and confidentiality for communicable diseases. While we cannot turn back the clock on HIV, we must prepare for the next emerging infectious disease. This will be most critical in states that crippled their

[35] See generally William H. McNeill, *Plagues and Peoples* (New York: Doubleday, 1976); more specifically Lemuel Shattuck, *Report of the Sanitary Commission of Massachusetts 1850. Facsimile Edition* (Cambridge, Mass.: Harvard University Press, 1948): 61.
[36] Shattuck, *Report of the Sanitary Commission of Massachusetts*.
[37] For a general discussion of this period, see Catharine Drinker Bowen, *Miracle at Philadelphia: The Story of the Constitutional Convention May to September 1787* (Boston: Atlantic Monthly Press, Little, Brown & Co., 1986).
[38] Edward P. Richards, 'The jurisprudence of prevention: society's right of self-defense against dangerous individuals', *Hastings Constitutional Law Quarterly* **16** (1989): 329.
[39] Alfred Yankauer, 'Sexually Transmitted Diseases: A Neglected Public Health Priority', *American Journal of Public Health* 84 (1994): 1896.

general disease control efforts in response to HIV. Scientists study-
ing emerging viruses such as Hanta virus and Ebola virus are raising
the alarm that we are no longer prepared to control a communicable
disease epidemic.[40] The gravest threat may be from the growing resistance of common bacterial illnesses to antibiotics.[41] We may soon
come full circle, returning to a world in which public health and
safety are dependent on disease-control practices rather than medical
technology.

[40] Llewellyn J. Legters, *et al.*, 'Are we prepared for a viral epidemic emergency?', in
Stephen S. Morse (ed.), *Emerging Viruses* (New York: OUP, 1993): 269–82.
    [41] See generally Paul W. Ewald, *Evolution of Infectious Disease* (New York: OUP,
1994).

6

Compensation and Consent: A Brief Comparative Examination of Liability for HIV-Infected Blood

DIETER GIESEN

Introduction

Many complex legal and ethical issues have been raised by the AIDS crisis.[1] As lawyers, scientists, and ethicists, it is vital that we collaborate in identifying and clarifying these issues and that we contribute thereby to rational public discussion of the problems associated with AIDS in society. This chapter will focus upon just one quite specific, but nonetheless significant aspect of this legal and ethical problem field, namely consent in relation to the obtaining and transfusion of HIV-infected blood and the liability of hospitals, blood banks, and others for the transmission of the virus in this manner.

Although doctors in the USA became aware of the acquired immune deficiency syndrome (AIDS) in 1981, it was not until 1983 that the AIDS virus was isolated by scientists. At the same time hospitals and blood banks concluded that the deadly virus could be transmitted by blood transfusions. Only in 1985, however, was the ELISA test developed which allowed donated blood to be tested for the presence of HIV antibodies. This was followed by the Western Blot test which provides confirmation of ELISA test results.

I gratefully acknowledge the cooperation during the course of the work on this chapter from John Harrington, BA (Dub.), BCL (Oxon.), Research Fellow at the Working Centre for Studies in German and International Medical Malpractice Law, the Free University of Berlin, 1992–4.

[1] Generally, M. L. Closen, D. H. J. Hermann, P. J. Horne, S. H. Isaacman, R. M. Jarvis, A. S. Leonard, R. R. Ivera, M. Scherzer, G. P. Schultz, and M. E. Wojick, *AIDS: Cases and Materials* (Houston, 1988).

Specifically, the Western Blot test helped to eliminate most of the 'false positives' yielded by the oversensitive ELISA test. Soon after it was put to use by blood suppliers in most developed countries, enabling the elimination by blood suppliers of the risk of contamination of the blood supply thereafter. Regrettably, in France, for reasons of economic nationalism and due to governmental incompetence, this opportunity to prevent infection was not taken sufficiently promptly, resulting in a wholly needless increase in the number of individuals with AIDS in that country.[2] In Germany also the public has recently been shocked to discover that, even after the introduction of the above-mentioned testing procedures, certain businesses engaged in the manufacture of blood products failed to test all incoming blood supplies for HIV, with evidently disastrous consequences.[3]

Nonetheless, we are chiefly concerned in this chapter with the two-year period between the discovery of the virus and the availability of the ELISA test. In this interim period the only means of preserving the blood supply from contamination was to ensure, as far as possible, that persons carrying the AIDS virus refrained from donating blood. This required an effective exclusion of individual members of groups at high risk of being infected with HIV, chiefly homosexual men and intravenous drug users. In several of the leading jurisdictions a body of important case law has arisen from this period, determining the extent of the precautions which could and should reasonably have been taken against infection in this manner by hospitals, blood banks, and the manufacturers of blood products. From this jurisprudence it is clear that the situation under discussion embodies a clash of interests between different groups of persons, which must be resolved if appropriate rules of civil liability are to be developed.

The question of the patient's informed consent in relation to the administration of blood transfusions has also gained in significance in the context of liability for HIV-infected blood. The general rules

---

[2] A brief chronology of relevant events in France at this time may be found in B. Dufort, 'French Doctors accused over HIV in Blood', *Bulletin of Medical Ethics* **74** (Dec. 1991): 13–15.

[3] *Cf.* S. Dauth, 'HIV—verseuchte Blutprodukte. Rückrufe, Firmenschliebung and Mahnung zu Besonnenheit', *Deutsche Ärzteblatt* **90** (1993): 1994; S. Dauth and H. Clade, 'Skandal urn HIV-verseuchte Blutprodukte. Die Lawine rollt weiter', *Deutsche Ärzteblatt* **90** (1993): 1945; *Der Spiegel* 45 (8 Nov. 1993): 272–85.

governing the duty of disclosure upon medical professionals vary considerably as between the various legal systems both within and beyond Europe.[4] This difference has furthermore been reflected in the legal regulation of disclosure in the context of transfusion of HIV-infected blood.

I shall therefore critically examine the differing approaches of British, German, and American courts to questions of consent and products liability in this field. Our discussion is focused upon this varied jurisprudence because of its crucial importance to the fate of such outstanding claims for compensation as may yet arise from infection with HIV by way of blood transfusions. In addition, and at a more abstract level, the outcome of those cases so far litigated reveals highly divergent attitudes to patients' rights and to the significance accorded to the goal of compensation within the various systems of delictual liability.

Liability for the Transfusion of HIV-Infected Blood

In many countries governments and health authorities have reached out-of-court settlements with haemophiliacs and others who have been infected with HIV as a result of blood transfusions.[5] Thus, for example, in the UK the Department of Health and the National Blood Transfusion Service settled with such a group before their case went to full trial.[6] The decision of the Court of Appeal in that case to uphold the plaintiffs' claim for discovery of documents, which concerned the proposal to make the British blood supply self-sufficient, is also important in itself.[7] It is clear that the determination and application of procedural and substantive rules will strongly influence the bargaining position of this group of people with HIV beyond the context of litigation.

---

[4] These rules are assessed in comparative light in D. Giesen, *International Medical Malpractice Law* (Tübingen, 1988): §§20–7.

[5] e.g. in Australia: *B C* v. *Australian Red Cross Society*, *Australian Torts Reporter* §9–195 at 15,333 (Vict. SC 1991).

[6] *Re HIV Haemophiliacs Litigation* (1990)140 NLJ 1349 (CA).

[7] *Cf.* M. A. Jones, *Medical Negligence* (London: Sweet & Maxwell, 1991): 146.

The basis of liability in American Law[8]

The most important Common Law developments in the area under discussion have taken place in the USA.[9] We shall see that courts and legislatures have cut off the clearest routes to compensation by virtually excluding recovery under contractual warranty or in strict liability. The plaintiff is left, therefore, to surmount the difficulties presented by the negligence action.

Breach of warranty

The first possible basis of a plaintiff's action in a case concerning HIV-infected blood in the USA would be in contract for breach of warranty. Since it is highly unlikely that express contractual negotiations have taken place, this warranty would have to be an implied one that the blood was of merchantable quality, i.e. safe for transfusion. American courts have, however, been firm in refusing to apply the law of warranty in this context.[10] This refusal is based upon the highly questionable premiss that blood is not a product and therefore not subject to the law of sale and warranty. Thus, in its 1954 decision in *Perlmutter* v. *Beth David Hospital*[11] the Supreme Court of New York held that the supply of blood was merely an incidental aspect of the general service provided by the defendant hospital. Although *Perlmutter*[12] concerned blood infected with serum hepatitis, the products–services distinction upon which it rests has been relied upon to preclude recovery for infection with HIV.[13] This decision

---

[8] *Cf.* generally, R. C. Greif, 'Hospital and Blood Bank Liability to Patients who Contract AIDS through Blood Transfusions', *San Diego Law Review* **23** (1986): 875–96; D. A. Roling, 'Transfusion Associated AIDS: Blood Bank Liability', *University of Baltimore Law Review* **16** (1986–7): 81–119; *D.H.J. Hermann*, 'AIDS: Malpractice and Transmission Liability', *University of Colorado Law Review* **58** (1986–8): 63–107.

[9] For a comparative discussion of German and American law on liability for contaminated blood and blood products, *cf.* D. Giesen and J. Poll, 'Zur Haftung für infizierte Blutkonserven im amerikanischen und deutschen Recht', *Recht der internationalen Wirtschaft* (1993): 265–71.

[10] *Uniform Commercial Code* 2–313 to 2–316.

[11] *Perlmutter* v. *Beth David Hospital*, 308 NY 100, 123 NE2d 792 (1954). *Cf.* also, *Community Blood Bank. Inc.* v. *Russell*, 196 So2d 115 (Fla 1967); *Jackson* v. *Muhlenburg*, 53 NJ 138, 249 A2d 65 (1969); *Samuels* v. *Health and Hospital Corp.*, 591 F2d 195 (2d NY 1979).

[12] *Perlmutter* v. *Beth David Hospital*, 308 NY 100, 123 NE2d 792 (1954).

[13] D. Louisell and H. Williams, *Medical Malpractice,* 4 vols. (New York 1993 with 1993 suppl.) §19A.06 at 19A–17.

essentially gives effect to policy considerations which have been a feature of civil liability in the field under discussion ever since. The Court's finding that the continued and sufficient availability of blood is of great importance to society is not open to dispute. The Court went further, however, in acting upon the unproven assumption that the imposition of civil liability upon hospitals and blood banks would endanger this availability.

Strict liability

Alternatively a plaintiff in the USA may allege strict liability in tort, relying upon §§402a of the *Second Restatement of the Law of Torts*. According to this provision, which has been adopted by the courts of most States, the vendor of a product which is unreasonably dangerous to users and consumers is made strictly liable for damage which it causes.[14] Again it is clear, however, that a plaintiff infected with HIV can only succeed if blood is characterized as a product rather than as a service.

In *Cunningham* v. *MacNeal Memorial Hospital*[15] the Supreme Court of Illinois held the defendant hospital strictly liable to a patient who had been infected with serum hepatitis as a result of a blood transfusion. The Court rejected the reasoning in *Perlmutter*,[16] holding that '[it would be] a distortion to take what is arguably a sale and twist it into the shape of a service, and then employ this transformed material in erecting the framework of a major policy decision.'[17] As the lower court held in *Cunningham*[18] blood is as much a product as pharmaceuticals, which have been held to come within §402a of the *Second Restatement of the Law of Torts*.[19] The decision of the Illinois Supreme Court sent hospitals and blood banks scurrying for legislative protection. Consequently, most of the USA enacted so-called 'blood shield statutes' which expressly classify the

[14] W. L. Prosser and W. P. Keaton, *The Law of Torts* (5th edn., St Paul [Minn] 1984) §§98–9.

[15] *Cunningham* v. *MacNeal Memorial Hospital*, 47 Ill2d 443, 266 NE2d 897 (1970).

[16] *Perlmutter* v. *Beth David Hospital*, 308 NY 100, 123 NE2d 792 (1954).

[17] *Cunningham* v. *MacNeal Memorial Hospital*, 47 Ill2d 443, 266 NE2d 897 (1970 per Culbertson J. at 901), adopting the words of the Florida Court of Appeal in *Russell* v. *Community Blood Bank, Inc.*, 185 So2d 749 (Fla App 1967 at 752) affd and modified *sub nomine Community Blood Bank* v. *Russell*, 196 So2d 115 (Fla 1967).

[18] *Cunningham* v. *MacNeal Memorial Hospital*, 113 IllApp2d 74, 251 NE2d 733 (1969 per McCormick J. at 738).

[19] e.g. strict liability may be imposed upon manufacturers of oral contraceptives: *Orecman* v. *G. B. Searle & Co.*, 321 FSupp 449 (1st Cir.1971).

supply of blood as a service 'for all purposes'.[20] Subsequent case law has put beyond question the application of these statutes to blood infected with HIV.[21] Purely from the point of view of doctrinal coherence this legislative adoption of a highly questionable judicial distinction is to be regretted. Furthermore, it bears out the considerable influence of the medical lobby, a phenomenon which is also observable in European countries.[22]

It must be made clear that the legislative and judicial stance outlined above drastically limits the right of the infected individual to compensation on the basis of a mere supposition as to the requirements of the common good. It may be added that there has been too little consideration of the important policy factors which favour the imposition of strict liability in cases of infected blood. As Traynor J put it in the path-breaking Californian case of *Escola* v. *Coca-Cola Bottling Co*,[23] public policy demands that responsibility be fixed wherever it will most effectively reduce the hazard to life and health inherent in defective products. It is evident that the manufacturer can anticipate some hazards and guard against the recurrence of others, as the public cannot.[24] It is submitted that this rationale for strict liability loses nothing when considered in the context of blood supply. Blood banks and hospital authorities were after all in a position to preclude members of high-risk groups from donating blood up to mid-1985 and later to test all donated blood for HIV antibodies. Furthermore, the 'blood shield statutes' represent a revival of the charitable immunity accorded to hospitals which was effectively abolished by judicial decision in the 1960s.[25]

Even if it can be said that the transfusion of blood by blood banks and hospitals is essentially an element of the provision of a service, this should not in our view preclude claims against the manufactur-

[20] e.g. in California, *cf.* §§3294, 3333.1 CC West Ann Cod (St Paul [Minn] 1970 [Suppl. 1992]). Statutory restrictions have also been introduced in Australia, *cf Australian Torts Reporter* §§ 9–195 at 15,323–15,324.

[21] *Kirkendall* v. *Harbour Insurance Company*, 887 F2d 857 (8th Cir. 1989); *McKee* v. *Cutter Laboratories*, 866 F2d 219 (6th Cir. 1989). They have also withstood constitutional scrutiny on the basis of the Fourteenth Amendment to the US Constitution, *cf. Samson* v. *Greenville Hospital*, 377 SE2d 311 (SC 1989).

[22] D. Giesen, *International Medical Malpractice* (Tübingen, 1988), §§1417–1526.

[23] *Escola* v. *Coca-Cola Bottling Co.*, 24 Cal2d 453,150 P2d 436 (1944).

[24] *Escola* v. *Coca-Cola Bottling Co.*, 24 Cal2d 453,150 P2d 436 (1944 per Traynor J. concurring, at 439–40).

[25] *Darling* v. *Charleston Memorial Hospital*, 33 111(2)d 326, 211 NE2d 253 (1965); *cf* D. Giesen, *International Medical Malpractice Law* (Tübingen, 1988) §§74–103.

ers of blood products based upon strict liability or warranty. The arguments in favour of strict liability are clearly stronger in the case of such producers. No possible charitable exemption can be justifiably claimed by these commercial enterprises and they, and not the recipients of their HIV-infected blood products, are best placed to absorb the cost of any losses suffered. Finally, the transmission of the AIDS virus may be viewed as an externality, an additional social cost generated by the manufacture of blood products but not reflected in the expenses incurred by the relevant companies.[26] It is now recognized that one of the major goals of a system of civil liability is to ensure that such externalities are reflected in operating costs. Haemophiliacs and others infected with HIV in this manner should not be left to meet the entirety of their expenses nor should the State, in the form of the social welfare system, be forced to bear the whole burden.[27] In this respect the manufacturers of blood-clotting agents such as Factor VIII and Factor IX should not benefit from a special, unmerited exemption. As it was put in a relevant decision from Maryland, '[o]ne can agree with John Stuart Mill that poetry provides a higher type of pleasure than does pushpin without accepting the defendant's [manufacturer of blood products] argument that it is a provider of poetry and therefore should be exempt from the Benthamite calculus providers of pushpins are subject to. Nor should it be. Those who choose to operate in the economic marketplace play by the rules applicable to all.'[28]

Negligence

It remains then for the plaintiff to make out a case in negligence against the hospital or blood bank. While the incidence of a duty of care in such cases is beyond doubt,[29] the appropriate standard of care is sometimes problematic. In an industry as highly regulated as

---

[26] *Cf.* generally, G. Calabresi, *The Cost of Accidents: A Legal and Economic Analysis* (New Haven, 1970).

[27] This argumentation is deployed most effectively in relation to the interpretation of the blood shield legislation in California in P. T. Westfall, 'Hepatitis, AIDS and the Blood Products Exemption from Strict Products Liability in California: A Reassessment', *Hastings Law Journal* 37 (1985–6): 1101–32.

[28] *Doe* v. *Miles Laboratories, Inc., Cutter Laboratories Division*, 675 FSupp 1466 (D Md 1987 per Ramsev DJ at 1480).

[29] In relation to hepatitis B: *Samuels* v. *Health & Hospital Corp.*, 432 FSupp. 1283 (SD NY 1977); *Jones* v. *Miles Laboratories, Inc.*, 887 F2d 1576 (D Ga 1989). In relation to HIV-infected blood: *Kozup* v. *Georgetown University*, 663 FSupp. 1048 (D DC 1987); *Jeanne* v. *Hawkes Hospital*, 13 MedLR 231 (Ohio Ct App 1991).

the one under discussion it is possible that a court will regard compliance with administrative requirements or customary practice as conclusive evidence that the defendant was not at fault in its screening or blood-testing procedures. It is important to recall, however, that the standard of care in negligence cannot be a mere summation of existing practice in any given area of society. Rather the courts are free, indeed they are obliged, in proper discharge of their functions, to determine what the particular defendant ought to have done in the circumstances, even if this involves condemning as negligent the practice of a whole profession.[30] Otherwise, as the Supreme Court of Colorado pointed out in *United States Blood Services* v. *Ouintana*,[31] there arises the danger that professional groups will be allowed to determine the incidence and extent of their own civil liability. Furthermore, it must be noted that the plaintiff in such a negligence action faces considerable evidential difficulties. The defendant benefits from an overwhelming superiority of expertise. In addition, given the various means by which HIV can be transmitted and, in the present context, the large number of blood suppliers, many plaintiffs will fail at the causation stage.[32]

German developments

In Germany, perhaps unexpectedly, it has primarily been the courts which have responded to the challenge presented by the AIDS epidemic.[33] Very much in the manner of Common Law judges, they have developed the law in the light of circumstances which the nine-

---

[30] D. Giesen, *International Medical Malpractice Law* (Tübingen, 1988), §§127–64.

[31] *United States Blood Services* v. *Ouintana*, 14 Med LR 122 (Colo SC 1992); cf. D. Giesen, *International Medical Malpractice Law* (Tübingen, 1988), §§1089–90.

[32] In Australia the burden of proving causation proved fatal to a claim in negligence arising from infected blood, cf. *E.* v. *Australian Red Cross* (1991) 31 PCR 310, *Australian Torts Reporter* §§9–195. On causation and rules of evidence in medical law generally, cf. D. Giesen, *International Medical Malpractice Law* (Tübingen, 1988), §§268–405, 851–82.

[33] I. Fahrenhorst, 'Die Haftung für HIV-verseuchte Blutkonserven', *Medical Law Review* (1992): 74–9; R. Eichholz, 'Die Bedeutung der arzneimittelrechtlichen Produkthaftung für das Blutspenden und den Vertrieb von Blutkonserven', *NJW* (1991): 732–5; E. Deutsch, 'Die neue Entscheidung des BGH zur AIDS-Haftung', *NJW* (1991): 1937–8; A. Spickhoff, 'Zur Haftung für HIV-kontaminierte Blutkonserven', *Juristen Zeitung* (1991): 756–60; J. Langkeit, 'Arztrechtliche Probleme im Zusammenhang mit AIDS-Tests', *Jura* (1990): 452–60; E. Reinelt, 'Die Haftung des Arzneimittelherstellers für die Übertragung von Viren durch Blutprodukte', *Versicherungsrecht* (1990): 565–72.

teenth century drafters of the Civil Code could not have foreseen. We shall see that they have not focused upon the arguably legalistic distinction between products and services, but have instead proceeded to a more realistic assessment of the relative positions of plaintiff and defendant.

In a very important decision of 1991 the German Federal Supreme Court established the fundamentals of liability for HIV-infected blood.[34] The defendant hospital had obtained infected blood from an HIV-positive donor in the period before testing was possible. This was transfused to a patient, who in turn infected her husband with the AIDS virus. The latter sought recovery in negligence under §823 I *German Civil Code*. At each stage of its decision the Court took cognizance of the plaintiff's considerable evidential difficulties. First it held that the defendant had breached its duty of care through its inadequate screening of blood donors. Although members of 'high-risk' groups were recommended not to give blood, the threat to life posed by their disregarding this recommendation was not made clear in a sufficiently vivid and forceful manner. The Court rejected the defendant's claim that compliance with this requirement would have led to criticism from interest groups and in the media. Furthermore, the need to protect patients' lives took precedence over the personality rights of potential donors. Thus, regardless of the practice of the rest of the profession at the time, the law required that blood suppliers do all in their power to exclude infected blood from the system where testing was impossible. This breach of duty having been established, the Court held that the burden of disproving that it resulted in the obtaining of defective blood rested upon the defendant. The lower instance had also held in favour of such a reversal of the burden of proof, but expressly based this upon judicially developed principles of product liability.[35] By contrast, the Federal Supreme Court refused to characterize blood as either product or service and looked instead to the basic principles of fairness which underlie these evidential rules. Essentially the burden of proof should be determined according to those areas under the organizational control of each party. In so holding the Federal Supreme Court progressed towards general rules of procedural fairness and just compensation regardless of the somewhat tenuous distinction between products

---

[34] BGH, 30 Apr. 1991 VI ZR 178/90 BGHZ 114,284, JZ 1991,785, NJW 1991,1948.
[35] OLG Hamburg, 20 Apr. 1990 1 U 34/89 NJW 1990, 2322.

and services.[36] Finally, the Court held that since neither the plaintiff nor his wife belonged to a 'high-risk' group they would be held to have made out a prima-facie case that they had become HIV positive as result of the blood transfusion and not otherwise.[37] We may conclude that German law, both adjectival and substantive, has been recast to take account of the real difficulties presented in cases involving blood contaminated with HIV.[38] Each of these developments accords, furthermore, with a leading decision of the Federal Constitutional Court which mandated the reshaping of the law of evidence in order to fully vindicate the plaintiff–patient's right to fair procedures.[39]

Duties of Disclosure in Blood Transfusion Cases

Another important area of law in this field relates to the informed consent of patients to the transfusion of blood. It is the law in all Western jurisdictions that, in order to respect his right to self-determination, the patient's consent must be obtained to any diagnostic or therapeutic procedure to which he is submitted. The right to self-determination embodies the fundamental value of individual autonomy which lies at the heart of the legal system in all open and democratic societies.[40] The extent to which this value is protected in the medical context will depend upon the standard of disclosure

---

[36] On the interaction between rules of product liability and medical liability in German law, *cf.* D. Giesen, *Arzthaftungsrecht*, 3rd edn. (Tübingen, 1990): 191–262.

[37] By contrast, in the Australian case of *Dwan* v. *Farquhar and Others* [1988] 1 OdR 254 (1987) Aust Torts Reps §80–096, the Full Court of the Supreme Court of Queensland rejected such a plaintiff's claim of *res ipsa loquitur*.

[38] *Cf.* generally, A. Laufs, Zivilrechtliche Fragen im Zusammenhang mit AIDS, insbesondere ärztliche Untersuchungs-Offenbarungs- und Behandlungspflichten, Berufshaftung, in *AIDS als Herausforderung an das Recht. Tagungsbericht über die Tagung vom 10–19 Oktober 1988 in der Deutschen Richterakademie in Trier* (Stuttgart, 1989): 278–303.

[39] BVerfG, 25 Jul 1979 2 BvR 878/74 BVerfGE 52,131. Note: although in that case the Court was divided evenly as to the precise impact of constitutional guarantees upon the law of evidence in medical negligence actions, both sides agreed upon the need for a re-evaluation of procedural rules in the light of the German Basic Law (Grundgesetz). *Cf.* D. Giesen, *Arzthaftungsrecht*, 3rd edn. (Tübingen, 1990): 196–9.

[40] *Cf. Schloendorff* v. *Society of New York Hospital*, 211 NY 125, 105 NE 92 (1914 per Cardozo J at 93); *Sidaway* v. *Bethlem Royal Hospital* [1985] AC 871, [1985] 2 WLR 480, [1985] 1 All ER 643 (HL per Lord Scarman at 649g); BGH, 9 Dec. 1958 Vl ZR 203/57 BGHZ 29,46 (49).

which the law imposes upon doctors and others. This standard, as we shall see in relation to blood transfusions, varies considerably.

England: Disclosure after Sidaway

In England the incidence and scope of the duty of care which a doctor owes to his patients is determined by the test laid down by McNair J in *Bolam* v. *Friern Hospital Management Committee.*[41] According to this test a defendant doctor will not be held liable if, in his conduct of treatment or diagnosis, he conforms to the practice of a responsible body of medical practitioners.[42] This was adopted (with certain qualifications) as the test of informed consent in England by a majority of the House of Lords in *Sidaway* v. *Bethlem Royal Hospital.*[43] Thus, in effect, the amount of information in relation to the risks accompanying any procedure which a doctor in England or Wales is required to disclose is determined by medical opinion, or at least a responsible section thereof and not by the distinctive needs of the particular patient. However, as Lord Scarman pointed out in his forceful dissent in *Sidaway,*[44] the decision to submit oneself to treatment is only partly a medical one, 'a patient may have in mind circumstances, objectives and values which he may reasonably not make known to the doctor but which may lead him to a different decision from that suggested by purely medical opinion.'[45] In short the principle of autonomy requires that patients be given sufficient information as to proposed or likely procedures to enable them to shape the course of treatment themselves and thus, ultimately, to determine the course of their own lives.

Regrettably, in its recent decision in *Re T*[46] the Court of Appeal has sanctioned the application of the doctor-centred and therefore, it

---

[41] *Bolam* v. *Friern Hospital Management Committee* [1957] 1 WLR 582, [1957] 2 All ER 118 (QB).

[42] For a comparative discussion of the weaknesses of the '*Bolam* test' in both the treatment and disclosure contexts, *cf. D. Giesen*, 'Medical Malpractice and the Judicial Function in Comparative Perspective', *Medical Law International* 1 (1993): 1–16.

[43] *Sidaway* v. *Bethlem Royal Hospital* [1985] AC 871, [1985] 2 WLR 480, [1985] 1 All ER 643 (HL).

[44] *Sidaway* v. *Bethlem Royal Hospital* [1985] AC 871, [1985] 2 WLR 480, [1985] 1 All ER 643 (HL).

[45] *Sidaway* v. *Bethlem Royal Hospital* [1985] AC 871, [1985] 2 WLR 480, [1985] 1 All ER 643 (HL per Lord Scarman at 652c–e).

[46] *Re T* [1992] 4 All ER 649 (CA).

is submitted, paternalistic approach of *Sidaway*[47] in the context of blood transfusions. The decision primarily concerned the question of consent where the patient in question is unconscious at the time of the proposed treatment. Additionally, however, in relation to conscious patients, it was held that consent to the procedure itself would only be precluded or vitiated in cases of direct coercion or complete deception.[48] By contrast, the incidence and scope of the duty to disclose risks accompanying blood transfusion, such as the possibility of contracting HIV or hepatitis B and the alternatives thereto would fall to be determined according to the ruling of the majority of the House of Lords in *Sidaway*.[49] More encouraging, from the perspective of patients' rights was Lord Donaldson MR's criticism of standard forms of refusal to accept a blood transfusion, which are increasingly used in British hospitals. Such forms are, he said, primarily intended to protect hospitals against litigation but will be 'wholly ineffective for this purpose if the patient is incapable of understanding them'.[50] Although the status of consent forms, as thus outlined, is accepted in most jurisdictions, very many medical professionals have persisted in the erroneous view that these forms suffice, ethically and legally, to vindicate patient's rights and to insulate professionals from liability.[51]

The patient-centred standard of disclosure

By contrast with their colleagues in England, judges in Civil Law countries and, indeed, the rest of the Common Law world have developed standards of disclosure which are sensitive to the informational needs of the patient and which seek to give primacy to his

---

[47] *Sidaway* v. *Bethlem Royal Hospital* [1985] AC 871, [1985] 2 WLR 480, [1985] 1 All ER 643 (HL); *cf.* also, *Gold* v. *Haringey Health Authority* [1987] 3 WLR 649, [1987] 2 All ER 888 (CA), revg [1986] CLY 2275, (1986) *The Times*, 17 June (Schiemann J). The Court of Appeal rejected a higher, patient-centred standard of disclosure in relation to non-therapeutic procedures such as sterilization and affirmed the unitary application of the '*Bolam* test' in all medical negligence cases.

[48] e.g. where the plaintiff is a Jehovah's Witness whose faith forbids him to accept blood transfusions, *cf. Re T* [1992] 4 All ER 649 (CA per Lord Donaldson MR at 662h663g). This holding is in accordance with that of the Ontario Court of Appeal in *Malette* v. *Shulman* (1990) 72 OR (2d) 417, [1991] MedLR 162, affg (1987) 63 OR (2d) 243 (Ont HC).

[49] *Sidaway* v. *Bethlem Royal Hospital* [1985] AC 871, [1985] 2 WLR 480, [1985] 1 All ER 643 (HL).

[50] *Re T* [1992] 4 All ER 649 (CA per Lord Donaldson MR at 663c–e).

[51] D. Giesen, *International Medical Malpractice Law*, §§813–26.

right of self-determination. Thus, in a very recent decision on the general question of consent to medical treatment, the High Court of Australia formulated a standard of disclosure based not upon prevailing medical practice, but upon the informational needs of the reasonable patient.[52] This 'reasonable patient' test was first adumbrated in Canada in the case of *Reibl* v. *Hughes*[53] and in the USA in the decision in *Canterbury* v. *Spence*[54] and has been adopted by most Common Law jurisdictions apart from England and Wales.[55] Ultimately, however, this objective or 'prudent patient' test is also found to be inadequate to the protection of the fundamental right at stake here. As it was stated by the Supreme Court of North Carolina, under such tests '[t]he right to base one's consent on proper information is effectively vitiated for those with fears, apprehensions, religious beliefs, or superstitions outside the mainstream of society.'[56] In the light of this consideration courts in the German-speaking jurisdictions have adopted a 'subjective patient' test which requires medical professionals to meet the informational needs of the actual patient at hand in order to comply with their duty of disclosure.[57]

Guided by this patient-centred approach the German Federal Supreme Court has recently outlined the scope of a hospital's duty of disclosure in relation to the possible need for blood transfusions and the risk of HIV infection entailed thereby.[58] It was recognized, as it has been in all major jurisdictions,[59] that a patient need not be informed of those risks accompanying surgical and other procedures of which there is general knowledge among lay persons. However,

---

[52] *Rogers* v. *Whittaker* (1992) 67 ALJR 47, (1992) Aust Torts Reps §81–189 (HC of A); for a discussion of this and other developments in Australian medical law, *cf.* D. Giesen, 'Vindicating the Patient's Rights. A Comparative Perspective', *Journal of Contemporary Health Law and Policy* 9 (1993): 273–309.

[53] *Reibl* v. *Hughes* (1980) 1 SCR 880, (1980) 114 DLR 3d 1, (1980) 14 CCLT 1, (1980) NR 361 (SCC).

[54] *Canterbury* v. *Spence*, 150 AppDC 263,464 F2d 772 (DC Cir 1972).

[55] *Cf.* D. Giesen and J. Hayes, 'The Patient's Right to Know–A Comparative View', *Anglo-American Law Review* 21 (1992): 101–22; D. Giesen, 'From Paternalism to Self-Determination to Shared Decision Making', *Acta Juridica* (Cape Town) (1988): 101–27.

[56] *McPherson* v. *Ellis*, 305 NC 266, 287 SE2d 892 (1982 per Mitchell J at 897).

[57] B.VerfG, 25 Jul. 1979 2 BvR 878/74 BVerfGE 52, 131; BGH, 9 Dec. 1958 VI ZR 203/57 BGHZ 29,46; BG,12 Jan. 1982 BGE 108 II 59 (no. 10), Pr 71 (1982) no. 122 at 299; *cf.* further, Giesen, *International Medical Malpractice Law*, §§590–601.

[58] BGH, 17 Dec. 1991 VI ZR 40/91 BGHZ 116, 379, JR 1992, 19 (D. Giesen), JZ 1992, 421 (E. Deutsch).

[59] Giesen, *International Medical Malpractice Law*, §§617–23.

the Court held that, while the possible necessity for blood transfusions during the course of an operation could be accounted part of that knowledge which a patient might be expected to have, the risk of infection with HIV in this manner could not. This was so since, at the time of the transfusion in question, the risk of infection was chiefly associated with sexual contact and the sharing of needles during drug use. Finally, the existential threat posed by the AIDS virus also had to be considered. Thus, the hospital was required to inform the patient of the risk of contamination of any blood used during the course of the operation. In addition it was also required to inform her of the possible alternatives (i) of donating her own blood in advance[60] or (ii) of obtaining a directed blood donation, from a member of her family, for example.

Causation in consent cases

Even if the plaintiff shows that doctors and hospital staff failed to meet the required standard of disclosure it remains for him to prove that this breach of duty was causative of his decision to allow the blood transfusion to proceed. Obviously the test of causation applied by the courts will be decisive to the success of such a plaintiff's claim. Thus, for example, in the Texas case of *Knight* v. *Department of the Army*,[61] the plaintiff was not properly informed of the risk of becoming HIV positive as a result of a blood transfusion. At the causation stage, however, it was held that, even if full disclosure had been made, a reasonable person in the plaintiff's position would not have forgone the transfusion. It is submitted that this objective test of causation, based as it is upon the concept of reasonableness, fails to give full effect to the right to self-determination. Rather, sufficient protection is only available where a subjective test of causation is applied in consent cases, as in several other Common Law and Civil Law

---

[60] It has been asserted by eminent German medical opinion that the use of such autologous blood transfusions enables patients to participate actively in the treatment process; *cf.* B. von Bormann and S. Aulich, 'Autologe Transfusionsverfahren: Nutzen and Risiko', *Deutsche Ärzteblatt* **90** (1993): 1958–62. This may help to forge the sort of 'therapeutic alliances' which commentators have proposed as a means of ensuring the vindication of patients' rights, *cf.* H. Teff, 'Consent to medical procedures: paternalism, self-determination or therapeutic alliance?' *Law Quarterly Review* **101** (1985): 432–53.

[61] *Knight* v. *Department of the Army*, 757 FSupp. 790 (WDTex 1991).

jurisdictions.[62] As the German Federal Supreme Court has put it, 'the patient's personal reasons for refusal must be respected. No generalizing yardstick is allowed: not that of a reasonable patient, and even less so that of medical judgement.'[63]

Conclusion

We have seen that civil liability for the transfusion of HIV-infected blood has been developed chiefly through case law in both the Common Law jurisdictions of the USA and the German Civil Law system. On the other hand, the intervention of State legislators in the USA has been a negative one, effectively bringing a guillotine down upon a feared extension of liability in such cases. Ultimately the varying doctrinal outcomes have been determined by differing assessments of policy considerations in this area. The need to preserve an adequate blood supply has been allowed by American lawmakers and judges to prevail over the right of HIV-infected plaintiffs to adequate compensation for the devastating injury which they have suffered. In Germany the reverse was found to be the case. There judges were seen to be willing to overcome the outdated distinction between products and services in order to ensure that the law remained responsive to the changing needs of individuals and of society. Thus, in the modern context of the AIDS epidemic, we have come upon an old and fundamental legal problem, namely, how far must the interests of the individual yield to the greater good? More specifically, is the solution arrived at in the USA consistent with the principles of a legal system which has the protection of the individual at its core, or must the claims of these individuals with AIDS be sacrificed in the interests of a speculative gain for society as a whole?

Quite what level of blood supply is deemed necessary varies from country to country. Many Third World countries, so far from

[62] England: *Chatterton* v. *Gerson* [1981] QB 432, [1980] 3 WLR 1003, [1981] 1 All ER 257 (Bristow J at 265g). New Zealand: *Smith* v. *Auckland Hospital Board* [1965] NZLR 191, 224–5 (CA). South Australia: *Gover* v. *State of South Australia* (1985) 39 SASR 543, (1985) 125 LSJS 342 (1985) Aust Torts Reps §80–758 (SA SC, Cox J at 365). Germany: BGH, 7 Feb. 1984 Vl ZR 174/82 BGHZ 90, 103 (112), JR 1985, 65 (D. Giesen). Switzerland: BG, 12 Jan. 1982 BGE 108 II 59 (no. 10), Pr 71 (1982) no. 122 (at 299). Austria: OGH, 23 June 1982 (3 Ob 545/82) SZ 55 (1982) 581 (no. 114), JBl 1983, 373.

[63] BGH, 7 Feb. 1984 Vl ZR 174/82 BGHZ 90, 103 (112), JR 1985, 65 (D. Giesen); *cf.* further, Giesen, *International Medical Malpractice Law*, §§685–93.

meeting their own needs, serve as sources of blood for richer countries. Even among the developed nations, Germany's use of blood and blood products is well in excess of those of its neighbours.[64] Beyond the questions of law discussed here there remain important issues of public health and distributive justice which society as a whole must begin to examine. For example, the deliberate stimulation of demand for arguably fruitless, but expensive medical procedures, which divert resources from primary care.[65]

We also found that the various standards determining doctors' general duty of disclosure were applied consistently in the context of informed consent to blood transfusions and infection with HIV. The case law in relation to those infected with HIV in this manner puts into particularly sharp relief the varying extent to which patients' right to self-determination is protected in different countries. It is submitted that a patient-centred approach, at both the fault and causation stages, which has been adopted in the German-speaking countries, is to be preferred to the amalgam of more or less objective tests which are applied in the Common Law countries, especially England. As we have seen, patients encounter great difficulty in proving specific negligent conduct or negligently organized procedures on the part of hospitals and blood producers. Given this, and the deadly nature of AIDS, it is essential that patients are fully informed of the risks accompanying blood transfusion, and the alternatives thereto. Otherwise the patient cannot be said to have consented to run the risk which has been realized and he should not, therefore, be burdened with the entirety of the loss resulting therefrom. For the courts to hold otherwise is to subordinate the rights to health and self-determination of the individual patient to the pecuniary interests of a paternalistic medical profession.

[64] *Cf. Der Spiegel* no. 45 (8 Nov. 1993): 272–85.
[65] *Cf.* I. Illich, *Limits to Medicine. Medical Nemesis: The Expropriation of Health* (Harmondsworth: Penguin, 1976).

7

Individual Responsibility for Health

INEZ DE BEAUFORT

> On the whole people want to be good, but not too good and not
> quite all the time.
>
> George Orwell

Introduction

In these times of limited resources for health care, different criteria
for the allocation of health care both on a micro- as well as on a
macro- (societal) level are being discussed by philosophers, physicians, and policy-makers. I will discuss one of the criteria that has
featured in the Netherlands,[1] in quite heated debates, that is the
responsibility of the individual for his or her own health. (More col-
loquially: does one have to pay for one's faults and unhealthy
habits?)

Some people have a chronic unhealthy lifestyle: they smoke, drink,
work too hard, eat junk food, and engage in 'unsafe' sexual adven-
tures. Others have dangerous hobbies like hang gliding, parachute
jumping, or participating in the Paris–Dakar rally.

On the other hand, other people live healthy lives: they eat moder-
ately, refrain from smoking and drinking, they exercise, and practise
'safe' sex. They, of course, do not go canoeing in Brazil or Belgium

I am very grateful to Charles Erin, John Harris, and Medard Hilhorst for their com-
ments on earlier drafts of this chapter. Of course, I'm entirely responsible for faults,
weak arguments, etc.

[1] Of course, as the vast amount of literature shows, this issue has received much
attention in other countries as well. See e.g. D. Wikler, 'Who should be blamed for
being sick?' *Health Education Quarterly* **14**/1 (1987): 11–25; R. E. Goodin, *No
Smoking* (Chicago: University of Chicago Press, 1989).

(a little less dangerous, but still adventurous), but collect stamps, go for walks, go bowling, or play golf in their free time.

A question that has arisen in the Dutch context is: is it fair that those who live healthily pay for (a part of the) health care for those with an unhealthy or risky lifestyle? If one claims a right to health care, should that not be based on the obligation to live a maximally healthy life? And can and should such an obligation be enforced by the government by imposing financial or other sanctions? Can society afford (morally as well as financially) to be like the Good, even Very Good, Samaritan who, without regard for persons' present or past lifestyles, provides care for those who need it. It is within the context of the discussion on priorities and choices with regard to health care that the problem of the *individual's responsibility* for his own health has been raised.

Different options have been discussed. First: excluding ill persons from certain health care facilities, in particular *scarce* facilities, if they were themselves responsible for their illness. Secondly: higher insurance premiums for health care[2] for those who live unhealthy lives. Of course, these solutions differ in the sense in which they influence the freedom and the health of individuals.

A Drastic Solution

I will first discuss what I consider as the most drastic proposal. Dupuis has defended the idea that it can, sometimes, be justified to exclude people from health care facilities.[3] She illustrates her view with the following example: in an intensive care department of a hospital a bed is reserved for an elderly lady who is scheduled to undergo cardiac surgery. Postponement of the operation may endanger her life. The night before the operation a drunken man drives his car into a tree and, seriously injured, is brought to the hospital.

Dupuis argues that the elderly lady should be treated and occupy the intensive-care bed instead of the drunken man, because the lady is ill through no fault of her own, whereas the man brought the situ-

---

[2] Another financial measure is to increase taxes for unhealthy products like tobacco, etc. I will not discuss this in this context, because with regard to AIDS it doesn't seem a realistic option. It seems rather difficult to find a 'product' that could be taxed.

[3] H. M. Dupuis, oral statement, congress record, *Verpleegkunde Nieuws* **23**/4 (8 Nov. 1990): 20–3.

ation upon himself. In a situation of scarce resources 'the blameless' go first. She has also defended the proposition that AIDS patients who, knowing the risks, have contracted the disease through unsafe sex or drug (ab)use should not get a *scarce* new drug.[4] In her view this is unfair towards those who are the victims of bad luck and could have done nothing to avoid it.

The same argument was raised when an ex-alcoholic sailor received a new liver in the Academic Hospital of Groningen, which was for a number of potential donors a reason to state that they did not want their liver to be implanted in an ex-alcoholic.

Guilt or Actual Suffering?

Suppose one could argue that if someone destroys his own health this may lead to some unfair consequences for others, couldn't one also argue that moral considerations other than justice based on past actions are more important when it comes to providing health care? Isn't the principle of solidarity based on the confrontation with human misery overriding in these situations? If you see, for example, how people with AIDS suffer physically, mentally, and socially, doesn't society have a moral duty to help, no matter whether the person contracted HIV as a result of 'recklessness' (a person who became HIV positive as a result of high-risk behaviour) or not (a person who contracted the virus by an infected blood transfusion, for example)? They both end up in a situation in which they need all the care they can get. It is not decisive *how* they ended up in this situation. What is important is that they are in this situation this very moment. Whether one finds this argument convincing depends, of course, on one's view of solidarity. (I will define solidarity rather loosely as the commitment of a person or a group of persons to share the burdens, financial or otherwise, of the problems of other persons.) Is not solidarity based on actual misery rather than on the causes of misery?

Of course, our feelings of pity may vary in relation to the causes of suffering. If a woman becomes HIV infected through rape we feel extremely sorry because she had so much suffering and a death

---

[4] I. de Beaufort and H. M. Dupuis, 'Selectie op microniveau', in I. de Beaufort and H. M. Dupuis (eds.), *Handboek Gezondheidsethiek* (Assen, Maastricht: Van Gorcum, 1989): 187–95.

sentence inflicted on her by the immoral behaviour of someone else. We may feel less pity with someone who engaged in careless behaviour and think 'how stupid, you could have prevented this', but we will also think (or ought to think) 'how terrible for him to be HIV infected. We ought to help.' I think this is a strong argument against the withholding of medical treatment. Even the drunken driver finds himself in a pitiful state.

One could argue that this may be true for the drunken driver and the AIDS patient but not for other health care facilities as, for example, IVF for persons who are infertile as a result of a venereal disease in the past. Some situations are sad (not being able to have children) but not as miserable as other situations. If someone is dying in the street, we should be good Samaritans and rush out to provide help, but other conditions do not motivate us in the same way to give help. This implies judgements on 'scales of misery' and on what calls for societal help on the basis of solidarity and what does not. In my view this issue should be solved in the discussion on priorities for health care. If IVF is considered to be a luxury and not a basic technology that should be available for all, it should not be included in the basic insurance. That should hold for everyone who needs it, not only those with infertility caused by a venereal disease. If, on the other hand, it is considered basic health care and therefore a reason for solidarity, it should be available to all who need it.[5]

If Only One Can be Saved

One could again emphasize that it would be unjust to use *scarce* resources that therefore cannot be used for somebody else whose plight is worse. A situation in which all of us have to make a certain financial sacrifice is quite different from the situation in which a particular person cannot get what he or she needs (the elderly lady) because the health care facility is used for someone else (the drunken driver). The elderly lady should not be sacrificed because of feelings of pity or solidarity for the drunken driver. She is, in her situation, at least as much (probably more) entitled to our help than the drunken driver. If their situations are equally miserable, but only one can be

[5] What one considers to be basic or not can, of course, vary in relation to the perspective chosen. I will discuss the issue from the perspective of an affluent society. A global perspective would lead to different priorities.

saved, the old lady ought to get the treatment. Choosing the drunken driver would simply be unfair towards her.

If on the basis of medical criteria her operation cannot be postponed (she is as likely to die when the operation is postponed as the drunken driver is when he does not receive care), then she ought to be treated. The presupposition then is that from the point of view of medical urgency they both are equally in need of urgent treatment. Then, in my view, maybe the lady should be helped first on a 'first come, first served' criterion. Not because she is not to blame for her illness, but because she was there first. If the ambulances bringing the elderly lady and the drunken driver to the hospital arrive at exactly the same moment, in my view a lottery device of selection ought to be used.[6]

Suppose, however, that the operation of the elderly lady can be postponed (for several hours or a day). In that case the drunken driver should be helped first. Why? Because it is very difficult to draw lines when a criterion of guilt or responsibility for health is used.

Coincidences and Triage

Suppose the car accident took place the next day. The lady had been successfully operated on and the intensive-care bed is again available. I think that few would defend that in those circumstances the drunken driver should *not* be helped but allowed to die. However, the view I feel uncomfortable about is that the moral judgement is not always made (all drunken drivers, all AIDS patients), but depends on coincidences (the absence or presence of 'competing' patients at time *t*). Of course, our lives are in many respects influenced by coincidences. ('If I had left two minutes earlier I would not have been in the car accident. If only I had flu on the night of the 20th, then I wouldn't have met this exciting stranger who has infected me. If only the tree hadn't

---

[6] I'm not altogether sure how far I would go. Suppose the drunken driver was a sober bank robber who first shot the old lady and then a child and all three of them were brought to the hospital at the same time in the same need of urgent treatment. Let's also suppose that there is no doubt that the bank robber did it. In that case the other patients are *his* victims, which changes the situation. In the original example the lady is not the victim of the drunken driver. If the drunken driver is helped, she may be the 'victim' of society's view on solidarity. What if the old lady was just having a nice picnic under the tree into which the drunken driver drove? Or his mother sitting next to him in the car not knowing he was drunk?

been there, I would just have driven into the ditch.') However, notwithstanding all the 'if-only-ing' we do, we have to accept that what happens to us is (also) dependent on coincidences. The fact that in some cases moral judgements on a person's responsibility with regard to his health status are made, whereas in other situations they are not made, bothers me in the case of, for example, the accident happening a day later. One could argue: such is 'lifeboat' life; it is even more unfair to use a lottery device because then the elderly lady suffers the consequences of chance instead of being given what she deserves.

Of course, one could develop a theory of deterrence and sacrifice some drunken drivers and AIDS patients in order to prevent others from engaging in the same behaviour. ('That is what will happen to you if you drink too much or have dangerous sexual liaisons.') It may have a deterrent effect. But that doesn't mean it is justified. There are other less invasive and less cruel measures available to convince people that it is better not to drink and drive and do everything you can in order not to get AIDS. And if we agree on the fact that the drunken driver should not be left to die when he can be helped, we face the problem of how to define when there is a situation of scarcity that would lead to unfair sacrifices of others.

The problem with examples like this is their (academic) lifeboat character. Useful to test one's triage-ethics, but they are not exactly the same as societal scarcity problems. I'm not denying that there may be situations of absolute and/or acute scarcity. Think of the limited availability of some donor organs. But when it comes to hospital intensive-care beds or expensive drugs for AIDS the situation is more complex, because these are forms of a relative scarcity that could be solved by spending more money on manufacturing drugs and expanding hospitals (or transportation of ill persons to other hospitals). One may not want to do that, of course, because other societal purposes are considered to be more important, but it is a complex scarcity. Even those who defend the Dupuis argument in a lifeboat situation could argue that it is not a good argument to accept other scarcities and not a good argument to keep the costs of certain health care facilities down. ('It's all right to restrict the manufacturing of drugs for AIDS and accept the scarcity because many AIDS patients attribute their situation to their own stupid behaviour.') I think that even in an absolute scarcity situation it is a very problematic criterion, for arguments having to do with responsibility that I will discuss later.

The Physician as Judge

Another problem for Dupuis's point of view is that it puts the doctor in a complex position.[7] He is expected to make a judgement on someone's culpability. Not only can there be circumstances in which there simply is no time to do so because emergency care is required and the patient would die while the doctor was deliberating, but more important: a doctor is not equipped for such a task. And if doctors took it upon themselves to make those judgements, that would seriously undermine the trust that is essential for a patient–physician relationship. A doctor should be a professional to whom you can go for treatment without having to justify your past and present lifestyle. If doctors were to pass judgements on lifestyles and treat conditionally[8] ('I'm very sorry, but you are guilty of dangerously promiscuous behaviour, so you have no right to a scarce treatment'), we would try to hide our pasts from them and would not trust them. (Except those who cannot hide their 'sins', but those people knowing they would be found guilty wouldn't bother to visit a physician. And those with perfect and blameless lifestyles who have nothing to hide may not need a doctor anyway. Well, maybe some psychiatric help, it must be very hard to be perfect.)

Maybe the drunken driver had lost his job that day and when coming home to tell his wife discovered that she had left him taking the children, the couch, and the video, only leaving him the beer which 'caused' the drunkenness. Maybe not. Maybe he was an irresponsible egoistic person who didn't care about the consequences of what he did. Anyway, he certainly deserves to be punished for drunken driving, but the doctor should not be the judge and the punishment should not consist of withholding life-saving medical treatment.

[7] In a Dutch research project regarding doctors', nurses', and physiotherapists' views on these matters, when asked if guilt for a disease could be a criterion for selection for scarce resources: 19% of the physicians answered 'yes, always', 56.4% 'sometimes', and 24.6% 'never'. See Tj. Tijmstra, H. C. M. Busch, and W. ScafKlomp, *Keuzen in de zorg. Meningen van beroepsbeoefenaren in de gezondheidszorg* (Groningen: Styx, 1991): 30.

[8] The only exception in my view would be the situation in which a certain treatment will not work unless a patient stops a certain habit (e.g. smoking). In that case the physician will not pass a moral judgement on the patient ('you are an irresponsible person, you don't deserve this treatment') but a medical judgement ('unless you stop doing x, I can't medically help you'). The fact that a treatment may possibly be (somewhat) less effective, in my view, is not a good reason for refusing it.

Doctors may warn their patients about the dangers of what they are doing, they may urge them to live differently (I'm not against a well-balanced dose of moralism when it comes to prevention), but when the worse comes to the worst they should treat and not punish by not treating.

Of course one could argue that doctors need not necessarily make the judgements themselves but they could just carry out decisions made by (special) judges specialized in health and guilt. ('We have these two candidates for a liver transplant, please let us know which one has a right to it.') This would be a possibility for non-acute situations. In my view this would not be a good idea, both on the basis of the misery argument (one ought to help very ill persons regardless of the causes of their disease) as well as for practical reasons. Imagine two AIDS patients. One of them infected by a blood transfusion because he was in an accident in Africa and had not brought—against all advice—his own sterile needles and blood products. ('Oh no, I'd rather travel light, nothing's going to happen to me. I don't want to take all that along.') Recklessness? As 'blameworthy' as the person who engaged in anal sex with unknown partners but always using a condom, but one fatal day the condom got torn?

In a Dutch TV programme on the liver transplant for the ex-alcoholic sailor referred to earlier, some alcoholics and ex-alcoholics stated that they would refuse a liver transplant because they themselves felt that by destroying their liver, they had lost the right to claim such an organ (in times of scarcity). Impressive as such statements are, to exclude oneself, however, is an altogether different situation from when others decide you do not deserve the transplant.

Why is Dupuis's example convincing for many? One problem it confronts us with is the possible sacrifice of a real person. I also think it has to do with the plain immorality of drunken driving, which involves the unacceptable endangering of other, innocent persons' lives. But suppose the same man did not drive but got drunk and then fell down a staircase and was brought to the hospital, heavily injured? Would we still say 'no treatment, this is your own fault'? And if we would not, where do we draw the line?

Those who argue that society cannot afford to help, should also ask whether it can afford *not* to help.

In view of these problems, excluding people from (certain forms of) health care is, in my view, not a defensible solution for the unhealthy lifestyle problem.

Van Asperen's Champagne Drinker

I will now discuss another solution, in the Netherlands defended by van Asperen. Van Asperen has developed a more or less Rawlsian-inspired view on health care.[9] She argues that it is a great good that people in our society have the freedom to choose their own lifestyle. However, it is not reasonable to expect society to pay for the consequences of an unhealthy lifestyle. She argues that we would not consider it reasonable if a person with expensive tastes and preferences was to receive financial support from 'collective sources' in order to pay for these luxurious tastes. The person who cannot live without champagne, caviar, or truffles should manage his financial situation accordingly or—poor soul—live without his champagne and settle for fish and chips instead. The same argument holds for health care insurance. Van Asperen states that the comparison is not frivolous as long as we are discussing *self-chosen* and *avoidable* preferences. It is unreasonable to expect other persons to show solidarity with daredevils. (Very interesting how the devil shows up in the English language if one discusses this kind of person; he doesn't, at least not literally, show up in the Dutch language, although of course he may be behind it all.) In van Asperen's view those with risky or unhealthy lifestyles should pay their own way by having extra insurance. They ought not be excluded from health care facilities, but others do not have to pay. This has to do with her view on solidarity. One cannot demand or even expect solidarity from others to soften the consequences of unhealthy living. The same holds for certain technologies or facilities on the moral acceptability of which people have strongly differing views. Those who feel, for example, that abortion is morally reprehensible cannot be expected to feel solidarity with (and pay for) those who choose an abortion. Solidarity with a person or a group that one thinks has the wrong moral standards or ideas is asking too much, according to van Asperen. And because there is a simple solution that protects individual freedom (extra freely chosen insurance), there is no need whatsoever to enforce solidarity.

Why is the idea of extra insurance attractive to many?[10] I think it

---

[9] G. M. van Asperen, 'Jouw geld of mijn leven', in G. A. van der Wal and F. Jacobs (eds.), *Medische schaarste en het menselijk tekort* (Baarn: Ambo, 1988): 50–78.

[10] In the above-mentioned research regarding the views of health care workers, 63.2% of the physicians said that persons who take health risks (smoking, alcohol)

derives part of its popularity from the examples given to support the idea which usually involve more or less luxurious pastimes. ('Well, if you can afford to go skiing, you can easily afford the ski-holiday insurance.') We don't pity the owner of a Rolls-Royce because he has to pay more for his car insurance than the owner of a modest Beetle. And we don't feel sorry for the champagne drinker who has to drink cheap sherry by the end of the month. But does this also hold for other situations and other habits or lifestyles? It may be a perfect system for skiing or hang gliding (freely chosen activities with risks for which an extra insurance can be bought), but it becomes more complicated in other situations. I think we would hesitate to ask all swimmers to pay for extra insurance, because swimming may involve the risks of diving into shallow water which may have serious consequences, like being paralysed for life.

A Practical Problem

One practical problem of van Asperen's view is that is it not simple to organize. There are many facilities and technologies on which people are (morally) divided. (This may even be considered a Dutch hobby.) Some are against prenatal diagnosis, others against modern procreation technologies, or against modern 'high-tech' medicine in general, some persons think that transplantation medicine is unacceptable. If for all technologies on which people disagree you would have to be able to choose, very little may be left that is collectively or societally organized and we might end up with a highly complex and bureaucratic system.

Regret and Misery

Suppose you are an old spinster and firmly oppose modern 'loose' sexual morals. Convinced that you will never have an affair, you have no insurance that covers sexually transmittable diseases. Why should you? You are an old spinster and intend to stay one. Not paying much for health care insurance you can afford to go to Malta for a holiday. There much to your own and his pleasure you are seduced

should pay a higher premium for health care; 19.9% did not agree (15.9% no opinion). Tijmstra *et al.*, *Keuzen in de zorg*: 29.

by the local gigolo, who as it tragically turns out when you have returned, has infected you with HIV. You have no insurance.

Here again we are confronted with the misery argument. Society should not say to you: 'Well, isn't that sad. If only you had insured yourself, but now we cannot help.' Van Asperen's idea rests on the presupposition that people rationally know what kind of health care they will need and want in the future and that they can reasonably judge their future needs and preferences with regard to health care.

I'm afraid I have seen people change their minds when confronted with new situations too often to support this presupposition: fathers violently opposing abortion who do accept it as the only possible solution when their teenage daughters get pregnant; people who say that transplant surgery exceeds acceptable boundaries, patiently wait for a kidney or heart transplant when they themselves fall ill. Shouldn't one be allowed to regret former decisions and change one's mind? In my view it is important that people should have second chances in life. (And that should not be restricted to those who can afford extra insurance that covers every possibility.) There are so many situations in which life itself is hard and offers no point of return: if you have AIDS nobody can make it go away. In life people are so often 'punished' for what they have done or not done, if a possibility for help exists, it should surely be offered. However, this misery argument only holds in the case of *expensive* health care: if the spinster returned not with HIV but with gonorrhoea, she could simply pay for the antibiotics.

Now of course one could, knowing human nature, change van Asperen's proposal of freely chosen extra insurance into a system of obligatory extra insurance at least for those facilities that are so expensive that the average individual could not afford them. That would prevent society from having to pay anyway if something happens which causes great misery. That would solve the dilemma *vis-à-vis* the spinster, but it would undermine the whole idea of choice. You'd be expected to show solidarity towards persons with different views and habits if these views and habits lead to expensive health care consequences. The idea, however, was that you didn't want to have to pay for these consequences, not (only) because of the costs, but because of the immorality of the choices or behaviour in question.

One could also question the notion of solidarity underlying her idea. Is it so absurd to defend solidarity also in the case of behaviour of which you don't approve, of lifestyles that are certainly not your own? Isn't it too easy to say: 'Well we only expect or demand you to feel solidarity with those with whom you agree? You don't have to pay for the ones with different opinions and lifestyles.' ('Just you and your "moral soul mates"'.) Isn't that a rather intolerant and, in a way, selfish kind of solidarity?

Freely Chosen and Preventable Preferences?

> You may say that it is your misfortune to be criminal; I answer
> that it is your crime to be unfortunate.
>
>   Samuel Butler[11]

We have so far assumed that people do freely choose their unhealthy lifestyles and habits, but do they? I seriously doubt this in many cases. Smokers and alcoholics often are addicted. They may, at one moment in time, have freely decided to try a cigarette or a drug, but now they cannot live without their drug. That is where the comparison with the (occasional) champagne drinker and the truffle gourmet, in my view, ends. It is not, at least not always, a matter of a simple (frivolous) preference that you can choose and change.

It is, I think, widely accepted that the so-called 'lower classes' of society generally have a more unhealthy lifestyle. To quote a Report by the World Health Organization,

There are also marked differences in health status between the more and the less privileged groups within countries. Irrespective of the means by which socio-economic groups are distinguished, it has always been shown that there are seriously disadvantaged groups with regard to health status as measured by classical mortality indicators with the widest gaps concerning the preventable causes of ill-health such as infections or behaviour related conditions.[12]

Dutch studies have also shown that close social relations and a close family life protect against certain diseases.

---

[11] S. Butler, *Erewhon* (London: Penguin, 1983; first published 1872). Fascinating reading for those who are interested in the subject of guilt and disease. It was brought to my attention by H. Crombag and F. van Dun, 'Moralisering van de gezondheidszorg of de actualiteit van een utopische satire', *Hollands Maandblad* **32**/522 (1991): 115.

[12] WHO, *Targets for All* (Copenhagen: WHO Regional Office for Europe, 1985): 25.

Next to the influence of the social situation, individual psychological factors are important. Some are prone to suffer from stress, others are not. I do not want to suggest that we are all the powerless victims of our bad habits because they are caused by factors that we cannot control or influence and that therefore moral virtues like moderation and self-control are nonsense, but I do think that the term 'self-chosen' preferences is too simple for many unhealthy habits and their 'victims'. Life is more complicated than that.

But, one could counter this argument: 'This is absurd. We cannot always support those who make a mess of their lives.' If I run a company and through my bad management the company goes bust, I will be held responsible for the mess I made. I don't have the right to a brand-new company because I came from a broken home. In my view, however, a person should not be left to die from starvation. People should be helped in order to survive and should have the chance to learn from their mistakes and try again. Health care and basic social security are essential provisions. Health is a necessary condition to start again.

It is important to emphasize that people do not live unhealthy lives in order to profit from the goodness of others who provide health care, to be pampered by doctors and nurses. The intention underlying their behaviour is not to profit from and enjoy the miracles of modern health care technology. (Nobody becomes an alcoholic because he always wanted a liver transplant. It is absurd to think that anyone would deliberately dive into shallow water because he wants to live his life as a paraplegic in a nursing home.) In fact those with unhealthy lifestyles or habits are usually very good at denying the possible consequences. ('Statistics, I don't care about statistics. I have an 80-year-old uncle who smoked all his life and still is working on his *magnum opus* on ethics.') They may be careless or stupid, but not fraudulent. (I do admit that knowing that adequate care will be available may be one incentive less to be careful. I doubt, however, that it will be an invitation to unhealthy behaviour: why bother living a Spartan life if you know you will be taken care of? People (often) enjoy their unhealthy behaviour, but definitely not the consequences.)

I'm not saying that the drunken driver should have a brand new Mercedes delivered the next day (with love from society) but that is quite different from not providing life-saving health care.

The same holds for the notion of 'preventable' behaviour. Between bad luck and one's own fault there is a wide area of unfortunate concurrences of circumstances with regard to which we have to recognize that persons made irrational or unwise or risky decisions. But we are not known for our continuous rationality, perfectness, etcetera. We do fall from staircases, we are known to suffer from erotic intoxications. We hold pit bull terriers or Pekinese dogs and get bitten by them. We serve delicious shrimp salmonella sandwiches on a beautiful hot summer day. Blind fate? Own fault? Neither? A little of both? Probably something in between. Bad habits and bad luck.

I think it is realistic and morally called for to base one's health care insurance on these presuppositions about human behaviour, knowing that persons 'want to be good, but not too good and not quite all the time'. For those who oppose there is always the question: 'Are you so sure that it could never happen to you?' (The 'those-without-sin-throw-the first-stone' test.)

How about Good 'New' Patient Autonomy?

But, one could argue, how about the autonomy of the (potential) patient? Isn't this a rather paradoxical or even self-contradictory view when in other contexts one defends the autonomy of the individual? One would expect a plea for responsibility of the individual based on this same autonomy. Why only autonomy to claim rights and not to accept responsibilities? Why not indeed? I think it is difficult to navigate between the ideal of the responsible autonomous individual with a strong mind and a strong will, and the reality of the fallible human being sometimes confronted with his weak flesh and wrong decisions. I'm inclined to think that most of us have our fatal attractions, although some attractions are more fatal than others. But I agree that there may be a limit to the excuses that one can adduce for irrational and dangerous behaviour. I also agree that understanding certain weaknesses is not the same as justifying them. The fact that people often don't do what is best for them and/or others is not a reason to decide that therefore they have now lost the right to decide over their own lives and bodies. (Divorcing one partner doesn't prove you're incompetent to choose your next partner.) Neither in my view is it a reason to leave them to drown in the consequences of their former choices. (Suppose someone in the first stage of a serious disease refuses all medical treatment, when the disease progresses he regrets this decision and comes for help. The treatment now is more expensive than it would have been had he accepted treatment earlier. We should surely not refuse help saying: 'Well you're an autonomous person. Face the consequences.')

There are more arguments that have been forwarded in defence of my view on health care insurance.

The Scapegoat Problem

As has been suggested by others, it may be very difficult, even impossible, to distinguish between different kinds of unhealthy behaviour. Of course, it is rather easy to tax tobacco or alcohol and relatively easy to raise the insurance premium for smokers and drinkers. But then they will be in a way the scapegoats, whereas others go 'untaxed' or 'unpunished'. Is that fair? Is it consistent? How about the workaholics, people with unhealthy eating habits, suntan fanatics, persons who refuse medical treatment out of fear, thereby worsening their condition and costing more to treat at a later stage.

I know that the fact that you cannot catch all crooks is not a reason to let the ones you can catch off the hook, but the point is that some habits are not even characterized as being 'unhealthy' or 'bad' (both *qua* health consequences as well as morally) and that others are, but at the same time are considered to be societally useful (working hard). And you can get away with it, whereas the scapegoats cannot. Attitudes towards certain ways of living may change according to the social climate. Besides there's a lot we don't know yet. What is your fault today, may be, after all, your genes tomorrow.

Another problem is that some habits or lifestyles are healthy (or at least not unhealthy) when practised in a certain moderate way, but not when practised in another way. (Two drinks of alcohol a day is apparently more healthy than being a teetotaller,[13] a happy sex-life is good for physical exercise and mental relaxation, sports are healthy in general but the costs of sports-related injuries are high.) Is it possible to incorporate this in an acceptable and practical system? People sometimes run risks because of a useful profession (firemen, war journalists). One wouldn't say to a physician who has contracted HIV while working in primitive conditions in an African hospital:

---

[13] I can't find the source of this important information. Well, the message suits me.

'Well, why did you become a doctor? Or why did you insist on doctoring in Africa?'

Privacy

Then there is also the problem of privacy. Imagine a behaviour-dependent health insurance, individually based on a behavioural anamnesis. 'How much do you smoke? How much do you sleep? With whom? Do you have a close family? etc., etc.' A first problem is that the premium would be based on your lifestyle now. If you decide to change it, start or stop smoking, for example, the premium would have to be adapted to the new lifestyle. Quite complicated.

Secondly, if one could solve the scapegoat problem, this kind of questioning could be an invasion of one's privacy. That is a high price for not having to pay for those who live unhealthily. Even if you don't agree with the lifestyle of an individual or a group, the perspective of a loss of privacy may be worse than having to accept differences. Of course, we have accepted these kind of questions for those who want to have life insurance, so why not for health care insurance? But even in the context of life insurance in the Netherlands we have debates on whether one can ask 'everything'. ('Are you a homosexual? Have you suffered from anal gonorrhoea in the past few years?')

Actuarial Gymnastics?

Finally there is the problem of the calculation necessary to allow for all the fair details. Suppose it would be considered unfair to have the non-smoker pay for health costs of the smoker. Wouldn't it then also be unfair if smokers paid for the costs of non-smokers? A non-smoker usually lives longer, he enjoys an old-age pension. When 80 he may suffer from a chronic disease and need long-lasting and expensive care. How expensive is smoking for society?[14] The irony of this argument, as has been cynically brought forward, is that because the cheapest patient is a dead 'patient', those who live very healthy

[14] See e.g. W. G. Manning *et al.*, 'The taxes of sin', *Journal of the American Medical Association* **261**/11 (1989): 1604–9.

lives should pay more because in fact they may, on the whole, cost more money to society.

Anyway, one should wonder if we do not all have our 'health sins' and, if so, whether we would not be even in the end so that we can spare ourselves the trouble and costs of the actuarial exercises. You may be so irritated by your neighbour's loose morals or gourmet lifestyle that you find yourself lying next to him in the hospital, the two of you, of course, both suffering from stomach ulcers. The proposal of van Asperen, in my view, leads to many practical and theoretical problems.

Don't Worry, Be Healthy

I think that an obsessive preoccupation with healthy living ('working out', dieting, and otherwise healthy living) can be rather boring and, although I cannot prove it, maybe not always as healthy as those who adopt that lifestyle may think.[15]

The missionary zeal of some 'health freaks' (immoderate in moderation? Methuselahmetism?), though (probably) based on respectable motivations, sometimes causes them to have harsh judgements on those with a different lifestyle, even morally ostracizing them. Quite an intolerant attitude.

I certainly do not want to defend that *savoir-vivre* can only be proved by taking risks or to defend the stance that everyone in an outburst of collective *carpe diem* ought to dance on the volcano and live dangerously and that we should applaud a kamikaze lifestyle. If one thinks of AIDS, we all know how much pain and suffering can be prevented by being careful and responsible. I also realize that sometimes not only the individual bears the consequences of his own behaviour, but also others—the most tragic example being children with HIV. But to picture those who in some respect live unhealthily as the 'moral lepers' of our time is carrying it too far. I do think that a moral duty to live a healthy life ought to be taken seriously. There are both convincing moral and self-interest-based arguments in defence of the view that one should not waste precious health. But there is more in life than health. And this duty should not be enforced by excluding persons from health care. I'd rather live in a Good

[15] *Cf.* G. Patzig, 'Gibt es eine Gesundheitspflicht?', *Ethik in der medizin* **1** (1989): 312.

Samaritan kind of society than in a society of a Pharisaic nature, although that may cost me money and although some parasites and 'health-hooligans' may profit from the goodness of that society.

So be it.

8

Is Society Responsible for My Health?

SØREN HOLM

One of the most important issues in the field of allocation of resources for health care is the question of whether a person is responsible for his own health state. This question has been posed many times, and has prompted very detailed and deep philosophical analysis.[1] At the same time it has often been presumed that the question put in this way has priority over the question of whether society is responsible for my health. That is, if it can be established that I am responsible for my own health, then it is at the same time established that society has no such responsibility.

This presumption has permeated the debate about liver transplants for alcoholics and has also surfaced in the public discussion about the huge sums of money health care systems are projected to spend on HIV-infected persons over the next decades. In the AIDS debate, the connection between a stigmatized (and in some countries even illegal) form of sexual practice, a deadly disease, and a set of very expensive treatments has set the scene for an especially pernicious form of the argument that personal responsibility for health, releases society from all health care obligations. Acceptance of this argument would lead to almost total abandonment of the HIV-infected persons, because very few would be able to shoulder the enormous economic burden themselves.

What I want to argue in this chapter is that this order of priority is misconceived! And further that modern societies (or at least societies of a certain type) have far-ranging responsibilities with regard to the health of their citizens, whether or not the citizens themselves have a similar responsibility.

[1] D. Wikler, 'Holistic Medicine: Concepts for Personal Responsibility for Health', in D. Stalker and C. Glymour (eds.), *Examining Holistic Medicine* (Buffalo, NY: Prometheus Press, 1985).

Am I Responsible for My Own Health?

Since antiquity, it has been claimed that there is no point of view so foolish that it has not been argued for by some philosopher.[2] And some will undoubtedly feel that the project of this chapter falls squarely within the category of foolish ideas.

How can society be responsible for my health? Given the relatively limited impact of health care on health status it seems absurd to argue for a societal responsibility for the health of individual citizens. If my own actions are the main determinants of my health status, then I must be the one responsible for my health!

This clear argument for personal responsibility seems convincing, but only because it has two important hidden premisses. The first is that society can or should only discharge a societal responsibility for health through health care, which is highly implausible. Relief of poverty, better education, or restriction of environmental pollution are also effective means to bring about better health in the popula-tion.[3] The second is that my actions must be *my* actions in a very rad-ical sense. I cannot here present a full analysis of the concept of personal responsibility for health, but would just like to point out that in order for the standard argument presented above to be valid my actions must be mine in the sense that they are all freely chosen, not instinctive, not conditioned by the society in which I live and have been brought up, and not constrained by any external factors. But how many of our health-related actions are ours in this radical sense? Not very many! The most clear-cut exemplars of the class of actions that can be said to be mine in this radical sense must be found among the cases of non-psychiatric self-induced illness, but such cases are few and far apart.

The question of personal responsibility becomes more difficult to answer when we come to the area of dangerous hobbies like moun-taineering, scuba-diving, or hang-gliding and even more difficult in the area of socially conditioned habits like smoking, sexual activities, or eating fatty foods. The philosophical analysis of personal respon-sibility for health is therefore stuck with an unfortunate state of affairs. The activities which have the greatest aggregate impact on

---

[2] *Nihil tam absurde dici potest, quod non dicatur ab aliquo philosophorum,* Marcus Tullius Cicero (*De Divinatione,* II. 58).

[3] T. McKeown, *The Role of Medicine* (Oxford: Blackwell, 1979).

health (i.e. our daily habits) are at the same time the activities where personal responsibility is most difficult to establish. In many of these cases the claim that I could have acted differently, although true in the logical sense, seems to miss the point when applied to a given action. Let us assume that it is true that every action I perform, I perform because I have made a decision to perform it. From this it does not follow that I just could have acted differently. Limiting the area of your search for pertinent facts is also a part of what it means to be rational and deliberate in a rational way. It is well known from the debate about act-utilitarianism that any attempt to assess the full range of consequences of each individual action performed through the day will be immensely time-consuming and lead to virtual paralysis. It is therefore rational not to scrutinize all of one's actions to the full extent possible, but to perform the more routine ones guided by the 'automatic pilot' and habits one has acquired in the course of one's life. These actions are of course chosen by me, they are rational, but they are not the result of any decision in the true sense of that word. Maximizing might be good in theory, but a satisfying strategy seems more suited for real life.

Is Society Responsible for My Health?

After this short detour into individual responsibility, it is time to get back to the main topic of the chapter, i.e. the question of societal responsibility. An argument for societal responsibility for the health of individual citizens can be approached from at least two complementary points of view:

(1) as a question of allocative ethics; or
(2) as a question of political philosophy.

There are of course interesting interconnections between these two approaches, but in the present context I will allow myself to go straight to the political philosophy. The long-standing debate about the future of American health care has produced many intriguing arguments based on theories of just allocation,[4] but perhaps not *the* argument which is necessary to establish a comprehensive societal obligation for health care.

[4] e.g. N. Daniels, *Just Health Care* (Cambridge: Cambridge University Press, 1985).

Security, Needs, and the Social Order

Any society needs to maintain the allegiance of its members in order to function as a society. If allegiance cannot be maintained, the stability of the society will be in danger and everybody will (at least in the short term) suffer. Allegiance can, however, be maintained in many ways, e.g. through ideology, repression, or protection, and the proper way of maintaining allegiance is a classic problem in political philosophy.

A further consistent feature of the modern State is its monopoly on the use of violence, but such a monopoly obviously has to be legitimated, beyond the mere claim that 'power is right'. What is therefore needed is an explanation of why the individual citizen should (*a*) recognize this monopoly and (*b*) show allegiance towards the State. In this context reference to ideology, or as Habermas terms it 'hypostatized violence', will not suffice. Many solutions to this problem have been suggested based on implicit or explicit consent, on rules of fair play, or on ideas about natural duties.[5]

One of the early modern philosophical contributors to this debate was the English philosopher Thomas Hobbes[6] who based his political philosophy on the idea that the main reason for establishing and continuing a society was the need for protection from internal strife and external enemies.[7] For Hobbes, life in the state of nature prior to the establishment of the state is: Solitary, poore, nasty, brutish, and short.[8] Given this description one can wonder, whether life being short in this state of nature should be taken as a disadvantage or whether it would really be a benefit.

For Hobbes, the only way out of this predicament is that Everyman relinquishes his freedom and powers to an absolute sovereign. This sovereign should have almost unlimited powers, but only as long as he is able to provide protection for his subjects, for as Hobbes writes:

The Obligation of Subjects to the Soveraign, is understood to last as long, and no longer, than the power lasteth, by which he is able to protect them.

[5] J. Waldron, 'Special Ties and Natural Duties', *Philosophy and Public Affairs* **22**/1 (1993): 3–30.

[6] I was first pointed in the direction of the political philosophy of Thomas Hobbes by John Harris.

[7] T. Hobbes, *Leviathan* (London: Penguin Books, 1987).

[8] Ibid., part I, ch. 13: 186.

For the right men have by Nature to protect themselves, when none else can protect them, can by no covenant be relinquished.[9]

and

And thus I have brought to an end my Discourse of Civill and Ecclesiasticall Government . . . without other designe, than to set before mens eyes the mutuall Relation between Protection and Obedience; of which condition of Humane Nature, and the Laws Divine, (both Naturall and Positive) require an inviolable observation.[10]

Hobbes's further arguments are based on an idea about an original covenant or contract entered into by the people in the original state of nature and binding all their descendants. We know that no actual contract of this kind was ever established, and its value as a philosophical construct is also doubtful, but this does not touch Hobbes's original insight that (part of?) the legitimation of the sovereignty of the State must lie in its ability to protect its citizens from harm. The mutual relation between protection and obedience has two aspects. On the one hand the protection of the sovereign gives rise to a duty of obedience, on the other protection is a sign of citizenship. Anybody who is deliberately and publicly denied protection is at the same time denied citizenship and cast as an outlaw. This is relevant in the context of HIV and AIDS. If society denies protection and treatment to HIV-positive persons, it thereby also severs their connection to society and makes them 'outlaws'. An outlaw is outside of the law in two senses. He is not protected by the law but he is at the same time not bound by the law. If we abandon HIV-positive persons, we also abandon our claim that they should behave responsibly.

In his *Anarchy, State and Utopia*, Robert Nozick has taken Hobbes's point of view to its extreme and argues that the *only* possible legitimation of the State is the protection it can offer against violence, and that the only legitimate function of the State is to provide such protection.[11] He thereby seeks to provide both a legitimation of, and a limiting principle for his 'Night-watchman state', essentially restricting the legitimate functions of the State to policing, sentencing, and punishing. The Nozickian approach is based on an extremely thin conception of morality, and would require an extensive dismantling of the State in virtually all present societies if

[9] Ibid., part II, ch. 21: 272.   [10] Ibid., A review and conclusion: 728.
[11] R. Nozick, *Anarchy, State, and Utopia* (Oxford: Blackwell, 1974).

applied as a normative principle.[12] I cannot here present a full argument against this line of reasoning, but I want to note two main problems in Nozick's analysis. Not only does the analysis proceed from a very thin conception of ethics where only negative rights (i.e. rights of non-interference) are recognized, but it is also based on a very narrow conception of action and of the ways in which people may harm each other. There are many other ways to harm people than through direct physical violence or direct economic exploitation, and any serious political philosophy will have to take account of this. This can perhaps best be illustrated by an example.

Let us assume that someone at my place of work contracts the flu but decides to go to work anyway, thereby spreading the contagious agent to me, so that I fall ill and become unable to work for a couple of days. In this situation I have been harmed in a very palpable way if I have no insurance against my loss of wages, and even if I am insured, my feeling ill and miserable will be a harm. But I have not been physically attacked or economically exploited, and membership of a Nozickian protection agency will not be of much help to me. The minimal State is ill-suited for the rectification of harms of this kind, something more is required.

In the world of today, many societies have progressed beyond the point where it is reasonable to construe the protection against internal and external enemies as the *raison d'etre* of the State. If sovereignty, or allegiance from the citizens towards the State, is to be based upon the ability of the State/sovereign to protect the citizens, then the nature of the salient threats must be taken into account. If the State is only protecting me from events that I don't fear and leaves me vulnerable to events that seriously harm me even though it could have protected me, then my propensity to show allegiance to such a State will be diminished. In a setting where external enemies are few and natural disasters rare, other 'enemies' such as poverty, pollution, and ill-health pose greater threats to the security of the individual citizen and the relationship between citizen and sovereign must be reformulated and restructured to take these factors into account.

How far should the scope of protection then reach? To be able to answer this question we need to look more closely at the aim and purpose of protection. What makes protection the paramount good for

---

[12] A. Brown, *Modern Political Philosophy* (London: Penguin Books, 1986).

Hobbes is the connection between protection and security. Without the sword of the sovereign to maintain order man will revert to a state of nature characterized by the war of Everyman against Everyman and all security will be lost. In *Leviathan*, he writes about this state of nature:

> In such a condition, there is no place for industry; because the fruit thereof is uncertain: and consequently no culture of the earth; no navigation, nor use of commodities that may be imported by sea; no commodious building; no instruments of moving, and removing, such things as requires much force; no knowledge of the face of the earth; no account of time; no arts; no letters; no society; and which is worst of all, continual fear, and danger of violent death.[13]

For Hobbes, physical security is thus a necessary prerequisite for all other pursuits of man, and therefore it becomes more important than liberty or freedom. In this connection it is important to notice that Hobbes is not an ethical egoist, as he has often been portrayed. He recognizes the existence of many other ethical motivations apart from egoism or self-interest, but his claim is that in a state of nature it is irrational to act on such motivations because it will be too dangerous. If I show beneficence towards somebody this will leave me vulnerable because I cannot expect them to act in the same way. Only after the establishment of the State can I safely act on my non-egoistic moral intuitions because the protection of the sovereign will ensure that my acts of goodwill are not taken as opportunities to harm me.[14]

It can therefore be argued that the connection between security, submission, and sovereignty is established by (or mediated through) the concept of need. The value of security is that it provides the necessary environment for the fulfilment of important substantive human needs.

Hobbes sees the need for security from violence as the prime need in a state of nature and the satisfaction of this need as the prime responsibility of the sovereign and as the initial rationale behind the sovereign's claim to sovereignty, but when the danger of reverting to a Hobbesian state of nature is remote, and no external enemies are at hand, the need for physical protection diminishes in importance and other needs may take its place and *become* the (prime) responsibility

[13] Hobbes, *Leviathan*, part I, ch. 13: 186.
[14] T. Sorell, *Hobbes* (London: Routledge, 1986); R. Tuck, *Hobbes* (Oxford: OUP, 1989).

of the sovereign. Traces of such an extension of the concept of protection can be found in Hobbes's elaboration of the office of the sovereign in chapter 30 of *Leviathan*, where he writes: 'But by safety here, is not meant a bare Preservation, but also all other Contentments of life, which every man by lawfull Industry, without danger, or hurt to the Common-wealth, shall aquire to himselfe.'[15] And, further on in the chapter, in a paragraph on 'Publique Charity': 'And whereas many men, by accident unevitable, become unable to maintain themselves by their labour; they ought not to be left to the Charity of private persons; but to be provided for, . . . by the Lawes of the Common-wealth.'[16] For Hobbes, the external enemies are other human beings or other States, but is it not equally relevant to construe infectious diseases or pollution as external enemies?

Lawrie Reznek argues convincingly that when we talk about disease we do it within a natural-kinds semantic.[17] Diseases are conceptualized as natural kinds, as entities, which can afflict, attack, or strike human beings. This way of talking is especially prominent when we talk about infectious diseases, and it is also in this area that the congruence between our natural-kinds semantic and the medical facts is best. Our body is really invaded by a foreign organism when we acquire an infection, and the micro-organism *is* in some real sense the disease, although many factors intervene between the exposure to the micro-organism and the final manifestation of disease. It simply makes more sense to talk about a person being attacked by plague or AIDS than to talk about someone being attacked by gout or sunburn.

In the case of infectious diseases it is therefore possible to argue that the diseases or perhaps more accurately the micro-organisms in question are external enemies, from which a good society ought to shield us. This argument has been made by Charles A. Erin and John Harris and I will not try to elaborate on their exposition.[18] Some would claim that natural disasters and fire are also enemies in this sense, and since most societies leave insurance against such misfortunes to the discretion of individual citizens, establishing that something is an external enemy in the requisite sense is not sufficient to show that society ought to help us against it. The argument is, how-

---

[15] Hobbes, *Leviathan*, part II, ch. 30: 376.   [16] Ibid., part II, ch. 30: 387.
[17] L. Reznek, *The Nature of Disease* (London: Routledge, 1987).
[18] C. A. Erin and J. Harris, 'AIDS: Ethics, justice, and social policy', *Journal of Applied Philosophy* **10** (1993): 165–73.

ever, fallacious because (*a*) in most countries society does provide some kind of protection or help against such natural enemies, and (*b*) it does not follow that a society should not take a certain responsibility upon itself from the fact that it has not yet done so.

Other diseases or environmental pollution could also be construed as external enemies but with considerably greater difficulty. I will therefore leave this line of argument aside and instead pursue a more general line based on the connection between needs and the legitimation of the State.

In philosophy and especially in health care economics the attempt to differentiate between needs and wants is often scorned, and it is claimed that the use of 'need' instead of 'want' is only a way to add rhetorical emphasis to one's claims. It may well be true that one of the functions of 'need' statements is rhetorical, but this does not prove that it is impossible to differentiate between a 'need' and a 'want' concept. Much of the confusion stems from a conflation of the first personal and the third personal use of 'need' and 'want'. In the first personal use, 'need' and 'want' have very similar meanings. There is not much difference between the two statements: (1) I *want* the new compact disk by Michael Jackson and (2) I *need* the new compact disk by Michael Jackson, and very few parents would be convinced that there was any significant difference between the states reported by the two sentences if they were used by their teenage daughter. It is of course possible to profess to need something you don't want (e.g. 'I need to go to the dentist, but I don't want to') and want something you yourself claim not to need (e.g. 'I don't need a new dress, but I want this one'), but an effective use of first personal need statements in the strong sense mentioned below requires reference to an external criterion to acquire rhetorical force.

In the third personal use, this is different because here a 'want' statement always refers to the presumed mental state or expressed wishes of the subject in question, whereas a 'need' statement may have two different meanings. One that is equivalent with the similar 'want' statement and one that refers to the speaker's assessment of some lack pertaining to the subject or his/her environment. This difference comes out in sentences like: (1) He *wants* a health check-up and (2) He *needs* a health check-up, and perhaps even better in sentences like: (1) He *wants* plastic surgery and (2) He *needs* plastic surgery.

The same difference in use is brought out when we ascribe needs to inanimate things like plants. A statement like 'This rose wants water' can only be taken as metaphorical, whereas the comparable need statement 'This rose needs water' describes an objective assessment of the state of the plant.

But can we really distinguish between these two different third-personal uses of 'need' in an objective sense? A first approximation could be that 'objective' need statements refer to states in which a person lacks something which is fundamental for the pursuit of any (or perhaps only most?) of the activities that are common for a person to pursue in a given society. That is, he or she lacks something without which he would be significantly harmed. This would connect need with function and not with well-being, satisfaction, desires, or pleasure, thereby establishing a semi-objective foundation for this kind of need statements.

In the area of health and health care, such a conception of need could align itself with the concept of disease put forward by Christopher Boorse, who sees disease as a deviation from species-typical levels of functioning,[19] but, in contrast to Boorse, it would not focus exclusively on biological functioning but would also consider social functioning. But would this concept of need be able to limit the needs correctly ascribable to people, or would needs still be unlimited as the health care economists often claim?[20]

In some areas this explication of need seems to provide a limitation on the legitimate use of need statements. On this view it would be correct to claim that I need food, but incorrect to claim that I need to dine at a three-starred restaurant. It would (at least in some areas of the USA) be correct to claim that I need a car, but incorrect to claim that I need a Mercedes, because a Skoda could perform the same essential function. I need decent living conditions, but I don't need a penthouse apartment on Fifth Avenue. These examples are simple, because the essential functions of nutrition, transportation, and housing can be fulfilled at a fairly low level of cost, but what about education or health care where the relationship between function and cost is very different? In education the duration of the day as well as the intrinsic limitations of the human mind with respect to information-processing and ability to maintain attention puts natural limits

[19] C. Boorse, 'On the Distinction between Disease and Illness', *Philosophy and Public Affairs* 5 (Fall 1975): 49–68.

[20] G. H. Mooney, *Economics, Medicine and Health Care* (London: Wheatsheaf Books Ltd, 1986). Already Hobbes observed that 'the estate of Man can never be without some incommodity or other' (*Leviathan*, part II, ch. 18: 226), so that desires would always be unlimited.

on the amount of resources that can be deployed in the education of any given pupil, but the concept of need developed here does not entail that there is an individual need for this level of education. Normal individual functioning in society requires some education (i.e. a certain level of literacy and numeracy) and there are undoubtedly present needs in this sense that are not fulfilled, but the need is not unlimited.

In health care this seems to be different. Being alive must be taken as one of the most basic prerequisites for being able to function and pursue one's (earthly) goals, and modern medicine is able to consume seemingly unlimited sums in the pursuit of prolongation of life. Does this mean that medical needs must always be unlimited, and that a societal duty to fulfil those needs thereby would be undischargeable and presumably void (using the 'ought-implies-can' rule contrapositively)?

A first point to notice is that the concept of need used here refers back to social functioning, and although being alive is a necessary prerequisite for social functioning it is not a sufficient condition. Not all life is connected with social function and not all life needs to be prolonged. It could further be suggested that although even a tiny prolongation could be of use for some persons to finalize their life-project, in most instances this is not the case. There is in most cases some lower limit to the amount of lifetime which it is useful to get, and this in itself could limit the amount of resources to be deployed.

Secondly, a partial discharge of a duty to fulfil health care needs is in most cases better than no discharge of such a duty. Delivering health care or applying preventive measures is not an all or nothing endeavour; it is often better to do something than to do nothing, even in the case where I can't do everything. A primitive lower limb prosthesis may be functionally inferior to a modern prosthesis, but it is far better than no prosthesis. A fifth-generation cephalosporin may be the drug of choice for my infection, but giving me the slightly less effective (but much less expensive) combination of penicillin and an aminoglycoside is still worth doing. If society cannot afford Retrovir for its AIDS patients, it should still offer them treatment for their *Pneumocystis carinii* infections. A society which maintains a basic health care system, but cannot afford to provide heart and liver transplants to those few who would benefit substantially from such transplantations, has not failed. It is true that there is more to be done, but what is being done now will in its own right contribute to the social functioning and the feeling of security among the citizens, i.e. society ought to do what it can and work towards doing what it cannot yet do. Or to put it in another way, it really does not matter in this context whether medical needs are unlimited or not. A society has a duty to provide as much health care as is compatible with the discharge of other societal duties, including, as I have argued elsewhere, the important duty to secure that differences in social class do not create differences in health status.[21]

But isn't this just an evasion of the real issue? If health care needs are unlimited, how can we then secure justice in health care allocation? This could be a valid objection, but it is an objection to another argument than the one which is being put forward in this chapter. What is argued for here is that society has a duty to protect the health of its citizens through health care or other means, that this duty is based on the fact that being in good health is a basic need, and that this duty is not void if it cannot be completely fulfilled. How this duty should be discharged, and how resources should be allocated to health care is a separate question, and not the subject of this chapter.

Apart from the external factors mentioned above (poverty, ill-health, etc.) the individual may also be harmed by his or her own stupidity or negligence. Does the societal responsibility extend to these internal factors? Or, to rephrase more explicitly: does society have a responsibility to protect me against my own stupidity? This is an area where political philosophy and ethics inevitably engage. If I am to be protected from my own stupidity, it necessarily entails some restriction of my liberty or some modification of my state of mind (taken in a broad sense). In this area the societal duty to protect must therefore be balanced against the individual interest in the greatest possible liberty. A continuum exists between compulsory use of seat belts and crash helmets on the one hand, and compulsory use of special diets or prohibition of certain sexual activities on the other. As with most balancing exercises there seems to be no obvious optimal general solution but each stupid case or foolish activity must be considered on its own merits (so to speak).

This is, however, not true, when we consider the duty to warn instead of the duty to protect. Although my peace of mind can be disturbed by a warning, opening my eyes to previously unseen or repressed dangerous aspects of one of my favourite activities, this

[21] S. Holm, 'Sundhed og socialklasse—en etisk analyse' ('Health and social class—an ethical analysis'), *Bibliotek for Læger* **185** (1993): 66–79 (in Danish).

does not infringe my liberties (taken in a strong sense). I am free once more to engage in repression or neglect of the unwanted knowledge, and thus to re-establish my mental equilibrium, but I am, on the other hand also free to mend my foolish ways and thereby free to rid myself of one of the dangers threatening my life.

A Special Problem

In health care systems of the Scandinavian or British type a further Hobbesian argument can be adduced to support a societal responsibility for health and health care. Health care systems of these types are not only characterized by the fact that they get their revenue through taxation and seek to provide comprehensive care for all, they are also characterized by their distorting effect on the market in health care. The state functions as both an exclusive monopsonistic health care buyer and an exclusive monopolistic health care provider. That is, the State is the major health care buyer and it buys only from its own institutions and these institutions are not allowed to sell to others. In such an environment the capital costs necessary to establish new private health care facilities may become very large, and the initial marginal costs for private health care prohibitive. When this is combined with the State offering health care services at zero-price at the point of consumption, entry into the market becomes almost impossible for the new private health care provider. This is demonstrated by the economical problems private hospitals in Denmark are experiencing. The structure of the system therefore in fact prevents citizens from obtaining health care outside of the public system. Hobbes (for obvious reasons) didn't envisage this situation, but he did speculate about the limits of the Soveraigns' powers and came to the following conclusion:

> If the Soveraign command a man (though justly condemned,) to kill, wound, or mayme himselfe; or not to resist those that assault him; or to abstain from the use of food, ayre, medicine, or any other thing, without which he cannot live; yet hath that man Liberty to disobey.[22]

What is presently the case is most often not a sovereign command to abstain from medicine, but the net effect is precisely the same. Through its policies the State prevents the individual citizens from

---

[22] Hobbes, *Leviathan*, part II, ch. 21: 268–9.

obtaining health care in any other place than the public health care system, thus *de facto* denying the citizen access to health care that he may want. This is no great problem if the public health care system truly provides the care that the citizens need. But if this is not the case the citizen seems to have a prima-facie right to try to obtain such health care in whatever way it may be obtainable, even through illegal means.[23] In an ordered society such an approach must be considered suboptimal, and, given the explication of 'need' presented above, two different solutions are possible. The health care system could be enhanced so that all legitimate needs were covered (which would be difficult if needs are unlimited), or it could be reorganized so that the *de facto* exclusion of citizens from obtaining needed health care privately was removed. A monolithic health care system can have many advantages in terms of justice in the allocation of public resources and low transaction costs, although the experiences in the former Eastern European countries have shown that these advantages are not realized in all monolithic health care systems. Any solution to the problem outlined above should try to maintain these advantages and one suggestion could be for the State to sell health care in those areas where it cannot provide it for free. This obviously brings out all sorts of slippery-slope scenarios depicting the inevitable erosion of public health care. I am sceptical about these scenarios, but the limited space of this chapter does not permit me to go into details.

Two sets of arguments have been put forward here to establish the proposition that society is responsible for my health. One argument claimed to be valid in all societies where protection from external enemies or the forces of nature can no longer be the prime responsibility of the sovereign, and another argument with a more restricted scope only pertaining to those societies where the structure of the public health care seriously distorts the function of the health care market.

Although these arguments are sufficient to establish such a responsibility on the part of the State, some further explication is necessary to delimit the exact nature and content of this responsibility.

In both cases the validity of the argument presented is based on certain contextual and empirical claims about a given society (e.g.

---

[23] Hobbes makes this point with respect to food or other things necessary for life: 'When a man is destitute of food, or other thing neccessary for his life, and cannot preserve himselfe any other way, but by some fact against the Law; . . . he is totally Excused' (*Leviathan*, part II, ch. 27: 346).

that physical protection from external or internal enemies is no longer a major consideration). There are many societies where these empirical claims are not valid (i.e. in many Third World countries), and even in countries where they have once been valid they may lose this validity. A very topical example of this is the situation in the former republic of Yugoslavia at the time of writing this chapter. Before the present war in Bosnia both sets of empirical claims were true, and the State therefore had an extensive responsibility for the health of its citizens. In the present situation with Sarajevo and Srebrenica under siege, the empirical claims are no longer true. Now the foremost obligation of the Bosnian State is to protect its citizens against foreign invasion, and the responsibility for health, education, and other social goods must be put aside in order to achieve the more important and immediate goal of simple physical protection. This does not mean that any state of war will automatically release a society from its obligations to secure the health of citizens. Only wars which threaten the survival of the State itself or which threatens the life or social functioning of many citizens will make this obligation void. The responsibility of the government of the UK did therefore not disappear during the Falklands War or during the campaign against Iraq since both of these engagements were of a limited nature. At no time could these 'wars' be described as the primary concerns of citizens, CNN coverage not withstanding.

9

HIV/AIDS and the Point and Scope of Medical Confidentiality

ANTON VEDDER

Introduction

It is generally assumed that workers in the field of health care and health research have a duty to respect the confidentiality of personal medical information, meaning that in principle they should not pass this information on to third parties, unless the person whom it concerns explicitly agrees or requests that such is done.[1] The duty of medical confidentiality has a relatively long tradition and is deeply entrenched in the practice of health care and health research. Now, sometimes personal medical information can be literally of vital interest to third parties, so that disclosure to them would seem highly desirable. This seems to be the case with information resulting from HIV testing and screening which indicates that a person is HIV positive. Armed with such information, the sex contacts of that person might protect their own health and the health of others. First, they might abstain from sex or turn to 'safe sex' in order to avoid HIV infection, and, in case they are maintaining sexual contacts with others, to avoid the infliction of the disease on other sexual partners. Secondly, the information is of importance for the sex contacts of the infected person who considers the possibility of having children. An HIV-infected woman has a 30–40 per cent chance of transmitting

---

[1] The duty to respect personal medical information is explicitly mentioned in several professional ethical codes. See e.g. the Hippocratic Oath, the European Medical Ethical Code, the International Council of Nurses, Code for Nurses, etc. In many countries there are legal regulations securing the confidentiality of personal medical information and specifying conditions under which the duty to respect the confidentiality of personal medical information may be suspended.

HIV to the newborn child during pregnancy.[2] Therefore, information about the HIV status of (one of) the partner(s) might make a person choose not to have children. Thirdly, the sex contacts of that person might, if they themselves turned out to be HIV positive already, perhaps sooner or later call upon the possibilities of early intervention by way of treatment with AZT and prophylactics of opportunistic infections in order to slow down the development of AIDS. (It should be noted here that the possibility of early intervention, as well as situations in which the sex-contacts of the infected person maintain sexual relationships with others, and situations in which the partner of an apparently HIV-positive person considers the possibilities of offspring with another person than this apparently HIV-positive person, make it desirable that she not just abstain from sex or turns to safe sex, leaving the partners ignorant about the reason for this change of behaviour, but that these contacts are actually *informed* about their chance of having been infected.) Now, does the opportunity to provide third parties with this vitally important information justify a breach of the alleged duty of health care and health research professionals to respect the confidentiality of personal medical information?

Confidentiality and Harm to Others

Let us begin by considering the view developed by M. E. Winston who favours a positive answer to the question.[3] Winston presumes that the duty to respect the confidentiality of personal medical information derives from a more basic duty to respect the autonomy of individuals.[4] Because it is generally assumed that the autonomy of individuals may be legitimately restricted in cases where they expose others to risk of harm, so, Winston argues, it may likewise be assumed that medical confidentiality may be restricted in cases where the individuals concerned put others at risk of harm. Winston then goes to specify the circumstances in which the duty to avoid possible

---

[2] European Collaborative Study, 'Mother-to-child transmission of HIV-infection', *Lancet* **ii** (1988): 1057–8.

[3] M. E. Winston, AIDS, 'Confidentiality and the right to know', *Public Affairs Quarterly* **2**/2 (1988): 91–104.

[4] In this, Winston relies heavily on the view put forward by Sissela Bok in *Secrets: On the Ethics of Concealment and Revelation* (New York: Vintage Books, 1983): esp. 123–30.

harm to third parties may be thought to outweigh the duty to respect the autonomy of individuals. He stipulates that the duty to protect them from harm should be considered to have this strength in contexts where there exists large disparity of power or abilities among the parties involved to protect their own interests. According to Winston, this applies to situations such as those envisaged by our initial problem, where ignorance of the third parties pertaining to the HIV status of their partner constitutes a large disparity among the parties involved. The specific vulnerability of the third parties, therefore, should be considered to yield sufficient justificatory grounds for putting aside medical confidentiality, not only in cases where HIV-infected persons evidently refuse to protect their partners by informing them, but as general policy, whether or not HIV-infected persons appear to be willing to take measures in order to protect their partners from contracting the disease.

The argument put forward by Winston is, to my mind, problematic. If we presume that individual autonomy is the motivating reason behind medical confidentiality, and that confidentiality, like autonomy, may be overruled by the duty to protect third parties, then there still remains an important problem as to the specification of the harms justifying infringements of autonomy, or, for that matter, medical confidentiality. The criterion of vulnerability does not seem to be of very much help in this respect. Although it draws attention to the kinds of contexts in which a duty to protect third parties from harm is likely to occur, it does not yield determinate criteria as to the assessment of the kinds of harm which might justify infringements of autonomy, *qua* character, e.g. extent and seriousness, and probability of occurring. Now, of course, if anything is to count as a harm, as to extent and seriousness sufficient to justify infringements of autonomy, then it surely must be the harm consisting in loss of health and life. What are we to think, however, of the probability of this harm occurring? In the case of HIV/AIDS, as opposed to many other contagious diseases, the probability of transmission of the virus, or, put differently, the probability of the harm occurring, depends largely on the willingness of the person already infected to change her habits or inform her partners. Because of this, agreement on the subject of probability could perhaps be obtained in situations where HIV-positive individuals explicitly tell a professional that they will neither inform their partners about their HIV status, nor change their sexual behaviour in order to protect them from contracting the

disease. With regard to all persons who have come to know about
their HIV status, irrespective of their apparent (un-)willingness to
inform their partner and to change their sexual behaviour, such
agreement seems to be impossible.[5] Therefore, whereas the possible
harm to be done to sex contacts may be thought to justify infringement of confidentiality on particular occasions; that is to say, in situations where the infected individual is evidently unwilling to inform
his or her sex contacts and to take safety measures, the question
which remains to be answered is whether the possible harm might
justify a general policy of partner notification.

Why should this question matter? In order to see this, a closer look
at the basic reasons for medical confidentiality is appropriate. Why
is individual autonomy regarding personal medical information
important? Is it the only rationale for medical confidentiality?

The Point of Medical Confidentiality

In maintaining medical confidentiality, by leaving to the individual
the discretionary authority over access to her personal medical
information, one shows reverence for the autonomy of the individual
in a significant respect. There are two sides to this autonomy. First,
respecting autonomy has to do with considering the individual to be
the master of her own well-being. Autonomy regarding personal
medical information puts the individual in a position to look after
certain vital interests of his, which cannot adequately be looked after
by others without risk of harm. In order to explain this, we must have
a look at the special character of personal medical information, and
information concerning the private sphere in general.[6] Information

---

[5] On the subject of HIV antibody knowledge and behaviour change, see
J. McCusker *et al.*, 'Effects of HIV antibody test knowledge on subsequent sexual
behaviours in a cohort of sexually active homosexual men', *American Journal of Public
Health* **78** (1988): 462–7; D. G. Ostrow *et al.*, 'Disclosure of HIV antibody status:
behavioural and mental health correlates', *AIDS Education and Prevention* **1** (1989):
1–11.

[6] In this respect the rationale for medical confidentiality may be thought to derive
from a right to informational privacy. Because there exist large controversies on the
subject of such a right, it seems to be more appropriate to look for good reasons for
respecting the confidentiality of personal medical information straightaway—reasons
which, however, may partially coincide with those traditionally adduced in favour of
a right to privacy—than to argue indirectly in general terms via an alleged right to privacy. About the right to privacy, see: J. L. Johnson, 'A theory of the nature and value
of privacy', *Public Affairs Quarterly* **6**/3 (1992): 271–88; W. A. Parent, 'Recent work

concerning one's health condition or health prognosis is often of delicate character, in that, when imparted to others without the discretion of the person concerned, it may cause material and emotional harm to him. This is most obvious in cases where the third parties are insurers, bankers, or employers who may refuse an applicant on the basis of a bad health condition or bad health prognosis. There are, however, more intricate ways in which people may be harmed, when such information becomes known to third parties. Information concerning certain aspects of the body, or bodily condition of persons, at least in the tradition of Western cultures, is conventionally considered to be intimate, and therefore to be kept away from the public's eye. This applies most clearly, though not exclusively, to information pertaining to bodily functions which are surrounded by taboos, such as defecation and sexuality. Information concerning such diseases, when imparted to others, may harm the person whom it concerns in that he may be ridiculed by it or his moral reputation might be damaged by it. Now, the individual to which it pertains seems to be the most appropriate locus of control over the access to such information, because he, from his subjective point of view and with an eye to his particular situation, is in the best position to judge whether or not revealing certain information to certain persons may harm or benefit him.

To this, there may be added a more fundamental consideration about the significance of personal information in general. The information passed on to others concerning one's personal sphere seems to be a constitutive factor of the kind of relationship one has to others.[7] Personal relationships, such as those towards blood relatives, friends, employers, and employees, etc., in large part are differentiated by the degree to which personal information is communicated to the other parties respectively. Therefore, by controlling the transmission of personal information, one is (at least in part) able to be in control of the kind of relationship one has, which in turn seems to be an important aspect of one's life.

Although one might agree with this reason for respecting individual autonomy regarding personal medical information generally and

on the concept of privacy', *American Philosophical Quarterly* **20** (1983): 341–56; J. Rachels, 'Why privacy is important', *Philosophy and Public Affairs* **4** (1975): 323–33; T. M. Scanlon, 'Thomson on privacy', *Philosophy and Public Affairs* **4** (1975): 295–315.

[7] See Rachels, 'Why privacy is important'.

normally, one might question whether it suffices for maintaining medical confidentiality even in those particular cases where the health of third parties might be threatened. Does not the possible serious harm to be done to the health of others outweigh what intuitively appears to be the smaller harm, e.g. the one which is brought about by taking away the control over certain medical information? However, whereas it seems right to consider the possible harm to health and life of others as outweighing the violation of privacy of the tested person in case the latter is expressly indicating that she will not inform others, there seems to be little reason to think that *every* person subjected to the test and appearing to be HIV positive will take this stand.

Secondly, respecting autonomy may be viewed as an expression of esteem for the dignity of individual persons, because in doing so one takes them seriously as beings capable of taking up moral responsibilities. By not interfering in their choices and actions, one leaves them free to choose and act morally rightly. So, for instance, by not informing sex contacts of an HIV-infected person against her will or without her consent, one leaves to her the opportunity to do freely what certainly must be morally right, e.g. protecting others from serious harm. Of course, the problem with respecting autonomy, taken this way, is that the freedom to do what is morally right goes hand in hand with the freedom to do what is morally wrong. Although, ideally, it seems to be better that persons do what is morally right freely, and by their own accord, than that they are forced to do so, the question remains whether this opportunity to show oneself a morally responsible person is more valuable than the possible protection of the health and life of others. Should a person be respected as a free moral actor, when she clearly expresses the intention to do serious harm, or, rather, not to prevent serious harm, for instance by indicating that she will not inform her sex contacts about her HIV status? Perhaps it could be argued that persons who show explicit and specific serious disregard of the well-being of others, are placing themselves outside the bonds of morality, thereby warranting a suspension of the moral privileges normally permitted them.[8] So, for instance, one might say that a person expressing the intention not to inform sex contacts about her HIV status or not to change her sexual behaviour, thereby loses her entitlement to control over the

[8] Grant Gillett, 'AIDS and confidentiality', *Journal of Applied Philosophy* **4**/1 (1987): 15–20.

information concerning her HIV status. However, whereas this may rightly be thought so in those cases where a person indeed expressly indicates that she will not disclose the information to her partners, distrust of *all* people shown to be HIV positive, by looking at them as intentional wrongdoers, seems to be misplaced. Therefore, taking away their privileged status as autonomous persons, capable of taking up moral responsibilities, beforehand, cannot be justified.

Respecting individual autonomy, however, although being one reason for it, is not the exclusive reason for confidentiality. Confidentiality has another basic objective which is of a more pragmatic kind. It hinges on a functional aspect of confidentiality in health care and health research as social institutions. Since the information which people as patients or as research subjects have to entrust to health care and health research professionals often is of sensitive character, imparting such information to third parties might result in distrust towards these professionals. Because such distrust again might lead to a situation in which people no longer would be willing to take part in health research projects or to seek help in the health care system, in the long run, breaches of confidentiality might endanger public health.

This second objective of medical confidentiality seems to be of special importance in the context off HIV/AIDS. Persons whose HIV infection becomes known to third parties are thereby likely to be exposed to all kinds of discrimination. They will not only be confronted with obvious cases of unequal treatment when for instance applying for insurance and jobs; they will also have to deal with more subtle, almost elusive forms of discrimination: being evaded by friends, being looked upon as a moral pervert, etc. However, as much as one might regret these phenomena and tendencies in the attitudes of persons; their existence is a matter of fact. Because of this, however, if medical confidentiality is no longer guaranteed to them, people who might suspect themselves to be HIV infected, for instance, because they belong to a so-called 'high-risk group'[9] in fact would have strong reasons to refrain from taking part in, for instance, HIV-surveillance studies, or from seeking help in the health

---

[9] The so-called high-risk groups are social groups in which HIV/AIDS is comparatively more prevalent than in other social groups. The high-risk groups are homosexuals, bisexuals, intravenous drug users, persons born in the Caribbean and Central Africa, and persons who received blood transfusions and blood products before the middle of 1985 or in countries where HIV/AIDS is endemic.

care system. Putting aside confidentiality in cases of HIV/AIDS would, in other words, be a strong disincentive to voluntary testing. As a consequence of this, many people would stay ignorant of their antibody status, which in the long run might result in the uncontrolled spread of the disease.

Now, it might be objected that this argument, as applied to AIDS, hinges on the debatable assumption that, with respect to adequate and efficient control of the disease, voluntary testing is indeed the most promising option. Might not the opposite be true?[10] In this regard, it should be noted that any such policy, which makes use of mandatory HIV testing and screening in such a way that test results can be demonstrably traced back to particular persons in order to ensure the possibility of partner notification, still depends on the voluntary collaboration of the persons subjected to testing and screening. In this case, the voluntary collaboration does not pertain to the test itself, but to the provision of the names of sexual partners. From the perspective of the infected individuals involved, however, again the fear of being exposed to discrimination and scorn could be brought against such collaboration. Needless to say, sidestepping voluntary collaboration in this respect, by putting sanctions on the refusal to provide names, by investigating and surveilling the sexual behaviour of the individuals involved, or by completely sidestepping partner notification, and for that reason the need for collaboration, by enforcing screening programmes for the whole population every three to six months, would amount to absurd consequences, at least from the perspectives of practicality and financial costs.

Conclusion

Respecting the confidentiality of personal medical information has its point in respecting the autonomy of individuals, which shows reverence for them as beings capable of taking up moral responsibility and leaves to them the possibility of looking after vital interests in an appropriate way. Apart from this, medical confidentiality is an

---

[10] The history of public policies regarding sexually transmitted diseases, for instance, does not seem to yield justificatory grounds in support of either of the possible options in a clear-cut way. See e.g. A. M. Brandt, 'AIDS in Historical Perspective: Four Lessons from the History of sexually Transmitted Diseases', *American Journal of Public Health* **78**/4 (1988): 367–71.

important means to ensure the proper functioning of health care and health research systems in society. The first reason, perhaps, would allow exceptions to the rule of confidentiality in cases where an HIV-infected person is evidently unwilling to protect her partner(s) from the harm of contracting HIV infection. It does not allow of exceptions by means of a general policy of dispensing with medical confidentiality. The second reason should be taken to count as a strong argument against both occasional and systematic infringements of medical confidentiality via non-voluntary or involuntary partner notification.

It should be understood that the health care or health research professional who finds herself in a situation in which a person explicitly expresses her intention not to inform her partner about her HIV status, whereas the professional knows the name of the partner and has a way of reaching him or her, is confronted with a tragic dilemma.[11] On the one hand, she has her duty to respect confidentiality. On the other hand, she has a duty to prevent serious harm, a duty which could be fulfilled by violating the confidentiality rule. However much distress and sadness this conflict might cause to her, at the same time it might be an incentive to make extra efforts in persuading through counselling the HIV-positive person to do what is morally right.

---

[11] *Cf.* Bernard Williams, *Problems of the Self—Philosophical Papers 1956–1972* (Cambridge: Cambridge University Press, 1973): 166–86.

10

Can Health Care Workers Care for Their Patients and be Advocates of Third-Party Interests?

MEDARD T. HILHORST

Introduction

People who have AIDS, or are HIV infected, no doubt have moral duties towards other people to inform them and act in a responsible way, although the extent of these duties, and how strong they are, is open to discussion. It can be argued that health care workers (HCWs) also have moral obligations toward these 'third parties'. These professional duties can, however, be conceived of in different ways. I will defend the view that the duties can best be seen as 'derived' duties: derived from the duties that can be ascribed to the infected people themselves. This view underscores a doctor's responsibility to confront his or her possibly unwilling, irresponsible, or unreflecting patient, with justified third-party interests and be an advocate of those interests. A professional relationship should—on this view—leave room for some kind of 'moralizing', in which professional responsibilities can be exercised and society as a whole can be served in the fight against AIDS. The 'derived duties view', however, also implies the limits of these professional obligations and of a public policy that seeks to promote them. These limits can he found in the personal and moral views of the patient, and should be respected.

In the case of counselling with respect to HIV infection an HCW can face a dilemma when the care he wants to give to somebody seems to be at the expense of others. In the following, I will look at some of these dilemmas and try to characterize the moral duties of the counsellor.

Not a Simple, but a Manifold Obligation

Case 1

In a STD (sexually transmitted disease) clinic, counselling and testing is offered anonymously. Without the need of identification one is given information, advice, and help. A woman, asks for a test, because she wants certainty about her HIV-status after a period of risky behaviour during which she gave 'escort service'. What moral duties does the counsellor have?

In my view one can speak of a 'manifold obligation'. First of all a counsellor has the duty, in conformity with the standards of his profession, to inform the woman in a pre-test dialogue about the nature of the test, the advantages and disadvantages of knowing and not knowing of her HIV status, and its possible consequences. About the aim of the dialogue one cannot be mistaken: he hopes to ensure that she will come to an informed decision. His *duty to inform* finds its basis in a conception of self-determination and can be characterized as a 'role-based' duty: a duty that simply comes with the role or task of an HCW.[1] If one chooses to become a counsellor, one will also accept the duties appropriate to that role. Usually these duties are circumscribed by juridical and professional standards and it is to these standards that an HCW looks for his moral obligation.

There is a second type of moral obligation, providing the pre-test dialogue with yet another aim. In his role as an HCW, the counsellor is a member and part of a system of health care, as it is organized in society—nationally, locally, and institutionally. This system entails its own manifold aims and inherent values.[2] One can, besides the care for the individual patient, think of the promotion of health in general, the quality and efficiency of medical care, or, as in the case of HIV/AIDS, the prevention of its spread. These inherent values entail corresponding duties for the HCW, which are again 'role-based'. However, they do not have a specific person-related but a general, 'in rem'-related character. As the duty to inform consists of a specific duty towards the woman, the *duty to prevent the spread* of HIV con-

---

[1] e.g. Tom L. Beauchamp and James F. Childress discern 'role-specific' obligations of health care professionals from the 'general' obligations, which everybody has. See their *Principles of Biomedical Ethics*, 3rd edn. (Oxford: OUP, 1989): 197.

[2] R. S. Downie and E. Telfer, *Caring and Curing: A Philosophy of Medicine and Social Work* (London: Methuen, 1980).

cerns the promotion (or protection) of health, its efficiency, quality, etc., in general.[3]

Within the framework of this second type of general duties—in our case—the HCW faces so-called 'third parties', to the extent that the latter are affected directly or indirectly by the decisions of the HCW and the woman. These third parties can have their *own* (health) interests which do not coincide with the interests of the woman. For that reason, the duty of the HCW towards these third parties should be seen as a *different* duty: the HCW should consider these interests *separately*.

Because of this, the HCW should see it as his duty towards the woman to raise the subject of the risk and severity of HIV infection in general during a pre-test dialogue. He will then also inquire after her lifestyle and the existence of concrete, non-anonymous third persons: sex partners, drug contacts, etc., who might be involved. If concrete third persons are concerned and can be distinguished, the general obligation to prevent the spread of HIV can thus lead to duties with a much more specific character. This can be particularly pronounced in the case of a family doctor who is also the doctor of the woman's partner(s) who are therefore known to him. In such a case, where the risks these people run are severe, the existence of a very strong, specific 'role-based' *duty to warn*[4] is not in question.

In the STD clinic, where help is offered anonymously, the HCW has, in short, a *manifold 'role-based'* obligation with regard to the woman. This obligation can he subdivided into: (i) the specific duty to inform the woman; (ii) the general duty—as far as he has the capacity to take on this duty—to prevent the spread of HIV; and, where appropriate, (iii) the specific duty towards non-anonymous third persons to warn or protect them.

[3] By analogy with the ideas of in personam and in rem rights. See Joel Feinberg, *Social Philosophy* (Englewood Cliffs, NJ: Prentice-Hall, 1973): 59.

[4] Also specific, and in principle the same, although less strong, are his duties when the known partner lives outside his area of practice. Probably, depending on factors such as the need to inform him—can one suppose that he already knows of the risks?—and the trouble it takes to warn him. The example makes clear that the concept of role duties cannot simply be discerned from the duties human beings have in general. (With respect to this, there is a grey area—see Beauchamp and Childress, *Principles of Biomedical Ethics*: 205.) Although in this case the doctor has no formal contractual duties, he is, if necessary, by his knowledge and position, more than anybody else the one to warn a partner.

The Separate Position of an HCW

For an HCW, duties towards third parties do exist, because *different* interests of third persons or of society as a whole can be at stake in his counselling. The 'role-based' character of the duties of an HCW implies that he cannot fully identify himself with the interests of his patients/clients with respect to this, he always has his *own, separate position*. By nature, an HCW is related to society and to the system of health care in a different way from his client. This position gives his duties towards third parties a different character. I will elaborate on this a little more.

Although an HCW's primary task is to serve the well-being of his client, society has made arrangements specifying in which circumstances duties towards third parties should be considered and should possibly prevail. These concern situations in which serious dangers exist for others (infectious diseases, etc.) and he is confronted with a sharp dilemma. He then can, consciously and with good reason, decide to exercise his duty towards third parties at the cost of his patient and eventually break his duty of confidentiality. Attitudes to this subject, which over the years has received much attention, have recently been undergoing a shift. Nowadays, third-party interests are being brought to the fore.[5] The interests of society, especially, are increasingly seen to have a role in the health care system, as well as in the consulting room, and, as is shown in the following example, not as a 'sharp' dilemma only.

Example
In Article 14 of the so-called Model Doctor–Patient Regulation, the main emphasis is on the duty which doctor and patient have to 'jointly strive' for 'a control of the costs related to diagnosis and treatment'.[6]

The regulation concerns the duty of both doctor and patient to be sensitive to cost-related considerations and therefore to the general aim of health care—a just, qualitatively good, and efficient health

---

[5] B. Sluyters, *De arts en het belangenconflict* (The Doctor and the Conflict of Interests), in E. van Lennep *et al.*, *Quid luris* (Deventer: Kluwer, 1977): 167–86.

[6] Royal Dutch Society for Medicine and the National Patient and Consumer Platform, 'Modelregeling Arts-Patiënt', *Medisch Contact* **22** (1990) supplt.

care system—and to avoid the unnecessary, unsuccessful, unfriendly, unsafe, and unwisely expensive.[7]

The idea of a 'joint' duty (in mutual deliberation), however, is misleading or, at least, insufficiently precise. It seems to say that both parties have the duty to strive for cost moderation to the same extent in the same way. This view seems hard to defend. As we have seen, the HCW has, by accepting his special task, become a bearer of role-based duties, specific (person-related) as well as general (*in rem*-related) duties. Cost reduction within this perspective of the profession can be seen as a general role-based duty of each HCW, provided that this reduction aims at efficiency and justice. Can one possibly describe the patient's perspective in an equal manner? I do not think so. A patient has a different relation to the general aims of health care. The appeal to goodness and justice is, of course, as relevant to her as to anybody else: the value of good and just health care for everybody cannot leave her unmoved. In her 'role' as citizen, one can also appeal to her co-responsibility in a certain respect—for the functioning and continuity of a good and just health care system. In short, one can ascribe 'human' and 'civic' duties to her (which, of course, every HCW also has). This clarifies the difference in responsibility between a patient and an HCW: the latter has, on the basis of his own (professional) position, *additional* duties, i.e. his professional duties, which I described as 'role-based'. Even *if* we could speak of somebody's 'role' as a human or as a citizen, it would be a different role concept: one does not *choose* the 'role' of human or the 'role' of citizen in the same way as one chooses the role (and duties) of an HCW.

The perspectives of doctor and patient differ in yet another way. The (sick) patient—and her direct relatives—will primarily focus her attention on recovery or the preservation of health. In addition, the HCW will also be alive to the requirements of broader aims: conditions of carefulness (e.g. in case of experimental drugs; euthanasia; time needed, as with abortion, for a conscious choice). He is more aware of the conditions and regulations and is, as a professional, more sensitive to their importance and value, although they are not always in the direct interest of this particular patient. With respect to efficiency and justice of care, a doctor can also bring forward cost considerations that are outside the viewpoint of the patient. Should

---

[7] Also E. Haavi Morreim, *Balancing Act: The New Medical Ethics of Medicine's New Economics* (Dordrecht: Kluwer, 1991).

the patient disengage herself from her own perspective and subordinate her own interests to such considerations? I do not think so.
There is no need to deny the appeal of an ideal of ethics that is impartial and universal, to acknowledge that in such a situation, and from
a moral point of view also, a patient's charity may begin at home: it
is not always wrong for people, out of solidarity or compassion, to
first seek to care for themselves and their relatives.[8] However, the
conflict of loyalty, and the tension between patient and society, have
a much stronger impact on a doctor: even if he wants to meet the
wishes of the patient, cost issues will permanently and emphatically
accompany him.

Let us go back to the HIV case. It can be difficult for the woman
to pay attention to the possible duties she has towards third parties.
However, during the pre-test dialogue, the counsellor, independent
of her, has, on his own authority, the role-based duty to ask her to
consider the interests of third parties. His aim is to prevent the spread
of HIV and, if possible, to warn or protect third persons from the
risks they run, whether the woman likes this subject of their dialogue
or not. On account of his position, the HCW is related to the values
inherent in health care. He can appeal to those values as they form a
basis of his duty.

To summarize, the HCW has his own position and third parties
have their own interests: both considerations lead to the duty of the
HCW towards third parties as his own, different, if you like *independent* duty, which does not coincide with the duty of the HCW
towards the woman.

Own Responsibility and 'Empowerment'

Case 2

The woman consciously decides on the test. As is known, there is no
simple and clear answer to the question of whether this is for her own
good: the medical options of treatment are limited, the psychological

---

[8] A. W. Musschenga, *Mag het hemd nader dan de rok zijn?* (Is Charity Allowed to
Begin at Home? About the Limits of the Moral Requirement of Impartiality),
Inaugural Lecture, Vrije Universiteit Amsterdam, 1989. The central question, which I
cannot answer here, is whether the different roles which a person has, and the duties
implied by them, can be seen as a harmonious unity. See e.g. C. A. J. Coady, 'Politics
and the Problem of Dirty Hands', in Peter Singer (ed.), *A Companion to Ethics*
(Oxford: Blackwell, 1991): 375.

consequences differ per person, and the social consequences are uncertain and full of risks (exclusion, discrimination, etc.). Testing is not always better: therefore it is her decision, her responsibility to do it. It turns out that she is HIV positive. In the post-test dialogue, the HCW has of course the duty to help her as much as he can medically, psychologically, and socially, and help her find her way. But what duties does he have towards third parties?

Suppose the woman tells him that her escort activities were anonymous and that her clients can no longer be traced. With her own partners she has always had safe contacts. This information considerably limits the duty of the counsellor and changes the picture of the manifold obligation outlined above. As no concrete third persons can be indicated—and possibly warned—his only other duty is the *duty to try to convince* the woman to change her risky (escort) behaviour.[9] In what way should she change? Technically speaking she should have 'safe sex', so that others no longer risk infection.

What more can one say about this duty to convince? First, the duty does not concern concrete, discernible third persons, but the spread of HIV as such (in which anonymous persons are at stake). Second, the norm held before the woman, to have safe sex, is general in the sense that if the test had been negative, or if she had decided not to be tested, one would have pointed to the same norm. Obviously, the test and test result do not change this. Finally, it becomes clear that the duty towards third parties, to prevent the spread of HIV, can only be exercised by the HCW by addressing himself to the woman. The interests of third parties still exist, but hide behind the woman. Only through her can he try to protect third parties. *He* has the duty to point them out to her; she has to act accordingly. This situation constrains his moral obligation towards third parties; what remains is only *her* responsibility.

One can interpret the duty to convince in different ways, either in a more strict or in a more broad sense. Do we take the view that counselling should restrict itself as much as possible to the facts by giving information: the risks of HIV transmission and its consequences? Or should a counsellor also insist on a dialogue even if a patient does not want this and, if so, how strongly? Does he stress the possible dangers or her duty to change her behaviour, or, to put it differently, should he teach her a lesson in medicine or morality? Is

---

[9] If she appears to know that she does not intend to change her behaviour, again duties towards (anonymous) third parties will come up. See Case 4.

he, in the end, indifferent as to what she decides to do, even if she becomes pregnant, for example?

At stake is the prevention of the spread of a deadly disease and the infection of people, which is—no doubt—a highly moral issue. Even the most liberal HCW—philosophically speaking—will be convinced that the woman has no liberty to impose this harm on others. He should try to make clear to her that unsafe behaviour is immoral. Although an HCW is no more of a moral expert than anyone else, within his professional role he is *in the position* to bring forward these general moral considerations.[10] Because of the severe health risks it is therefore, in my view, his duty not only to give just technical information but also to add moral considerations to it, in order to convince her of the importance of safe contacts.

One can still go one step further and argue that, because third parties hide behind the woman, she herself is his main concern. Not only is it important that she realizes that interests of third parties do exist, but also that she sees the moral relevance of this and understands the need to act accordingly. Therefore, the HCW cannot avoid appealing to her moral consciousness. If necessary he will even try to develop her moral sensitiveness. One can speak of her 'moral empowerment' and his duty to contribute to it—as far as it is in his power to do so; in short: to help her to also get hold of her life in a moral sense.[11]

Seen as such, the interests of third parties come up only in a derived way. By 'derived', I mean that the duty of an HCW towards third parties in the counselling situation to prevent the spread of HIV has been changed to the duty to convince the woman to behave towards third persons in a safe way, and finally, and more precisely, to the duty to help the woman get moral hold of her life. If he succeeds in the latter, then he will also indirectly contribute to the former. The interests of third parties therefore appear to him in an indirect way, i.e. as the importance to induce the woman to safe and

---

[10] He has the role of a 'geographer of values and rights' and should know the secular pluralistic moral framework as well as that of particular moral communities, according to H. Tristram Engelhardt Jr., *The Foundations of Bioethics* (Oxford: OUP, 1986): 55.

[11] R. S. Downie, Carol Fyfe, and Andrew Tannahill, *Health Promotion: Models and Values* (Oxford: OUP, 1990). Chadwick's concept of counselling with respect to genetics, however, seems to be restricted to liberal concepts of advising and alerting, with respect to the alternative options—see Ruth F. Chadwick, 'What counts as success in genetic counselling?', *Journal of Medical Ethics* **19** (1993): 43.

moral behaviour. All attention should be given to her: therefore it is, in my view, no longer possible to fully squeeze the duty of the HCW into a (strictly) liberal model. He is a 'moralizer', and so he should be.

There are no Third Parties: the Moral Shortcomings of 'Safe Sex'

The idea of an indirect, 'derived' duty could suggest that to the HCW there are in fact no third parties and that he only has one simple obligation: the welfare of the woman. This is a mistake. Above I made sufficiently clear that a manifold obligation is still there. The persistence with which the counsellor can talk to the woman and point out to her her duty to have safe sex, until he is really convinced about her intention to change her behaviour, shows that not only she, but also third parties—although anonymously—are at stake.

There is still another way in which some HCWs deny the existence of responsibilities toward third parties. The message 'safe sex' gives rise to this misunderstanding. The argument is that nobody needs to be infected, if one has safe sex (S), uses clean needles (N), and acts hygienically (H): the 'SNH norm'. Therefore, HCWs can restrict themselves to their patient, and third parties should be confronted with their own responsibility to adhere to the SNH norm. There are several objections to this argument that SNH as a norm is sufficient and equals moral responsibility, and should be propagated in all situations: in hospital and in prison, among drug abusers, and among people from different cultures and with different lifestyles and attitudes. With such a view on 'safe sex' much remains to be said.

Case 3

The woman, who is HIV positive, does not tell her present partner. In her view there is no point in doing so: their contacts are safe and the reasons for her not to tell him are plenty (moreover, not everybody wants to know). Following an accident, a broken condom, she tells him about her status and insists he be tested. He is infected. Should she have told him earlier? Does she have a duty to inform any contact she has? And did the HCW have the duty to insist on her telling?

The example makes clear that the SNH norm, if considered only as a technical norm, is not waterproof. There are people who get infected although they have acted according to it: by accident or due to professional risks; as a prostitute, a surgeon, or a development worker in Africa. This is only one objection to the view that SNH is sufficient and makes other norms superfluous.

There are also moral objections: not everybody seems to be able to (always) behave responsibly (SNH); some, in retrospect, took risks that were too big. With sex and drugs this is no different from mountain-climbing, smoking, or car-driving. Furthermore, knowing about SNH does not mean behaving according to the SNH norm, in circumstances of prostitution, addiction, or in heterosexual contacts. These objections refer to the human condition and its weaknesses[12] and state that SNH, seen in a purely technical way, reflects an image of men and their behaviour which is unrealistic. Reality is less beautiful, and much more complex than is suggested by the SNH norm.

The conclusion is simple. In those complex and confused circumstances, people should, as much as possible, try 'to guard one another' from the spread of the virus and the suffering as a consequence of it. 'Own' responsibility cannot mean: 'I take care of myself, and others should do the same, and if everybody does what he should do (SNH) there is no problem. If somebody wants to run the risks, he should bear the consequences.' In that case, the 'third parties' would be eliminated and any responsibility for others would be denied. In my view, 'own' responsibility means more, namely, also helping others to guard themselves against dangers and risks: morally speaking, one cannot dispose oneself of others. The (moral) shortcomings of a technical conception of SNH are now clear. At first sight, the norm seemed to have a technical character, with a rather modest aim, restricted to the prevention of the 'transfer' of the virus and not including moralizing. On further consideration, however, it imposes a moral norm in the form of an ideal, which, if it does not accept other ideals beside it, becomes a straitjacket.

First, paradoxically, an ideal: if everybody behaves responsibly (SNH), then SNH is a *sufficient* norm. Despite this norm, people are infected. Therefore it can be argued that, beside the SNH norm, other *additional* duties should be formulated, for example the *duty of 'extra precaution'*. For the woman in our case, this could mean in general that it is better to inform her partner about her status than

---

[12] e.g. weakness of will and character, as analysed by Thomas E. Hill Jr., *Autonomy and Self-Respect* (Cambridge: Cambridge University Press, 1991): ch. 9.

not to. (The elements 'in general' and 'better' leave room for discussion and shading.)

Secondly, the SNH norm offers only one perspective on relations. If it is presented as the norm, one overlooks that relations can be diverse and can take many forms. Some have ideals based on the virtues of (marital) faithfulness, others plead for honesty and openness towards one another with respect to their status and risky past and subsequently decide whether they are safe or not. Such considerations will of course get particular weight in more permanent and non-anonymous relations, like in the case of a woman who, after thirty years of marriage, will feel deceived by her husband when she turns out to be infected by him. This as opposed to situations of anonymous and transient contacts, in which partners are expected to know the risks they take and in which information about their status probably does not add much. Suppose our woman has to go to the hospital to undergo, for some other reason, one big operation, should she then inform her surgeon about her status, or is it sufficient that he acts according to the hygienic norm? And what if she has to be nursed for a long time? One can argue that an *additional* duty (SNH as well as inform) does exist, but also that a *different* duty (inform and, in safe situations, no need for SNH) cannot and should not be excluded. Prima facie, and in general, SNH is probably better than no SNH. To inform is probably better—'better' with respect to the risk of infection. One risky contact is better than many risky contacts. However, taking it as the only norm for all situations would do injustice to other views on life, relationships, and circumstances. In short, SNH cannot be the only norm: it is neither a sufficient nor a necessary norm. Its perspective on human relations, as far as the spread of HIV is concerned, would be too small. An HCW can do nothing but take into consideration the specific situation of his client and her (also moral) convictions and considerations.

Thirdly, the SNH norm is too general (and too uniform) to sufficiently discern different situations. This we have seen, for example, in the HCW's duty to explain to the woman the importance of safe sex, which exists independently of whether she takes the test or not, and of its positive or negative result. This points to the inadequacy of the norm. Why would the information that she is positive only be relevant to her and not (never) to her partner? Why would the answer in the pre-test as well as post-test situations be limited to SNH only?

Safe Sex as a Normative Prevention Message

In the Dutch discussion, the limitation to one, uniform, clear general norm of 'safe' has been well defended by the argument that every emphasis on a different, additional duty, e.g. 'You should always tell your partner', will possibly have counterproductive and disadvantageous consequences for public health. People might behave in unsafe ways, unless they are warned. In that case the general norm would be undermined by the additional norm.

To do justice, however, to the diversity of situations, the norm 'to behave safely' has been defined not in the above-mentioned small and technical way, but in a broad and normative sense. 'Safe sex' is defined as 'being conscious of the risks related to sexual contacts and considering it as self-evident to speak about it and act accordingly.'[13] This broad definition with its elements of consciousness-speaking-acting (let's call this a 'CSA norm') enables a public policy to find a large amount of support among the population as a whole. Public policy then aims at differentiating the norm towards the various groups in society, and with respect to this, HCWs have a main role to play, especially in enlightening people. There is a great emphasis on the social environment, family, and friends, etc., who can support the individual to behave safely, on the differences in risk experience of the various groups, and on the importance of making it possible for everybody to make a personal risk assessment. In this definition, 'unsafe' sex, in a technical sense, is not excluded, provided people have convinced themselves of the acceptable (small) risks they run. The concept of an 'own' responsibility extends to partners, contacts, and (possible) pregnancies and children, and society as a whole. It is my opinion that, as a consequence, an HCW should pay specific attention to the situation and convictions of his client and his counselling should be equally broad and differentiated: information and education, both technical and moral. Here the effectiveness of a public policy and doing justice to individual people and their views go hand in hand.

Back to the case. Should this woman tell her partner about her HIV-positive status and should the HCW insist on this? One can summarize as follows. In general: (i) one should (always) take into account not

[13] *Werkplan Voorlichting en Preventie 1993 (Plan of Work of Information and Prevention)*, National Committee on AIDS Control, Amsterdam, 1993: 69.

only the weaknesses of condoms, but of people, and not trust them too much; (ii) there is a difference of situations in which people leave one another 'ignorant' and therefore assess the risks wrongly, e.g. compare a supposedly permanent partner since 1980 and a surgeon, who knows the risks of his job; and (iii) if she knows her HIV-positive status, it will be 'better' that he also does, 'better' from the point of view of 'double precaution'. These general considerations, however, do not lead the HCW, in the case of the woman, to a conclusive argument. For there are the particularities of her situation, in which she has to make her judgement: (i) the HCW knows that there can be good reasons not to tell her partner; (ii) he can, on the other hand, not hide behind the simple technical SNH norm, which does not cover—as we have seen—each particular situation; and (iii) his insight and judgement completely depend on what she tells him.

This last consideration suggests that an HCW cannot play his own role. Let us, finally, look at some new situations to see whether this is true or not.

What More should an HCW Do?

In order for an HCW to carry out his duty towards third parties he is dependent on the woman in two ways: on the information she gives, and on her readiness to entertain moral considerations.[14] An HCW can try to get more information and can try to convince her more emphatically. I will describe the possibilities he should consider in three situations.

Case 4

The woman shows bitterness and seems to seek revenge on her business contacts. She says she is consciously having unprotected contacts, or at least threatens to.

These rather exceptional cases have led to many, probably too many, discussions. At stake are situations in which somebody behaves in an evidently immoral manner and is not prepared for

---

[14] Boyd speaks of a wishful relation of 'mutual empowerment', under the condition that both parties have a good understanding of confidentiality, so that medical beneficence and patient's autonomy go along. In paragraph 2, however, we showed that 'mutual' does not imply a symmetrical relation. See Kenneth M. Boyd, 'HIV infection and AIDS: The ethics of medical confidentiality', *Journal of Medical Ethics* **18** (1992): 173–9.

change. Usually this type of situation becomes evident only in retrospect and the conflict can only take the form of a law case. In such
cases, what should be the role of an HCW? When somebody places
herself so evidently outside the moral order, all means seem justifiable to stop her. However, on second thought, most means are not
effective or not proportional in relation to its aim, and other
approaches, without the use of force, seem to be much more obvious.

In case of known third persons—think of the family doctor—there
can be, morally and juridically, sufficient reason to break confidentiality and warn these third persons. Although the doctor has to
make a conscious decision each time, and different loyalties are to be
weighed, it is necessary that clear regulations will give guidance, in
order to let all parties know where they stand. One should prevent an
HCW, out of uncertainty or wilfulness, and in the absence of regulations, from acting on his own account.[15] Regulation is important
from a point of view of carefulness and justice, but also from a point
of view of effectiveness. An unclear situation can lead to a higher
threshold to health care, in which people ask for help less easily, out
of fear of the consequences.[16]

In the case of anonymous third parties, warning is not possible.
Notification of the police cannot help much, unless unaccountability
is at stake and a person can be seen as a danger to society: then our
case is not AIDS-related, but psychiatry-related, in which in exceptional, clearly circumscribed cases—through the law courts—con-
finement and isolation can follow. All other suggestions, such as
observing a person or putting a person's photograph in a newspaper,
are a severe intrusion into that person's privacy, with no clear relation, and in no proportion to its purpose. In these cases (fortunately)
legal means are limited, and the role of an HCW cannot be a criminal investigator.

One should, furthermore, take into account that HIV is transmitted by voluntarily entering into sexual contacts (with exceptions such
as rape); trying to prove that a person has been behaving in a (legally)
culpable way will result in many complications.[17] The only option

[15] According to Engelhardt, *Foundations of Bioethics*, he is a quasi-bureaucrat, living in a pluralistic society, and not a religious counsellor.
[16] Sluyters, *De arts en het belangeconflict*.
[17] The range of the law cannot be very long, as we can see from the Amsterdam
(rape) case (*Tijdschrift voor Gezondheidsrecht* **61** (1991): 382–5, and **53** (1993): 368–82)
as well as the Leeuwarden (partners) case (Court of Justice, Leeuwarden, 21 Jan. 1993,
H764792).

that remains is a public policy in which much attention is paid to the role of an HCW. An effective control of the spread of HIV will largely depend on the capacities of the HCW to help his client to take hold of her life.

Case 5

Suppose, on the contrary, that the woman shows great responsibility for her partner(s) and contacts, but does not want to give information about them. What else should the HCW do than point out to her the above-mentioned conscious-speak-act norm, as it applies to her situation and convictions?

Not much remains to be desired here: the HCW can try to support her in her new circumstances and help her to apply the CSA norm to her situation. Third parties will only come up if the woman prefers not to give information about them, in a 'hypothetical' way, and for the HCW there will be no conflict of loyalties: he has to leave the weighing of interests (her interest and those of third parties) to her. There is, of course, no reason to insist on her giving more information, or even to ask—against her wishes—for a new dialogue: what purpose could it serve and what right to do so does the HCW have? If she explains that she will assume her responsibilities, no insistence or enforcement will in any way serve the prevention of future infections. The interests of third parties are protected if the woman does her duty and behaves safely. If she feels a sexual contact from her past should be warned, but she prefers not to do so herself, the HCW can act on behalf of her, as a 'lengthened' arm. But the weighing of interests is done by her, and there is no reason to think the HCW should be morally better 'equipped' to this than she. He can, like a 'geographer', sketch the map of 'values and rights', but should call a halt there and respect her views, considerations, and final decisions, which can been seen as part of the convictions of the 'moral community' to which she belongs.

Case 6

Suppose that things develop less smoothly and morally, which is more common, and that the (interests of) third parties are hardly considered by the woman. Her anguish plays a central role when she hears about her status, reactions of uncertainty and indifference with respect to her own life succeed one another, and her capability to get hold of her life—on the basis of the new facts—are heavily laden by circumstances such as prostitution, addiction, and finance. In this situation she lacks a clear view of the consequences and a moral sensibility for the dangers for others.

How can an HCW help the woman to put some moral order into her life? Nobody can coerce her to seek help, but an HCW is in a position to offer it to her. There is a variety of possibilities to make clear arrangements with addicts, on a voluntary basis, to undergo e.g. drug rehabilitation. However, help can only be effective when it is accepted: I see no other alternative than reliance on conviction. Third parties are dependent on its success. Even the appearance of coercion within an assistance relation, or the plea for only non-anonymous counselling, can have the effect that clients will lie about their situation, or stop seeking help. In that case, the problem for society shifts and becomes more difficult to address. In the end, this is of no avail to anybody: neither client nor third parties, neither health care system nor society.[18]

The HCW can exert all his power to convince, so long as a confidential relationship is guaranteed. Therefore, Case 6 demonstrates no (moral) affinity with Case 4, but should be seen against the background of Case 5: in Case 6, as in Case 5, we assume that the woman is morally approachable. Case 4 forms an exception and should be singled out by regulations, which concern only clear and well-defined harmful and immoral situations. Only then can an HCW, in Case 6, call forth all his skill to convince her. The HCW and the woman both know that the situation (and the circumstances of society as a whole) is sufficiently safe. The prerequisite here is that the HCW will not break his confidentiality.

This leads to the following conclusion. The more a society is liberal in its regulations (and is 'safe' in the sense that there is no threat of coercion, discrimination, or stigmatization, and with no threat of the HCW breaking his confidentiality), the less an HCW needs to be liberal: he can moralize without having the need to be afraid of counterproductive and negative consequences, such as people refusing tests, seeking help, and hiding from society. The combination of a more liberal society and a less liberal HCW will possibly serve, in an indirect way, third parties best.

---

[18] See Boyd, 'HIV infection and AIDS', and also Scott Dunbar and Susan Rehm, 'On visibility: AIDS, deception by patients, and the responsibility of the doctor', *Journal of Medical Ethics* **18** (1992): 180–5.

Conclusions

Public discussion has paid a great deal of attention to conflicts between parties in terms of rights: patients' rights, such as autonomy and privacy, and the related responsibilities of health care workers, such as (not) breaking confidentiality. It has been shown that there are other important themes to be considered, in situations in which conflicts arise less sharply. In those cases, third parties can be served best by an improvement of the caring relationship, in which the general health is promoted or protected by the 'empowerment' of people to choose and act in a morally responsible way. Without patronizing, an HCW can play a role in which moralizing is justified in a situation in which someone has to face third-party interests.

My argument can be summarized as follows. An HCW has a manifold role-based obligation, which can be subdivided into the specific duty to inform his client, the general duty to promote health, e.g. by preventing the spread of HIV in society, and possibly the specific duty to warn or protect third persons. The duty towards third parties is based on the fact that the latter can have their own, independent interests and that an HCW has his own, separate position within the health care system. If concrete third persons are unknown (and cannot be warned), the general duty towards society to prevent the spread of HIV (and to protect anonymous third persons) can be turned into a duty to convince the woman to behave safely, and eventually a duty to help her to get moral purchase on her life; a duty which cannot fully be squeezed into a (strict) liberal model. The suggestion that a strictly technical conception of the SNH norm (safe sex, needles, and hygiene) is sufficient and makes duties towards third parties redundant is mistaken: the norm is neither sufficient nor necessary, and should leave room for additional as well as alternative norms. On the other hand, a normative interpretation of safe behaviour in terms of consciousness of risks, speaking about it, and acting according to it (a CSA norm), enables us to take account of third parties, whose interests are always involved. Finally, I argued that immoral situations should be set apart by clear regulations, whereas in all other situations society should guarantee safe circumstances, according to liberal principles, in order to maximize the possibilities for HCWs to use their powers of persuasion.

11

HIV Infection and the Health Care Worker: The Case for Limited Disclosure

CALLIOPE C. S. FARSIDES

In 1993, a number of cases hit the press in which health care workers employed within the UK were found to have died of AIDS. This in itself was not the major issue. With the growing awareness of the virus, the public could only expect that members of most groups in society would at one time or another be affected. Rather, the public concern was over the risk to which these workers may have put their patients. On more than one occasion the name of the dead carer was widely publicized, former patients were contacted, and help lines set up to deal with patients' worries and fears. We have an interest both in terms of respecting the confidentiality due to health care workers who die of HIV-related disease, and in terms of sparing patients unnecessary alarm to make sure that such occurrences do not become commonplace.

In this chapter I wish to consider the duties of health care workers who believe or know themselves to be HIV positive, and the corresponding duties of others towards them. I am most anxious to couch the discussion in terms of duties as opposed to rights as I do not wish to endorse a 'right-to-know' policy with relation to an individual's HIV status.

Wherever possible details of a person's state of health should remain confidential, and this is particularly true in the case of HIV/AIDS where the social implications of the disease are sometimes as devastating as the medical ones. However, the facts that the virus is contagious, and the illnesses it leads to eventually kills a person, make it difficult to indulge in a fully fledged defence of absolute confidentiality. Having said this, it should he possible to show that the need to protect against infection does not necessarily entitle patients or co-workers to specific information about a carer's HIV status.

For some, the obvious response to hearing of the AIDS-related deaths of health service employees was to demand mandatory testing of all health care professionals, but both the GMC and the UKCC decided not to back this call.[1] There are very practical reasons behind their stand, as the UKCC points out routine testing can itself be harmful because it generates a false sense of security, which could lead in turn to a fall in personal standards of practice. And, despite being expensive, given the seroconversion time, such testing cannot be both completely reliable and practically feasible.[2]

Instead the UKCC appealed to the moral and professional consciences of its members and advised them that '[e]ach practitioner must consider very carefully their personal accountability as defined in the Council's Code of Professional Conduct and remember that she or he has an overriding ethical duty of care to patients'.[3]

It is this duty of care which sets the health care professional apart from most other individuals. In terms of our moral or ethical duties it is generally felt that the strongest claim upon us is that we should not cause harm to others. To refrain from causing harm often requires us only to hold back, not to act, or to use a phrase popular with moral philosophers, 'keep our hands clean'. This is usually less demanding than the requirement that we should do good, which invariably entails some positive action on our part.

In many, although admittedly not all, moral theories a duty of non-maleficence is given priority over the duty of beneficence, and a failure to do good is not judged as harshly as actually causing some harm. Similarly in one's work, whilst it is to be hoped that most of us will attempt to do the best by those we serve, the standards we are asked to maintain are usually minimum standards of honesty and probity. That is we are expected not to cheat or defraud even when we are not required to positively benefit those we deal with.

The 'duty of care' referred to by the UKCC is plainly a beneficence-based duty, and health care professionals are quite clear about the fact that they have a duty to help their patients, as opposed

---

[1] General Medical Council, 1993, *HIV Infection and AIDS: The Ethical Considerations* (hereafter referred to as GMC 1993); UKCC, 1994, 'Registrar's Letter and Annexes, Acquired Immune Deficiency Syndrome and Human Immunodeficiency Virus Infection, the Council's Position Statement' (hereafter referred to as UKCC 1994).

[2] UKCC.   [3] UKCC (1994): 5.

to merely being required not to harm them. Contractually and morally the health care professional is committed to alleviating current suffering, preventing avoidable future suffering, and improving health states, all of which go beyond the very basic demands of non-maleficence.

By stressing the importance of the duty of care in this context, the professional bodies might appear to be claiming that the first responsibility of the health worker who considers that they may be infected with the HIV virus is to assess the extent to which their health state affects their ability to discharge their professional duties. However, it would probably make more sense to say that the first responsibility of a worker who suspects himself to be HIV positive is one shared by *all* individuals with similar fears about their HIV status, and that is to consider whether or not their condition will cause harm to others. The answer to this is of course 'no'. Their HIV *status* in itself will not pose a danger to others, the potential danger lies in their choice of behaviour. Irresponsible behaviour triggers the risk of doing quite devastating harm to others, that is infecting them with the virus.

The Duty of Non-maleficence

It could be argued that the primary duty upon all health workers with reference to HIV is a two-part duty of protection, which breaks down into a duty to protect themselves from infection, and a duty to protect co-workers and patients. The two elements of this duty are complementary, and if both are acknowledged and acted upon the risk of infection is minimized. If all health care workers operated in such a way as to protect others from infection, whilst also taking on the responsibility of protecting themselves, the risks of even the closest contact would all but disappear.[4]

[4] I have argued elsewhere that all individuals should accept that they have a moral duty of self-protection with respect to sexual activity, as well as a duty not to infect others. There is no reason why the scope of this duty cannot be extended as long as one keeps a realistic perspective on the issue of risk. Furthermore, one could argue that in the health care setting there may be occasions on which health care professionals choose to take risks in order to promote their patient's welfare. An example would be the health care professionals currently working amongst those suffering from the Ebola virus in Zaire. In such cases we have to allow that they might justify the harm they and their families might suffer in terms of the promoting of some greater good.

Current evidence suggests that the behaviour of health care professionals to date has effectively safeguarded patients and co-workers from infection. There has only been one case in which a HIV-positive health care professional is believed to have infected his patients, whereas the figures for infection in the other direction are much higher.

It would be naïve to assume that this evidence *proves* that the adoption of universal precautions is an absolute guarantee of safety. Just as we no longer speak of safe but only safer sex, it is wise to remain sceptical about the possibility of complete protection in a health care setting. This is particularly true of areas of medicine where procedures are invasive and/or the behaviour of patients unpredictable. Nonetheless, the risk of harm does appear to be very slight, and this must be taken into account at the outset.

Despite having agreed that the risk is small, and after appealing in the first instance to individuals' consciences, neither the UKCC nor the GMC are willing to leave the matter of protecting others from the risk of infection entirely to the infected individual. Those who 'think they may be infected' are told to get tested, and once they know themselves to be HIV positive their behaviour in the workplace is no longer a matter for self-governance. The GMC advises that

[I]t is imperative, both in the public interest and on ethical grounds that any doctors who think they may have been infected with HIV should seek appropriate diagnostic testing and counselling and, if found to be infected, have regular medical supervision.[5]

After demanding that doctors go on to seek professional advice the Council then states that

Doctors must act upon that advice which, in some circumstances would include a requirement not to practice or to limit practice in certain ways. No doctor should continue in clinical practice merely on the basis of their own assessment of the risk to patients.[6]

The UKCC makes similar recommendations, and both bodies stress a further responsibility on the part of fellow workers to alert the relevant bodies if anyone known to be HIV positive is not acting appropriately.[7] This latter recommendation is made with surprising ease given the potential for conflict once colleagues are asked to monitor one another's behaviour.

[5] GMC (1993): 2.　　[6] Ibid.　　[7] UKCC.

Whilst it is relatively uncontentious to demand that an individual remove himself from the opportunity of infection, it is potentially problematic to advise one individual to monitor and report on another. One can understand the need to ensure that those known to be HIV positive act responsibly, but there is the possibility that colleagues will also intervene when they simply *suspect* a co-worker to be infected irrespective of that person's behaviour. This is particularly worrying given the lingering association in people's minds between membership of certain groups and the likelihood of infection, coupled with a fairly widespread prejudice against members of the groups in question. It is at least possible, for example, that a colleague might confuse observations about a co-worker's homosexuality with the issue of whether or not that person may be HIV positive, and in turn conflate this with the question of whether this poses a risk to patients. For this reason it is particularly important to establish that the *work-related behaviour* of *all* individuals should be subject to scrutiny, and that the primary issue is whether or not adequate safety precautions are observed.

Having chosen to go along the path of advocating limited disclosure, the professional bodies essentially prescribe a duty on the part of their members to voluntarily disclose their HIV status at least to the Occupational Health Service. This duty arises not out of a corresponding right to know, but rather out of the duty to protect others. This being so it could be claimed that the duty has only prima-facie force, such that disclosure must be shown to facilitate protection in order for the duty to have force. However, even if there were evidence to suggest that limited disclosure was an effective risk-reduction strategy, it might not be easy to get all relevant individuals to accept and act upon the duty to disclose.

This is where the recognition of reciprocal duties on the part of employers and professional bodies becomes crucial. To motivate the individual who is not motivated by a sense of duty alone, we have to show him that he will not lose out by being open about his HIV status. From a motivational perspective it would be even better if we could show him that he would benefit as the result of carefully managed disclosure.

For this to be the case one would have to ensure that voluntary disclosure did not open the way to discrimination and unfair treatment. This in turn necessitates at least the following commitments. First, the involvement of the Occupational Health Service must be seen to be governed by the strictest rules of confidentiality. For example, fellow workers should not automatically be informed of a colleague's status, and the duty of confidentiality should extend beyond the death of the health care worker if that is his wish. Secondly, the question of redeployment should only be raised if absolutely necessary, and if so, it must be sensitively handled. A person should be allowed to remain in post for as long as she is able to perform her tasks without posing a danger to others, and a team should be able to accommodate a colleague shedding those duties that it is no longer appropriate for her to perform. Thirdly, workers who willingly disclose their HIV status should be left believing that they have benefited from disclosure as a result of the support and guidance they receive. Having disclosed his status the health care worker should receive support from his institution in terms of medical care, employment, pension and insurance advice, and counselling. Fourthly, the employers should work constantly to foster an environment which is as free as possible from prejudice and discrimination, and sensitive to the needs of people living with HIV/AIDS. Only in such an environment can a climate of openness flourish.

If these commitments were met, the ideal case scenario might arise in which health care workers willingly disclose their status to an occupational health practitioner but remain in their current role for as long as they are able to perform their tasks. Their patients and colleagues remain protected from infection by good standards of practice, without needing to know of the particular individual's status. Whom to tell and whom not to tell reverts to being a matter of personal choice once the initial disclosure has been made.

However, in terms of his relationship to patients, we have already established that in discharging his duty of care the health care worker must do more than protect them from the risk of infection. Because his professional life is characterized by a duty of care, it is important that the health care professionals can still do good for their patients, as opposed to simply showing that they do no harm. We now need to consider whether the possibility, or reality, of a health care worker being HIV positive will in any way affect that individual's ability to care for a patient.

The Duty of Beneficence, Autonomy, and Consent

In caring for a patient a health care workers can do good in a number of ways. They can fulfil their clinical duties, narrowly defined in terms of treating or palliating, and in some cases they can perform a social function in terms of befriending or acting as advocate. Increasingly we believe that a large part of doing good for the patient involves performing the various functions involved in caring in a manner that demonstrates respect for the patient as a moral agent. Thus we place a high premium on respecting the patient's autonomy and acquiring his consent to proposed interventions. The question now arises as to whether a health care worker's HIV positivity would impede any of these functions.

Any serious illness will potentially affect an individual's ability to perform his professional duties, and once someone is seriously ill with any disease he must decide whether or not it is proper for him to continue practising. Presumably an individual and his doctor will monitor the situation, and decide if and when resignation on the grounds of ill-health is appropriate, just as they would in the case of a doctor or nurse with terminal cancer or chronic osteoarthritis. HIV and AIDS, however, raise further issues, most of which arise out of public perceptions and misconceptions about the virus.

Despite the evidence which suggests only very limited means of transmission, the severity of the suffering associated with HIV infection, and the unavailability of a cure for AIDS, means that people have a greater fear of being infected than the statistics and evidence would justify. Added to this is the almost unprecedented stigmatization of the disease and its sufferers. It is against this background of fear and lingering prejudice that the implications of testing and disclosure must always be judged, and the reactions of patients anticipated.

Were a patient to become aware that someone involved in her care was HIV positive it is highly likely that this would cause her some anxiety, irrespective of the real risks involved. However, anti-paternalist arguments might suggest that the desire to avoid such anxiety is not necessarily grounds for withholding information about the carer's status if it is any sense relevant to the patient's care. Learning of the possible side effects of various treatments and procedures can often be distressing, as can knowledge of a terminal prognosis, but considerations around consent and autonomy are usually considered decisive in such cases, and the truth is told.

The question now arises as to whether a patient needs to know about her carer's HIV status for us to be able to claim that their autonomy has been respected and they have fully consented to treatment. One could argue that the issues at stake here are somewhat different from those involved in disclosure of clinical side effects, but it is probably worth exploring the analogy with side effects a little further nonetheless.

Consent

For certain procedures there are a list of side effects that are statistically possible. Of these some are relatively trivial, others more serious, some are fairly likely to occur, others are highly unlikely to happen. When acquiring consent, some sort of balance has to be struck between adequately informing the patient, and not causing unnecessary alarm. The patient must know enough to make an appropriate decision, but need not know of possibilities too remote to require serious consideration.

If a health care professional is offering non-invasive care to a patient the risk of transmitting the HIV virus is negligible. However, the anxiety which could be caused by even discussing the risk is disproportionately high. If, as claimed here, the adoption of universal precautions renders the risk of infection very small, it is not necessary in this context to disclose the information for the purposes of acquiring consent. The patient has been adequately informed by being told of risks which are statistically more probable. Indeed, in such contexts there might be more mundane facts which are much more relevant to the consenting procedure because they potentially affect the carer's judgement and competence. For example the state of the carer's marriage, or how much he drank the night before. Although few patients would demand such information before giving consent, the effects of heavy drinking or stress could realistically pose a greater risk to the patient than the carer's HIV status.

Certain procedures increase the likelihood of infection, and were an individual to continue carrying out such procedures it could be argued that the patient needs to know of the additional risk attaching to *this* person offering *this* procedure when consenting to his carrying it out. In a surgical context, for example, with the risk of needle-prick injuries, the risk of infection is statistically higher and therefore relevant to acquiring true consent.

Here, there would appear to be a choice of how to proceed. Either, infected individuals withdraw from such procedures and engage only in those where the risk is too small to be relevant to the acquisition of consent, or the patient should be informed of the additional risk involved—allowing that the patient may withhold consent to the health care worker performing the procedure.

Given the erosion of confidentiality involved in the second approach, coupled with the burden you place on the patient by asking her to make such a choice, it would immediately appear preferable to follow the first course.

Autonomy

In terms of the way in which knowledge of a carer's HIV status bears on a patient's autonomy the argument develops in the following way. Unless the patient has been given the opportunity to give or withhold consent on the basis of adequate information her autonomy has not been respected, and she has been wronged. But we can also look at another type of example relating to patient autonomy.

Consider a case where disclosing is not an issue in relation to consent because the risks of infection are not real enough to make a carer's HIV status relevant to consent. Instead the patient claims that they do not want to be treated by a carer who is HIV positive, even if the treatment is completely risk-free.

If a patient rejects a carer on the basis of knowledge or suspicion that he is HIV positive, the carer may well be hurt or angered, but it is the patient's prerogative not to be treated by a particular individual. To force the patient to be treated by that individual would be to undermine the patient's autonomy. The real issue arises when the institution within which care is being offered has to decide whether to reinforce the patient's attitude by readily offering an alternative carer.

Given that a carer is not afforded the right to withhold care from a person known to be infected with HIV, despite a higher statistical risk of infection,[8] it would surely be inequitable to afford the right to be selective to the patient. However, the patient may persist in argu-

---

[8] UKCC (1994): 6.

ing that as a result of being treated by this person their well-being is being threatened both actually, because of the anxiety they are suffering, and potentially because of the risk of infection (despite reassurances to the contrary). In the case of this particular patient the claim is being made that the carer cannot (through no fault of his own, but rather because of the patient's attitudes) effectively discharge their duty of care.

There seems to be only one way around this problem. If, as previously demanded, all health care professionals who knew or suspected themselves to be HIV positive withdrew from procedures where the risk of infection was real albeit small, patients could be told that the fact of the carer's HIV status was irrelevant up to the point at which his illness affected his ability to carry out his tasks. Similarly, if a health care worker withdrew from practice altogether as soon as his illness prevented him functioning effectively, a patient could not complain of receiving inadequate care.

If an individual patient then refused to be treated by the carer because she was (or thought to be) HIV positive he would be discriminating against that person, that is he would be treating her unequally for what should be morally irrelevant reasons. In other words, in the absence of risk, the presence of the virus is irrelevant in the same way as race and sex should (usually) be, and to replace the carer would be as morally objectionable as replacing a black or female carer because of a patient's racist or sexist views.

The duty to respect someone's autonomy should not require us to pander to views that can be shown to be bigoted or prejudicial. Were this to be the case we could be accused of placing too high a value on individual autonomy, and ignoring demands arising out of considerations of equality and social justice. If a health care worker poses no real risk to a patient, the fact of his HIV status cannot justifiably be used as a reason for rejecting his care.

However, it could be argued that the cases of discrimination on grounds of race and sex are always going to differ in an important respect from those based on HIV status because a female worker, for example, is never going to pose a *direct* risk to a patient's health by virtue of being female. One can respond to this in a number of ways. First, if the precautions and procedures advocated here are followed, an HIV-positive health care worker will not pose a *direct* risk to a patient's health. As stated above it is their behaviour which puts others at risk of infection, not their status. Secondly, the direct–

indirect dichotomy is not always morally relevant. Some people would argue that women doctors or male nurses can *indirectly* damage a patient's health if for cultural reasons or reasons of age that patient feels particularly uncomfortable with members of the opposite sex. In these cases a sympathetic response to a refusal to be treated might be justified on the grounds that the patient's well-being would suffer as a result of being treated by an individual of this type.

Admitting this second point raises rather difficult issues when the discussion moves back to HIV-positive health workers. Some patients may well argue that despite being told of the negligible risks involved, they would not *feel* safe if they knew their carer was HIV positive, thus the carer poses an indirect threat to the health of the patient. The patient's well-being might suffer in just the same way as that of the old lady who does everything she can to minimize contact with her young male nurse.

Far from being a reason to withdraw the health care worker from service, this might be offered as a further reason not to disclose the carer's status. Unlike a person's race or gender someone's HIV status remains invisible until the signs of disease are unmistakable. Unusually, given our general commitment to truth-telling within the context of health care, one might be justified in following the old adage 'what they don't know can't hurt them'. Knowledge of a health care worker's status may be detrimental to the effective delivery of care, and for as long as it can be shown that a patient's lack of knowledge does not increase risk, there need be no sense in which the decision to conceal such information is considered morally dubious. It might nonetheless be regrettable that such secrecy is called for.

The real difficulty arises when the patient claims to be suffering because she *believes* her carer is HIV positive, maybe because she assumes that members of a particular group are quite likely to be so, or because she thinks she can 'spot the signs'. The visible 'signs' of HIV-related disease are now recognized by many, and their appearance might, in and of itself, be enough to cause a shift in the attitude of the patient. In the film *Philadelphia*, the main character's problems begin after he fails to conceal the signs of Kaposi's sarcoma, and a health care worker might confront a similar situation.

In such cases the truth of the matter is almost superfluous, the issue is how to respond to the patient's claim of suffering. To this question there is no easy answer, and any solutions one might suggest have more to do with long-term education and attitude adjustment than changing the mind of this particular person. Cultures are capable of adapting in order to accommodate new forms of contact across old barriers of gender, race, and class but the process can be slow. In the meantime it is important, in all but a few cases, to challenge the views which run contrary to such change. In the case of HIV/AIDS it is particularly important to challenge prejudicial views now in the relatively early days, before individuals can claim to have become irredeemably encultured.

By tackling the real issue of risk of infection, one is immediately on surer ground from which to tackle the problem of irrational fear and/or prejudice. If we can be sure that the direct risk is almost non-existent, we can concentrate on combating the causes of the indirect risks posed by the patient's misplaced anxieties.

Conclusion

On the basis of the preceding arguments there seems to be a strong case to be made in favour of voluntary testing and liaison with occupational health practitioners, as long as an individual is assured that his employers and colleagues will not treat him unfairly once he is known to be HIV positive. If such assurances are not available, the individual still has a moral duty to act responsibly in the face of even a suspicion that he may be HIV positive. Even if he chooses not to disclose his status, he should act in such a way as to protect others from harm by voluntarily avoiding potentially risky practices.

The main advantage of limited openness is this. If the managers in a hospital or other health care setting can state that nobody who is HIV positive is engaged in significantly risky practices, neither staff nor patients can claim a right to know who if anyone is infected with the virus. Such knowledge is irrelevant to the proper provision of care and the maintenance of a safe working environment (assuming the adoption of universal precautions). Patients will not need to be told, and in many cases withholding this information will avoid unnecessary anxiety and harm. Patients or co-workers will not be able to refuse to be cared for, or to work with, an individual known or suspected of being HIV positive using the risk of infection as an excuse.

Those who make more generalized claims about threats to their well-being could be treated less sympathetically than some of those who object to female doctors or male nurses, for two main reasons. First, AIDS is still a relatively new disease, and although patterns of discrimination are emerging individuals still have a real choice whether to adopt or reject prejudicial attitudes. Secondly, the Muslim woman who cannot bear to be examined by a male doctor is saying nothing derogatory about the doctor by refusing his care. The person who rejects the HIV-positive health care worker—real or supposed—infers either that the person cannot be trusted with her safety and well-being, or that his very being offends her. This is the same in essence as the man who demands a male as opposed to female surgeon because women can't be good doctors, or the person who doesn't want to be touched by someone of another race because all members of that race are dirty. All such cases require a vigorous response on the part of the institution involved on behalf of the person discriminated against. In the case of the HIV-infected health care worker such a response can only be expected if the individual concerned can be shown to have removed the issue of risk from the agenda.

If those infected with the virus refuse to take seriously the duty to protect others from harm, they give more force to demands to disclose information because it is relevant to consent, and they strengthen the case of those who refuse to be treated by anyone suspected of being HIV positive. This is true even if they do not infect any other individual.

12

Fiduciary Relationship: An Ethical Approach and a Legal Concept?

MARGARET BRAZIER AND MARY LOBJOIT

Introduction

The HIV epidemic has graphically illustrated society's continuing inability to agree on the fundamental nature of the relationship between health professionals and their patients. Traditional notions of paternalism have been eroded and discredited. Respect for the patient's autonomy is much trumpeted. Yet at the same time many practitioners argue that informed consent is a myth[1] and English law largely continues to endorse medical paternalism.[2] Screening for HIV has revealed the contradictions in our response to the debate on patients' rights and professional responsibilities in a stark fashion. On the one hand it is contended that any professional testing for HIV without the patient's informed consent commits a criminal offence. On the other, the government endorses a programme of unlinked anonymous testing for epidemiological purposes where, as we will show, consent truly is a myth. Moreover, the Royal College of Surgeons, not an institution given to incitement to crime, advises its members that in certain circumstances they can, and should, proceed with non-consensual testing.

This chapter seeks to argue that a fruitful response to the ethical and legal dilemmas posed by screening for HIV is best obtained by recognizing that patients and professionals form a partnership.

We would like to thank Maureen Mulholland for her constructive and critical advice in the preparation of this chapter.

[1] H. K. Beecher, 'Consent to clinical experimentation—myth and reality', *Journal of the American Medical Association* **195** (1966): 39.

[2] See generally M. Brazier, *Medicine, Patients and the Law*, 2nd edn. (London: Penguin, 1992): ch. 4.

Paternalism degrades the adult patient and risks achieving a result where the disease not the patient is treated. Reduced to the status of child, the patient may not fully collaborate in a relationship in which he or she is denied equality. Treating diseases, not patients, is especially dangerous in the context of HIV where at present the 'disease' is in the majority of cases still considered ultimately incurable. Yet patients need professionals, and need them at times of extreme vulnerability when they can no longer operate as an entirely independent entity.[3] That need should prompt, not a take-over of the patient by the professional, nor a 'take it or leave it' response from the professional, but a true therapeutic alliance.[4] That therapeutic alliance, we believe, is best represented by developing the concept of the fiduciary relationship between patient and professional. Recognizing the fiduciary nature of the relationship between professional and patient will have several benefits for health care generally, as well as in the context of screening for HIV. (i) Partnership will be placed at the centre of the agenda between the parties to the relationship. (ii) Within a partnership the focus shifts from patients in general to that particular patient[5] with whom partnership is forged. (iii) Recognition can be given to the fact that both partners have responsibilities as well as rights. Reciprocity of obligations[6] can be given real meaning. (iv) Establishing the parameters of the partnership between individual patients and professionals allows society to make a better-informed and more reflective judgement on when, if at all, obligations derived from that partnership may be overridden by obligations owed to society.

We shall begin by examining briefly the current legal principles in England governing screening for HIV. Then we analyse the ethical debate on fiduciary relationships and attempt to see how far the ethical principle could be given legal 'teeth'. Finally we hope to demonstrate the benefits fiduciary relationships would generate in the context of screening for HIV.

---

[3] See A. Campbell, 'Dependency revisited: the limits of autonomy in medical ethics', in M. Brazier and M. Lobjoit (eds.), *Protecting the Vulnerable: Autonomy and Consent in Health Care* (London: Routledge, 1991): 101–12.

[4] See H. Teff, 'Consent to medical procedures: paternalism, self-determination or therapeutic-alliance', *Law Quarterly Review* **101** (1985): 432.

[5] See M. Brazier, 'Patient autonomy and consent to treatment: the role of the law', *Legal Studies* **7** (1987): 169.

[6] See C. A. Erin and J. Harris, 'AIDS: Ethics, justice and social policy', *Journal of Applied Philosophy* **10** (Sept. 1993): 165–73.

Common Law Chaos[7]

Gather two or three lawyers together to debate screening for HIV and you are likely to gather four or five different opinions on whether testing for HIV without express consent constitutes an assault. It is not that they will disagree on what *ought* to happen between patient and professional. In general, no patient should be tested for HIV without a specific and full understanding of what she is agreeing to and its implications for her socially, emotionally, and financially. The problems derive from the general principle of common (judge-made) law governing consent to treatment, and from the relationship between HIV and other forms of screening. In *Chatterton* v. *Gerson* (1981)[8] a patient complained that she had not been warned that the procedure to which she had agreed to relieve intolerable pain might result in long-term loss of sensation and consequent mobility in her leg. She contended that her apparent consent to the procedure was invalid because she lacked the necessary information on which to give a real consent. She sued for damages in the tort of battery.[9] The judge held that her consent was not vitiated by lack of information about potential risks or implications of the procedure. As long as a patient is informed in 'broad terms' of the nature of the procedure which is intended, her consent is real and effective and the doctor is protected from a claim in battery. Subsequent judgments confirmed that actions in battery for failure to give proper advice on treatment were to be deplored.[10] Sir John Donaldson MR, President of the Court of Appeal, said: 'only if the consent is obtained by fraud or misrepresentation of the nature of what is to be done can it be said that an apparent consent is not a real consent'.[11]

[7] See further M. Brazier, 'Common Law Chaos: Screening for HIV', in W. Kennet (ed.), *Parliaments and Screening* (Montrouge: John Libbey, 1995): 29–59.

[8] [1981] 1 All ER 257.

[9] Miss Chatterton brought a civil claim for damages against Dr Gerson. In such a claim where it is alleged that physical contact took place without a valid consent, the correct title of the tort committed is battery not assault. Lord Devlin once commented 'doctors batter their patients rather than assault them'! However, to confuse the non-lawyer even further, exactly the same conduct generally also constitutes the crime of assault.

[10] *Hills* v. *Potter (Note)* [1983] 3 All ER 716.

[11] *Sidaway* v. *Governors of the Bethlem Royal Hospital and Maudsley Hospital* [1984] 1 All ER 1018, CA. For an example where the defendant's misrepresentations and bad faith did suffice to vitiate the patients' consent see *Appleton* v. *Garrett* [1996] PIQR P1.

The technical legal debate then turns on what is meant by the nature of what is to be done in relation to HIV screening. Consider this scenario. The patient agrees to blood being taken. She knows that it is done to test for disease in a general sense. Perhaps blood is taken prior to surgery. If the patient asks, she is told that blood is needed to ensure cross-matching should she need a transfusion, and to ensure there is no condition present of which her surgeon should be aware before he operates. She is *not* told that an HIV test will be performed. What is the fundamental nature of the procedure to which she has assented? Is it simply to give blood for general unspecified testing? Or is it to an HIV test? Counsel advising the General Medical Council and the British Medical Association advised that as a diagnosis of HIV, and even agreeing to an HIV test which proves negative, has such profound consequences for a patient's financial and insurance status, as well as his or her psychological welfare, tests for HIV are quite different in nature from other routine blood-screening tests.[12] A consent to the taking of blood given without express agreement to test for HIV is thus invalid.

The trouble with that argument is this. Express information on the type and purpose of diagnostic tests is rarely given to British patients. Pregnant women are routinely tested for syphilis. Until recently, few were expressly asked to agree to that test and many never knew that it had happened. They would simply have assumed that blood was taken for further checks that they were not anaemic or diabetic. Pregnant women are tested for raised levels of alpha-protein to see if there is increased risk that the foetus is affected by spina bifida. Again until very recently the first a woman often knew that she had 'agreed' to this test is when she was counselled about the possibility of amniocentesis to confirm or dispel the suspicion raised by the blood test.

If it is right that testing for HIV without express consent renders that consent invalid, then either we must be certain HIV testing is entirely different in nature from testing for syphilis or genetic defect, or we must conclude that obstetricians across the land were acting unlawfully.[13]

The heart of the difficulty for the common law is that once it is determined that failure to tell the patient expressly of any intent to

[12] M. Sharrard and I. Gatt, 'Human Immune Deficiency Virus (HIV) antibody testing', *British Medical Journal* **295** (1987): 111.
[13] See J. M. Keown, 'The ashes of AIDS and the phoenix of informed consent', *Modern Law Review* **52** (1985): 790.

test for HIV invalidates any consent given, then the professional is not only in breach of his obligation to the patient, he has committed a crime. He can be sued for battery and prosecuted for assault. Is it appropriate to invoke the criminal process to police HIV screening? And if non-consensual screening constitutes assault how does such a conclusion affect anonymous unlinked testing for epidemiological purposes? The UK scheme provides that the residue of blood taken for other purposes, in amongst other places, antenatal clinics and general practitioners' surgeries may be forwarded for epidemiological screening. The test sample will not carry any means of identifying its source, the patient from whom the sample comes. The location of the source will be identifiable so that different trends in HIV incidence across the country generally, and between different groups of patients, can be monitored. Professionals taking blood in clinics which are part of the screening programme will know that a residue will be ultimately sent on for HIV screening. The patient will not be expressly told that this is the case.

Notices and leaflets are patchily available in the NHS explaining the screening programme and inviting the patient to object, to opt out, if she objects to any remnant of her blood sample being tested in this way. Is the programme lawful in the light of the arguments above about assault? Two arguments are deployed to justify the legality of the scheme. First, the Department of Health advises that a valid consent has been given to the initial tests agreed between patient and professional and that all that is later tested for HIV is left-over blood which would otherwise be discarded. The patient has given his blood away. He has no remaining property rights in the residue.[14] The trouble with that argument for a legal pedant is that from the moment blood is originally taken it is always intended that it be tested for HIV. Is the initial agreement to taking blood at all real, if the nature of HIV testing differs so radically from any other form of screening? Second, it is argued that as patients have the opportunity to object, to say 'no, you may not send on any of my blood for HIV testing', she does in fact consent. Quite apart from the evidence that many patients never notice the relevant notices, passive consent, consent implied by silence is a concept quite alien to English law.[15] If we offer to buy an elegant mansion in Belgravia for £500 and tell the current owner that we presume that he agrees unless he tells us otherwise

---

[14] See *New Scientist* (29 Jan. 1994) at 6.
[15] *Felthouse* v. *Bindley* (1862) 11 CBNS 869.

within twenty-four hours, we cannot claim a right to move in the next day!

Criminal prosecution for assault and civil claims for battery are of course not the only means by which the law enforces professional obligations to patients. In *Chatterton* v. *Gerson*, while the judge held lack of information on inherent risks of treatment did not invalidate a patient's consent, he found that such a failure could constitute a breach of the professional's duty of care to his patient. The professional's duty to provide treatment embraced a duty to offer adequate advice on the inherent risks, side effects, alternatives to and implications of treatment. Such a formulation of the professional obligation has immediate attractions in the context of screening for HIV. For it demands more than a bare warning of intent to test for HIV. It requires effective counselling to assist the patient to reach a considered judgement on how to proceed. Advice must be adequate for its central purpose. The patient's needs must be met. The flaw in the argument alas comes again from the interpretation of professional obligations by the courts.

Who defines whether advice is adequate? Who decides what the patient's need for information comprises? In England the answer remains that the professionals define adequacy; the professionals define the patient's needs. In *Sidaway* v. *Board of Governors of the Bethlem Royal and the Maudsley Hospital* (1985),[16] the House of Lords held by a majority of 4 to 1 that patients had rights of self-determination in relation to medical treatment, but that prima facie if a doctor conformed to a responsible body of medical opinion in deciding how to advise a patient and how much information to disclose to him, he was not negligent, not in breach of his duty to his patient. Lord Bridge[17] and Lord Templeman[18] asserted that the courts retained control over the scope of professional obligation to disclose information. If disclosure were clearly essential to an informed choice by the patient, the courts could still intervene to overrule professional opinion. It has only happened once,[19] twelve years after the judgment in *Sidaway*.[20]

---

[16] [1985] 1 All ER 643, HL.   [17] Ibid. 663.   [18] Ibid. 666.

[19] In the rather extraordinary case of *Smith* v. *Tunbridge Wells H.A.* [1994] 5 Med LR 334.

[20] The professional standard was unquestioningly endorsed in *Blyth* v. *Bloomsbury Health Authority* [1993] 4 Med LR 151, *Gold* v. *Haringey Health Authority* [1987] 2 All ER 888 and *Moyes* v. *Lothian Health Board* [1990] 1 Med LR 471. Judicial acquiescence in professional control over disclosure of information to patients is not common

Concern about the application of the professional standard in information disclosure may however be rather less acute in the context of screening for HIV than in other areas of health-care practice. The health care professions themselves proclaim the need for openness and a full exchange of information prior to HIV testing. Perhaps in this context the professional and the patient standards are one and the same? But what then of the Royal College of Surgeons' policy on non-consensual testing?[21] The RCS has issued guidelines authorizing members to go ahead and test for HIV without consent if an accident occurs in the course of surgery risking blood-to-blood contact between patient and surgeon and there is reason to suspect that the patient may be HIV positive. A responsible body of medical opinion thus does endorse non-consensual testing albeit in exceptional circumstances.

An assault or not, negligent or good practice: the law does not seem to offer any clear opinion. The chaos in the legal debate on HIV testing has at least three related causes. (i) The jurisprudence which has developed in England in relation to professional–patient relationships has its origins in the law designed to constrain violence, hence the emotive language of *assault* and *battery*. The mechanisms for defining a highly complex and sensitive relationship are crude in the extreme. (ii) English judges persist in viewing the doctor–patient relationship as adversarial perceiving doctors as under threat from an avalanche of medical malpractice litigation. The spectre of the malpractice crisis is never far from the judicial mind.[22] Whatever the reality of the malpractice crisis in general, evidence shows that only a tiny minority of claims relate to advice and consent.[23] (iii) The law's

to other common law jurisdictions. The Supreme Court of Canada and the High Court of Australia have both rejected the professional standard; see *Reibl* v. *Hughes* (1980) 114 DLR (3d) 1 (Canada) and *Rogers* v. *Whitaker* (1992) 67 AJLR 47 (Australia).

[21] A. Walker, 'Surgeons and HIV', *British Medical Journal* **302** (1991): 136.

[22] 'The principal effect of accepting the proposition advanced by the plaintiff would be likely an increase in the numbers of claims for professional negligence against doctors. This would be likely to have an adverse effect on the general standards of medical care.' *per* Sir John Donaldson MR in *Sidaway* v. *Governors of Bethlem Royal Hospital and Maudsley Hospital* [1984] 1 All ER 1018 at 1030–1, dismissing arguments that the patient standard should determine how much information professionals should disclose to patients.

[23] A survey commissioned in the USA for the President's Commission for the Study of Ethical Problems in Medicine showed only 3% of malpractice suits related to 'informed consent': see *Making Health Care Decisions* (Washington, DC: US Govt Printing Office, 1982): 22.

options are currently very limited, and the nature of professions' obligations tend to turn on very fine and technical points of law.

That last problem is well illustrated by the debate on the legality of unlinked anonymous testing and the RCS guidelines. The lawyer will say that it all turns on such matters as the definition of the nature of the procedure and property rights in left-over or spilled blood. The realist will say that what is truly at stake is whether the Department of Health can justify epidemiological screening *for the public good* and whether the RCS can justify testing in '*self-defence*' to protect surgeons from the consequences of a risk of infection. The RCS argues that immediate testing allows surgeons who have had contact with HIV-infected blood to start immediately on prophylactic treatment. The law is asking the wrong questions in the wrong language. The law paints the professional and the patient as adversaries in a battle which one must lose and one must win outright.

Fiduciary Relationship: An Ethical Approach

Ethical debate on the nature of the relationship between patient and professional has moved sharply away from the paternalist model. Yet undiluted and crude perceptions of autonomy have attracted criticism too. The patient lives in society. What he or she does, or does not do, affects others. The professional cannot view the patient as an isolated entity. The welfare of HIV-positive patients is bound up with their relationship with others, not always members of their blood-kin. Their responses to judgements on, and the consequence of, screening will affect others, including sexual partners, and in certain exceptional circumstances those with whom they work. Just as the RCS fears patients may infect surgeons, so patients fear surgeons may infect them.

Within the patient–professional relationship itself, a dynamic exists which over time changes the roles the parties play. An originally assertive independent individual who took full charge of his or her decision to undergo screening may subsequently need substantial support and for a time at least, a degree of paternalist care. He or she may need someone else to take responsibility from them while they adjust to their new circumstances. None of us is wholly autonomous all of the time.[24] Categorizing professionals and patients as adver-

[24] See A. Campbell, 'Dependency Revisited'; O. O'Neil, 'Paternalism and partial autonomy', *Journal of Medical Ethics* **10** (1984): 173–8.

saries one of whose 'rights' must triumph, isolating the relationship from wider relationships within society, does nothing to enhance that relationship. Recognizing that relationship as a *partnership*[25] is which professional and patient work together towards common goals enhances both the relationship of the individuals' concerned and the relationship between those partners and society at large.

Dyer and Bloch[26] have argued cogently that partnership resting on a fiduciary principle offers a resolution to age-old conflict between autonomy and paternalism. It is trite to describe the health professional's relationship with his or her patient as a relationship of trust yet the description encapsulates the very heart of the relationship. Patients trust doctors, nurses, and other health professionals with intimate details of their lives which they may even conceal from their families. The trust reposed in the doctor remains qualitatively different from the trust reposed in solicitors. Sentiment, even affection, are engaged.[27] The greater the trust, the greater the betrayal if trust is breached. Erosion of trust too affects not only the doctor or nurse who betrays that trust but her colleagues at large. The patient will not easily trust again, and erosion of trust in doctors may truly be one cause of the rise in rates of medical litigation.

Dyer and Bloch develop their model of the fiduciary principle largely in the context of psychotherapy. They stress the need for trust to promote effective care. Patients must feel confident that they can entrust all relevant information to their doctor and rely on the doctor acting on their behalf and meeting the highest professional standards. To provide the care the patient requires, mutual understanding is crucial: frankness on the part of the doctor is as important as frankness on the part of the patient. Doctors and patients cannot collaborate if one deceives the other or conceals information essential to advance their partnership.

The fiduciary principle sees the health care relationship as a whole and as an ongoing enterprise. Consent and confidentiality cease to be

---

[25] But note the partnership may be a multimember partnership involving not just doctor and patient but several members of the health care team; see J. Wilson-Barnett, 'Limited autonomy and partnership: professional relationships in health care', *Journal of Medical Ethics* **15** (1989): 12–16.

[26] A. R. Dyer and S. Bloch, 'Informed consent and the psychiatric patient', *Journal of Medical Ethics* **13** (1987): 12–16.

[27] Ibid. 15. Dyer and Bloch emphasize that terms such as trust, sincerity and 'loving care' suggest a 'dimension of ethical responsibility that is omitted in the modern ethical vocabulary of minimalist operational guidelines.'

separate concepts but are seen as inextricably linked within that fiduciary relationship. *Real* consent based on effective communication between the partners is not possible without the trust that confidentiality will be respected. Dyer and Bloch focus primarily on psychiatric care but undoubtedly confidentiality plays an equally crucial role in creating the climate of trust in which real consent is possible in the context of HIV testing. Patients will only be prepared to collaborate with doctors if they trust those doctors to preserve their confidences. Moreover the classification of the relationship as fiduciary on the model offered by Dyer and Bloch stresses the need to consider the 'dimension of time'. Within the patient–professional relationship, patients' needs change. As they put it: 'The static formulations of the doctors as paternalistic or of the patient as autonomous are characterisations which reflect a given situation at a particular moment, but say nothing about that relationship over time.'[28]

Although developed in the context of psychotherapy, Dyer and Bloch themselves contend that the fiduciary relationship offers a model for health care generally and others have advanced the argument beyond the field of mental health.[29] The benefits of partnership in terms of improved patient care are invoked to reinforce its ethical base. Partnership however is not a one-way street, creating only rights for patients and obligations for professionals. Partnership envisages a reciprocity of obligations. The patient is perceived as owing obligations towards the professional as well as enjoying rights against the professional.[30] This may not be an immediately popular notion to patients! However, reciprocity of obligations is an inevitable consequence of classifying the professional–patient relationship as a partnership collaborating towards a common end. Obviously the patient must accept responsibility for her share of the enterprise. She must ensure that the professional has the necessary information on which to exercise his professional judgement and offer professional advice. The professional obligation to preserve confidentiality can be seen as derived from the patient's obligation to surrender her privacy in order to promote the professional–patient partnership.

---

[28] A. R. Dyer and S. Bloch, 'Informed consent and the psychiatric patient', *Journal of Medical Ethics* **13** (1987): 16.

[29] See J. Wilson-Barnett, 'Limited autonomy and partnership'.

[30] M. Osinga, 'but the patient has responsibilities as well', *Journal of the Medical Defence Union* (Winter, 1989): 55–6.

Reciprocity of obligations goes much deeper than simply a duty of confidentiality generated by a duty to 'be frank'. If we argue that the patient-partner must seek to ensure that the professional receives the information which he needs to play his role in the partnership, then it follows that the professional must equally seek to ensure that the patient receives from him the information which she requires to fulfil her partnership role. As people differ, so partnerships differ as the information needs of each particular patient should be negotiated and assessed. The principle at the heart of the relationship though is beautifully expressed by Knoppers:

[R]eciprocity implies an exchange. The personal privacy of the patient which he entrusts to a certain extent to the physician must be met with a corresponding openness and full disclosure . . . Personal privacy and access to medical information are not incompatible partners but interchangeable rights.[31]

Once the professional–patient relationship is firmly founded on an open and equal exchange of information then the partners can negotiate the next stage in their alliance and agree what action to take. Marijka Osinga in her article on patients' responsibilities proposes a duty to collaborate and to limit injury.[32] Such a duty out of context tends to sound like an injunction to 'obey doctor's orders or else'. In a true partnership the outcome of the preliminary exchange of information will not be 'orders' but 'agreements'. Patients who wish to take equal responsibility for their health care must necessarily accept a responsibility to honour those agreements. They cannot blame the professional if they unilaterally abandon their side of the bargain.

In the context of HIV reciprocity of obligation goes yet a stage further, prompting the question of whether the patient may ever be said to have a responsibility *for*, as well as *to*, the professional. The professional obligation to care for the patient is unquestioned. The doctor must act in the patient's interests putting his interests before her own. No one doubts that the professional who had reason to believe that he or she might be HIV positive yet continued to engage in surgery risking blood-to-blood contact breaches relevant professional obligations.

---

[31] B. Knoppers, 'Confidentiality and Accessibility of Medical Information: A Comparative Analysis', *R. Dus.* **12** (1982): 431: cited in *McInerney* v. *MacDonald* (1992) 93 DLR (4th) 426.

[32] Osinga, 'But the patient has responsibilities as well'.

The General Medical Council[33] has made it absolutely clear that doctors who are, or suspect that they may be, HIV positive must seek testing and counselling. In those rare cases where there is a real risk of doctor-to-patient infection they must cease to practise. A doctor who ignored such guidance would be very likely to be found liable in negligence if a patient or patients successfully establish that he or she infected them in the course of surgery. Reciprocity of obligations requires that patients who are, or suspect that they may be, HIV positive act to protect professionals offering them care.

The mutual obligations of patient and surgeon to disclose their potential HIV status clearly illustrate too another crucial aspect of the debate on HIV. Neither patient, nor professional, nor the partnership of the two of them can be treated as an entity entirely isolated from the rest of society. The obligations which they owe each other cannot be totally divorced from obligations owed to others. The rights engendered by those obligations cannot be defined without regard to the rights of third parties. Consider again the position of the patient who knowing himself to be HIV positive withholds that information from professionals operating on him. In the course of surgery a mishap occurs and blood from the patient comes in contact with blood from the surgeon. The latter becomes infected. It may be that well before she appreciates her predicament the surgeon in her turn infects other patients. The patient's failure to accept responsibility for himself and his surgeon breaches much more than his obligation to her alone. We will return at the end of the chapter to the delicate relationship between the patient–professional partnership and society at large.

Fiduciary Relationship: A Legal Concept?[34]

It may be argued that it is all very well to adopt a partnership model, a fiduciary relationship, as an ethical ideal to define the profes-

---

[33] General Medical Council, see now GMC, *HIV and AIDS: The Ethical Considerations* (1995) updating their original *Statement on AIDS and HIV* (1988).

[34] For a comprehensive analysis of the current state of English law in relation to doctors and fiduciary obligations see A. Grubb, 'The Doctor as Fiduciary', *Current Legal Problems* **47** (1994): 311; I. Kennedy, 'The Fiduciary Relationship and its Application to Doctors and Nurses', in P. Birks (ed.), *Wrongs and Remedies in the Twenty-First Century* (Oxford: Clarendon Press, 1996); P. Bartlett, 'Doctors as Fiduciaries', *Medical Law Review* **5** (1997): 193–224.

sional–patient relationship. The truly important question is whether such a model, such an ideal, can ever be clothed with legal reality. In England, at present, the omens are poor. In *Sidaway* v. *Governors of the Bethlem Royal Hospital and Maudsley Hospital*[35] Dunn LJ in the Court of Appeal unequivocally rejected any concept of doctors standing in a formal fiduciary relationship to their patient. He refused to endorse any extension of the equitable fiduciary principle beyond the field of property law asserting:

[T]his doctrine has been confined to cases involving the disposition of property, and has never been applied to the nature of the duty which lies on a doctor in the performance of his professional duties. In any event, I do not find it helpful in considering the duty of the doctor to his patient to draw analogies, which are in any case ill-founded from other branches of the law which have developed in different circumstances and for different reasons.[36]

Dyer and Bloch recognize some of the difficulties in transposing a legal concept, primarily concerned with the protection of property interests, to meet the needs of the professional–patient partnership. In particular the fiduciary relationship is often perceived as essentially paternalistic. The trustee of a great estate acts for the infant beneficiary. Asserting the existence of a fiduciary relationship between doctors and patient in the Canadian Supreme Court in *McInerney* v. *MacDonald*[37] La Forest J cited an earlier judicial acknowledgement of the fiduciary nature of that relationship: '[i]t is the same relationship as that which exists in equity between a parent and his child, a man and his wife, an attorney and his client, a confessor and his penitent, and a guardian and his ward.'[38]

The analogies of parent and child, of guardian and ward, prompt fears, eloquently voiced by Kennedy,[39] that legal recognition of a fiduciary relationship between doctor and patient marks a retreat from autonomy and a return to paternalism. Recognizing the fiduciary relationship as a legal concept in this context demands that we first demonstrate that the fiduciary principle can be freed from its origins in the law of property and second that, if it were so freed, the

---

[35] [1984] 1 All ER 1018 at 1029: and see per Lord Scarman at [1985] 1 All ER 643 at 651. Their Lordships' sentiments were, alas, recently endorsed by Popplewell J in *R* v. *Mid Glamorgan FHSA* ex *Martin P,* (1993) 16 BMLR 81 affirmed on appeal [1995] 1 WLR 110 (The Court of Appeal remained silent on the issue of fiduciary duty; see Bartlett, 'Doctors as Fiduciaries' at 203–8).

[36] [1984] 1 All ER 1018 at 1029.   [37] (1992) 93 DLR (4th) 415 at 423.

[38] *Henderson* v. *Johnston* [1956] OR 141, CA.

[39] Kennedy, 'The Fiduciary Relationship'.

ethical approach and the legal concept would be compatible and not conflicting. Both purposes can best be served by examining the judgments of the Canadian Supreme Court in *McInerney* v. *MacDonald*[40] and *Norberg* v. *Wynrib*.[41]

In *McInerney* v. *MacDonald*, Mrs MacDonald who had suffered from a thyroid condition for several years became concerned about the care and advice which she was receiving. She sought access to her complete medical record. There was in New Brunswick no relevant legislation governing access to health records.[42] Dr McInerney offered to release her own notes but refused Mrs MacDonald access to any records from other professionals who had shared in her care. Mrs MacDonald then commenced legal proceedings. Argument in the lower courts centred on who owned the records and, if the physicians owned the records, whether the patient could claim a contractual right[43] to access to those records. The Supreme Court conceded that 'the physician, institution or clinic compiling the medical records owns the physical records.' They found argument about an implied contractual term guaranteeing access to records unhelpful.

La Forest J, giving the judgment of the court, ordered that Mrs MacDonald be given access to her full medical records. He first examined the reality of the doctor–patient relationship and the crucial importance in that relationship of a frank exchange of information. He stressed that the patient 'entrusts' information to the doctor fundamental to his personal integrity and autonomy. He went on to say:

The doctor's position is one of trust and confidence. The information conveyed is held in a fashion somewhat akin to a trust. . . . The confiding of the information to the physician for medical purposes gives rise to an expectation that the patient's interest in and control of the information will continue.[44]

    [40] (1992) 93 DLR (4th) 415.
    [41] (1992) 92 DLR (4th) 449. And see the analogous case of *Taylor* v. *McGillivray* (1991) 110 DLR (4th) 64.
    [42] In the UK a patient may now seek access to records compiled after Nov. 1991 under the Access to Health Records Act 1990 but access is subject to certain limitations and accompanied by inadequate remedies, see M. Brazier, *Medicine, Patients and the Law*: 62–5. In *R* v. *Mid Glamorgan FHSA* ex p *Martin* (1993) 16 BMLR 81 Popplewell J expressly declined to follow *McInerney* v. *MacDonald* to allow access to records compiled prior to Nov. 1991; affirmed on different grounds [1995] 1 WLR 110, CA.
    [43] An absolutely untenable argument in the UK for any NHS patient. No contract exists between patients and professionals with the NHS; see *Pfizer* v. *Ministry of Health* [1965] AC 512, HL.
    [44] *McInerney* v. *MacDonald*: 424.

Classifying the relationship as fiduciary not only imposes a duty of confidentiality but a duty of disclosure too: 'the trust reposed in the physician mandates that the flow of information operates both ways.'[45]

The Canadian judges appeared to find no difficulty in freeing fiduciary relationships from their historic link with overtly proprietary interests. Linking a duty of disclosure to the duty of confidentiality helps explain why no such difficulty was encountered in Canada, and why the difficulty perceived in England is largely artificial. The origins of the duty of confidentiality lie themselves in property interests. Protection of intellectual property in the form of trade secrets still remains in practice one of the prime concerns of the law relating to confidences. The obligation of confidentiality is a creation of equity.[46] The common law in England has, however, found no problem with extending and enforcing an obligation of confidentiality to health professionals.[47] The fiduciary nature of the relationship is implicitly, if not expressly recognized, in the context of judgments defining the patient's right to confidentiality.[48]

The subsequent judgments of McLachlin J and L'Heureux Dubé J in *Norberg* v. *Wynrib* extend the concept of fiduciary relationship much further, well beyond the sphere of information disclosure. Ms Norberg became addicted to painkillers. Ultimately she consulted Dr Wynrib who agreed to prescribe for her the drugs she craved in return for sexual favours. He did nothing to help her overcome her drug addiction. She continued to get drugs from him for over two years as long as she complied with his sexual demands and she also found other sources of supply. She was finally convicted of drug-related offences.

Three of the judges in the Supreme Court struggled (successfully) to classify the parties' sexual contacts as battery finding that the doctor's 'undue influence' negated any apparent consent given by Ms Norberg. Sopinka J classified the doctor's conduct as a breach of his contractual or tortious duty of care. He rejected the notion of fiduciary duty as applicable save in relation 'to disclosure of confidential

---

[45] Ibid. 426.

[46] See *Seager* v. *Copydex* (No 2) [1969] 1 WLR 809, CA; *Clerk and Lindsell on Torts* (17th edn.) 1995: ch. 26.

[47] See M. Brazier, *Medicine, Patients and the Law*: ch. 3.

[48] See the instructive judgment of the Supreme Court of Appeals of West Virginia in *Morris* v. *Consolidated Coal Co.* (1994) 446 S.E. 2d 648; and *Commentary* (1995) 3 Med. L.Rev. 217.

information or something like that'. The doctor's duty was 'to treat the patient in accordance with the standards of the profession'.[49] The tortuous arguments advanced to enable the judges in the majority to fit the plaintiff's claim for damages against Dr Wynrib into a conventional legal pigeon-hole illustrates yet again the inadequacies of battery and negligence as means of defining the obligations owed by health professionals to their patients.

McLachlin J boldly rejects her colleagues' more limited concept of the fiduciary relationship. Analysing the fundamental nature of the interaction between doctors and patient she regards the trust between the two as demonstrating the hallmark of the law's concept of the fiduciary relationship and expressly acknowledges the innate inequality of power between the parties. She argues that the relationship entails:

[T]he trust of a person with inferior power that another person who has assumed superior power and responsibility will exercise that power for his or her good and only for his or her good or in his or her best interests. Recognising the fiduciary nature of the doctor–patient relationship provides the law with an analytic model by which physicians can be held to the high standards of dealing with their patients which the trust accorded to them requires.[50]

Limiting the law's recognition of the fiduciary principle in the doctor–patient relationship to obligations akin to the duty of confidence is, the judge suggests, to take a 'closed commercial view of fiduciary obligations'[51] which cannot be sustained in principle or by reference to the authorities. Dr Wynrib's liability to Ms Norberg flowed quite simply from his breach of her trust, a breach which went much deeper than her reluctant submission to his sexual demands and embraced the whole of his exploitative conduct and failure to honour the faith she placed in him.

McLachlin J breaks the chains which bind fiduciary relationships to proprietary or quasi-proprietary relationships. But there is a sting

---

[49] Once again abrogating definition of professional standards to the profession alone.

[50] *Norberg* v. *Wynrib*, 486–7.

[51] Ibid. 495. And note *Reading* v. *Attorney General* [1951] AC 507 HL where the House of Lords found a fiduciary relationship unrelated to any proprietary interest to exist. See too *Frame* v. *Smith* (1987) 42 DLR (4th) 81 at 104 per Wilson J '[t]o deny relief because of the nature of the interests involved, to afford protection to material interest but not to human or personal interests would, it seems to me, be arbitrary in the extreme.'

in the tail of her argument. It is the inequality in power between the parties that she sees generating the fiduciary nature of the relationship. Does it then follow that for the law recognition of the fiduciary principle implies acceptance of paternalism—that doctors act on behalf of, and not in partnership with, patients? We believe that it does not do so. There are classic fiduciary relationships which of their nature are paternalistic, notably that of parent and child or guardian and ward. But fiduciary relationships are themselves variable in nature. In *McInerney* v. *MacDonald* La Forest J acknowledges the mutability of the fiduciary relationship: 'not all fiduciary relationships and not all fiduciary obligations are the same: these are shaped by the demands of the situation'.[52]

McLachlin J in *Norberg* v. *Wynrib* concedes that certain fiduciary relationships result from an innate inequality in status between the parties. Fiduciary relationships, she contends, always entail an element of dependency:

[B]ut the scope of that dependency is usually not as all-encompassing and pervasive as that obtaining in a status relationship. The beneficiary entrusts the fiduciary with information or other sources of power over the beneficiary, but does so only within a circumscribed area. . . . Although fiduciary relationships may properly be recognised in the absence of consent by the beneficiary. . . . they are more typically the product of the voluntary agreement of the parties that the beneficiary will cede to the fiduciary some power.[53]

The fiduciary relationship does not enable the fiduciary to dominate the beneficiary. It enables the fiduciary to satisfy the needs of the beneficiary. Fiduciary principles redress the inequality of power between the parties and protect the dependent partner. Inequality and dependency are to a greater or lesser degree, as we have argued earlier, inevitable because patients seek health professionals' help out of vulnerability and need. There is in crude reality all the difference in the world between a consultation between the wealthy well-dressed client and her solicitor, and that between the fearful semi-naked patient and his doctor. Your solicitor may control your finances. Your doctor enjoys powers of life and death.

[52] *McInerney* v. *MacDonald*: 423.
[53] *Norberg* v. *Wynrib*: 487. See also the interesting but inconclusive analysis of doctors' obligations to their patients by the Australian High Court in *Breen* v. *Williams* (1996)186 CLR 71 discussed by Bartlett, 'Doctors as Fiduciaries'.

The Fiduciary Partners and Society

We have sought to show that the fiduciary relationship can take shape as a legal concept as well as an ethical approach. The fiduciary principle can be liberated from its property-based origins, and does not necessarily reduce the patient to child-status. Nor does the fiduciary principle grant unlimited 'rights' to patients. We have argued that a reciprocity of obligation is inherent in the ethical approach to fiduciary relationship and that in the course of such a relationship the degree of patient autonomy and control within the relationship may be negotiable over time. The Canadian judgments suggest that the legal fiduciary relationship may mirror that ethical approach. In *McInerney* v. *MacDonald* asserting the patient's right to frank disclosure of information on the part of her doctor La Forest J nonetheless allows of an exception to the 'rule': '[n]on-disclosure may be warranted if there is a real potential for harm either to the patient or to a third party.'[54]

He goes on to warn that non-disclosure in the interests of the patient will only rarely be justifiable. The Canadian courts at least will not rubber-stamp paternalistic assumptions about patients' interests. There must be proved to be 'a significant likelihood of a substantial adverse effect on the physical, mental or emotional health of the patient or harm to a third party.'[55]

The Canadian approach, moving cautiously towards open recognition of the fiduciary nature of the relationship between professional and patients, offers yet another pointer towards recognition too of some degree of reciprocity of obligations. Issues of consent and confidentiality are brought within a common legal framework. Confidentiality is perceived, rightly, as an essential prerequisite for the process of obtaining a meaningful consent. In England already the courts have endorsed both the key role of the obligation of confidentiality and the limitations reciprocity must, of necessity, impose on that obligation where others are endangered by an absolute respect for that obligation.

In *X* v. *Y*[56] two general practitioners had tested positive for HIV and were receiving advice and counselling at a local hospital. Somehow a tabloid newspaper received evidence of their existence

---

[54] *McInerney* v. *MacDonald*: 429.   [55] Ibid. 430.
[56] [1988] 2 All ER 648.

and identities. An employee of the health authority breached his duty of confidence. The newspaper proposed to publish the story. The health authority obtained an injunction preventing them from doing so. Lawyers for the newspaper argued that in the circumstances a breach of confidence was justifiable. The patients of the doctors concerned had a proper interest in knowing the HIV status of their doctors. There was a legitimate public interest in debate on HIV-positive health professionals. Rose J dismissed the newspaper's arguments. He reviewed the evidence on the risk of a general practitioner, who had received proper advice on practice when HIV positive, transmitting HIV to a patient. He found that that risk was negligible and that a far greater risk of harm to others would be generated if those who might have contracted HIV would not seek professional advice. He argued: 'confidentiality is vital to secure public as well as private health, for unless those interested come forward they cannot be counselled and self-treatment does not provide the best care.'[57]

Note that the judge did not find that a medical practitioner would *never* be justified in disclosing a patient's HIV status. He found that to justify such a breach of trust there must be clear and substantial evidence of significant risks to others.

That degree of risk to others, justifying a breach of confidence was successfully established on the rather different facts of *W* v. *Egdell*.[58] W had been convicted of the manslaughter of five of his neighbours in a shooting spree. He was ordered to be detained indefinitely in a secure mental hospital. Only the Home Secretary could ultimately order his release if his condition improved so that he was no longer a threat to public safety. As a stepping-stone towards that goal, W sought a transfer to a regional secure unit. The Home Office refused to sanction the transfer and W (as he was entitled to do) applied to a mental health review tribunal. To support W's case his solicitors commissioned an independent psychiatric report from Dr Egdell. However, when Dr Egdell examined W he concluded that he remained an extremely sick and dangerous man, with psychopathic tendencies, who had manipulated his doctors at his current hospital into endorsing his application for a transfer. W, in his opinion, remained a danger to others. W's solicitors withdrew the application to the tribunal but refused to release Dr Egdell's report either to the tribunal, or the hospital or the Home Office. Ultimately Dr Egdell

---

[57] Ibid. 653.   [58] [1990] 1 All ER 835 CA.

himself did send a copy of his report to the hospital and agreed that a further copy be forwarded to the Home Office. W sued Dr Egdell for breach of confidence.

The Court of Appeal found in Dr Egdell's favour. In the face of what he considered to be 'a real risk of consequent danger to the public [Dr Egdell] is entitled to take such steps as are reasonable in all the circumstances to communicate the grounds of his concern to the responsible authorities.'[59]

W v. *Egdell* is instructive not simply because it demonstrates the level of risk to others which may justify abrogation of a patient's interests. Two other matters are crucial. The court stressed that Dr Egdell did owe W a duty of confidence. It mattered not that he was not W's personal physician. The obligation to W arose from his professional status. And a key factor in establishing the parameters of Egdell's relationship of confidentiality with W was the public interest. There is as powerful a *public* as a private interest in maintaining in all but the most exceptional circumstances the obligation of confidentiality.

In the context of that part of the professional relationship relating to keeping confidences then, the common law in England has recognized that absolute respect for patient autonomy would abrogate the fundamental interests of others.[60] The public interest cannot always be separated from definition of private interests. The patient cannot abdicate all responsibility to others, or at least cannot force the professional to endorse such an abdication of responsibility.

A Way Forward

Conventional common law principles dependent on the torts of battery and negligence have proved inadequate to vindicate patient autonomy in the context of health care generally. Nor have they been able to accommodate any realistic analysis of the public interest in maintaining health, and in particular in controlling the spread of infection.[61] The HIV epidemic has highlighted the law's inadequacies

---

[59] [1990] 1 All ER 853 *per* Bingham LJ.

[60] Note Bingham LJ's reference to the justifiability of breach of confidence under the European Convention on Human Rights (ibid. 853).

[61] See M. Brazier and J. Harris, 'Public Health and Private Lives', *Medical Law Review* **4** 171 (1996).

to address the fundamental ethical issues inherent in screening for HIV. The primary need is to give legal force to the creation of the necessary relationship of trust within which professional and patient can cooperate to promote both the welfare of the patient and the common good. Within such a relationship of trust, it may on occasion be necessary to impose some limit on patient autonomy. Within such a relationship of trust, consideration of the welfare of others may sometimes be relevant.

Limiting patient autonomy may sound heretical but at present in England the law does little more than pay lip-service to autonomy. The Canadian Supreme Court has offered in the development of the fiduciary relationship a model for providing substantive recognition of autonomy. It is a model which avoids unrealistic divisions of the total professional–patient relationship into issues of consent and confidentiality, as though the two matters were totally divorced the one from the other. The relationship between the two, the need to guarantee confidentiality to obtain real consent, is acknowledged. In England, the courts have endorsed the value of confidentiality in the clearest of terms. Yet they have conceded that, exceptionally, there are limits to such a right. We would argue that the time has come for the fiduciary principle to extend to the whole doctor–patient relationship and for express recognition of a limited reciprocity of obligations within their relationship.

In the context of screening for HIV it may be that the extent of such reciprocity is properly a matter for legislatures rather than for development by judges on a case-by-case *ad hoc* basis. The role of the courts is to create the mechanism through which the law can give full force to a relationship of trust. Within that relationship the strongest of presumptions must operate that the professional acts with and for that individual patient. Consent must be more than form-filling and more than simply a device to protect the doctor's back from litigation.[62] The professional's responsibility should be to promote understanding and insight, not solely to convey information.[63] On such a foundation reciprocity of obligations can begin to be debated by lawyers as well as ethicists.

[62] Quite contrary to Lord Donaldson's perception of consent as a 'flak jacket' for doctors as expressed in *Re W (Minor: Refusal of Medical Treatment)* [1992] 4 All ER 627.
[63] See another instructive judgment from the Supreme Court of Canada, *Ciarlariello* v. *Schacter* [1993] 100 DLR (4th) 609.

13

Ethical Aspects of the Use of 'Sensitive Information' in Health Care Research

SØREN HOLM AND PETER ROSSEL

Introduction

During the second half of the twentieth century we have experienced an explosive growth in the broad area of technology which, for want of a better name, is often called 'information technology'. This has affected society in many ways, but in this chapter we will mainly be concerned with the specific set of problems this development has created in medical and epidemiological research.

Information has always been a valuable asset and, since ancient times, States, cities, guilds, and other bodies have registered information about citizens or members in order to predict and control. The amount of information that could be collected and stored, and perhaps even more important, the speed with which it could be retrieved and linked, was, however, severely constrained by the available storage media. Very little development occurred in this area between the clay tablets of Assyria and the paper files of the British Empire. All this changed with the invention of the computer. Vast amounts of data can now be stored, transmitted, retrieved, and, most importantly, linked by means of computer. This has raised new fears in the public about the use (and misuse) of the information about citizens which is stored in computer registers. Many countries have enacted 'data protection acts', and international bodies like the European Community and the Council of Europe are also interested in regulating such registers.

Within the health care field these growing abilities to store, retrieve, and link large amounts of information from different registers have been used both in research and in health care administration. The advances of modern epidemiology could not have been made if these technological abilities had not been available. But the technology in itself is not sufficient to ensure scientific progress in this area; without the raw material, the information to be produced, retrieved, analysed, and linked, the technology is barren. Many epidemiologists and other health care researchers are presently worried that the possibilities to produce and access personal information could be severely curtailed in the future if the regulation of registers becomes too rigid and formalistic.

Regulation of registers is usually aimed at two distinct kinds of possible 'misuse' of stored information, and it is only one of these which is of interest in this context. A large part of the proposed regulatory measures are aimed at preventing *unauthorized* access and use of stored information by means of rules about proper data-security (passwords, encryption of data, physical access to data media, etc.). In the context of the present chapter, we will allow ourselves to assume that such data-security problems can be solved, so that unauthorized access to and misuse of stored information can be prevented.[1]

Our focus will instead be on the *authorized* collection and use of personal information within the field of health care, and thereby on a completely different type of misuse of information, i.e. misuse by authorized use in ways which are harmful to the individuals concerned or which constitute an infringement of their rights.

Discussion in this area often refers to 'sensitive information' without explicating what is meant by this term. By scanning newspaper articles, a catalogue of items of sensitive information can be made, and it is evident that one of the most sensitive bits of information is taken to be information about the HIV status of individual persons, but many other pieces of information are also described as 'sensitive' and it is seldom explained why. Our first aim will therefore be an analysis of the concept of 'sensitive information'.

What is 'Sensitive Information'?

Many pieces of information can be deemed sensitive, but we will mainly be concerned with the sensitive information that is

---

[1] All arguments in this chapter are based on the assumption that we live in a democratic society with societal and judicial control of administration and research.

information about persons, because this is presumably the dominant type of sensitive information within health care.

As a first approximation one could define 'sensitive information' in the following way: *A specific item of information is sensitive iff [2] it could harm the person described in this item of information if it becomes known to other specific persons or if it becomes more widely known.*

There are three immediate problems with this definition:

1. It is not sufficiently sensitive to the context in which a given piece of information becomes known. If I had two wives, it would be a very sensitive piece of information, because the revealing of this fact could harm me significantly, but this is only so given my Danish citizenship and my residence in Denmark. In many Muslim countries, this information would not be sensitive, and it might even enhance my social status. In the same way, information about HIV status is very sensitive in society in general, but loses its sensitivity within an organization like Body Positive.

2. It is too encompassing. Many items of information which are plainly visible (race, gender, etc.) would be sensitive according to this definition as would many items of information which we necessarily have to share with others in our daily social life (age, first name, etc.). Having a markedly 'foreign-sounding' name, for instance, may not be very conducive to one's employment prospects in Denmark. Such an item of information is therefore sensitive according to the tentative definition above. Many other similar examples can be found. Only a hermit can live without spreading sensitive information about himself. The rest of us constantly 'emit', 'store', 'process', and 'convey' such information about ourselves and others.

3. Information may be purely statistical and thereby not directly attributable to any specific person, but only to a group of persons, but may nevertheless be very harmful to specific persons. Assume, for instance, that research based on fully anonymous questionnaires shows that the proportion of members of the Conservative Party who engage in homosexual intercourse with minors is much larger than that of members of the Labour Party. This piece of information is not information about some specific person, but it is certainly harmful to each specific member of the Conservative Party as well as to the party as a whole. If 'sensitive' has any meaning at all, this is sensitive information.

---

[2] Where 'iff' expresses 'if and only if'.

Can the tentative definition be changed to take account of these three problems? The following revised version could be an attempt in this direction: *A specific item of information is sensitive iff it could harm someone if this item of information becomes known to specific persons or becomes more widely known, provided that the sharing of such information is neither inevitable nor necessary in normal social life.*

This version takes care of problems 2 and 3, but the 'sensitivity' of a given piece of information is still context-dependent, so that problem 1 has not been solved. It is, however, more worrying that a new problem has been created. A careful reading of the first part of the definition shows that the whole definition can now be collapsed to read: *A specific item of information is sensitive iff its dissemination could harm someone, provided that the sharing of such information is neither inevitable nor necessary in normal social life.*

This seems to be the same as saying that 'sensitive' is just a technical term for 'potentially harmful'. Harm is a central concept in moral philosophy, and we will therefore suggest that this concept should be used instead of the more nebulous and potentially misleading 'sensitive'.

There is still one remaining problem in the analysis, i.e. the context sensitivity of 'potentially harmful' information. Why is some person-related information harmful in a given context but not in another? A core element in the context-dependency seems to be the more or less widely accepted norms and/or prejudices about personal characteristics and proper behaviour which are prevalent in a given society or group. Information about deviation from those norms and prejudices can get other people accepting those norms or under the sway of those prejudices to act in ways that harm the deviating person or group of persons. If this is correct, no piece of information is *per se* harmful.

The distinction between potentially harmful and innocuous information is, however, still useful, as long as the context in which the item of information is produced, stored, used, etc., is clearly specified.

The researcher and the regulatory agency in charge of data-protection should therefore evaluate each item of information on its own, taking account of both content and context. This has, however, the disturbing and controversial implication that the researcher and the regulatory agencies have to take into consideration not only the norms of a given society but also widespread prejudices.

What is My Relation to Information about Me?

In the previous section we have argued that the concept of 'sensitive information' should be replaced by a concrete, case-by-case evaluation of the possible harm caused by spreading given pieces of information. That analysis is based on the point of view of the outsider who possesses information about somebody else, but would it not be better to start with the person in question, the person about whom this information is information? Would it not be better to analyse what rights I have to control information about myself? As suggested above the reason why some piece of information can be harmful has to do with the norms and prejudices in a given society. To approach the questions of rights to control the generation and use of information about myself let us, unrealistically, suppose that we lived in a society without those norms and prejudices causing some people to harm others. Would there still be some kinds of information about myself which I would want to control, even though this information couldn't possibly harm me? Or, to put it in another more realistic way, even if my behaviour falls well within the accepted norms and prejudices, would there still be ways of gathering and using information about me which I would like to control? It is to the analysis of this question we now turn.

Ownership

How should we conceptualize the relationship between a person and a given item of information about that person? One possible relationship could be ownership. I presumably own my own body, and I can own various physical objects as well as immaterial objects like ideas, literary works, etc., but can I own information about myself?

In one sense I clearly *can* own different pieces of information about myself. When I agree to participate in a piece of marketing research in return for a monetary reward I even sell such information (in this case information about my preference structure regarding a certain class of products). But does it make sense to extend this analysis to the more usual situations in which we exchange personal information with others? Do I retain the right to control or restrict the use of such information in the same way as we (the authors of this article) retain some limited control over the use of the intellectual property in this chapter once it is printed?

Normally we do not assume that such a right is present. If I tell you my age, my annual income, or the details of how I cheated the taxation board, you are free to remember this information and use it in your own future conversations with other people, unless I make it explicit that this information is given in confidence and should not be conveyed to others. But would it not be wrong for someone to tell the taxation board of how I cheated them last year? Well, it would certainly be bad form, not because I owned the information and should be allowed to control its use, but because (i) conveyance of this information to the taxation board would harm me, and (ii) social conventions hold that certain pieces of information are given in implicit confidence.

If we really had strong property rights in information about ourselves, life would become very complicated. For each given piece of information known to me about other persons I would have to keep track of the manner in which I had acquired this information and from whom. Do I know your age, because you yourself told it to me, or because somebody else did? And if somebody else did, who is then the owner of this information? Me, you, or this other person?

There is another important difference between personal information and the kind of 'objects' in which one can hold intellectual or other immaterial property rights. Whereas the plays of Shakespeare, the symphonies of Mozart, and the ideas of Newton are all, in a very real sense, produced by their original owner, this need not be true of the different items of personal information about a person. It is true that I have the blood type which is recorded in my hospital records, but this piece of information was not produced by me. It was produced by the employees of the hospital. I consented to its production, but did not take any part in it. I delivered the raw material for the production, just like the Danish medieval historian Saxo Grammaticus delivered the raw material for Shakespeare's *Hamlet*, but this does not in itself give me any property rights in the information produced.

Interesting problems occur if the hospital could sell the information it had derived from my blood sample, and in that case it could be argued that I had a right to a share in the profit. When information is used for research, there is seldom any (monetary) profit to share, so we will allow ourselves to leave these problems aside.

Integrity, Autonomy, Privacy, and Harm

If I do not hold property rights in information about myself, how can we then justify the intuition that I have some right to control the generation and use of such information? One possible approach would be to look for a justification in the cluster of moral rights (and correlative duties) that protects a person against unwarranted interference from others. Three rights seem important in this context: the right to personal integrity, the right to autonomy, and the right to privacy. Traditionally, the right to autonomy has assumed a central position in Bioethics, especially within the American tradition, but, as we will argue below, an exclusive focus on autonomy will not bring us far in the analysis of the present problems.

The Danish Council of Ethics has stated that there is a direct deduction from the right to personal integrity to an extensive right to keep personal information secret. In the opinion of the Council, the right to integrity entails that no personal information can be generated, stored, used, or reused for research unless there is explicit, present, informed consent. It is not obvious how the Council reaches this conclusion, and it seems to us that it rests on a mistaken understanding of the notion of 'personal integrity'. If there is to be any sense in distinguishing between integrity, autonomy, and privacy (and we do believe that this distinction is useful—see below), then the right to personal integrity must be understood as my right to be the person I am, i.e. my right not to have my personality changed or be forced to do what is against my innermost feelings.

In one sense a right to integrity is a strange right to posit. Is it not just in the cases where a moral agent is most under pressure from others, that he or she can display integrity? Is it not in the cases where he or she withstands such pressure that we speak of 'a person of great personal integrity'? How can he or she then have a right to be protected from the pressure which tests integrity and moral fibre?

At this stage of our discussion it is important to distinguish between two slightly different notions of integrity. When we talk about 'personal integrity' as a moral trait, basically we use 'integrity' in a way which has been admirably analysed by Bernard Williams:

What about concern with one's own *integrity?* The simplest thing to say about this would be that integrity is one case of a virtue . . . But I think that this would be wrong . . . It is rather that one who displays integrity acts from those dispositions and motives which are most deeply his, and has also the virtues that enable him to do that. Integrity does not enable him to do it, nor is it what he acts from when he does so.[3]

But there is another, psychological concept of integrity, where it makes sense to say that 'his integrity was destroyed' without thereby referring to any (immoral) acts performed by the person in question. If other persons, by way of force or subtle manipulation, try to brainwash me or change my personality, it seems quite clear that I have a right to be protected from this. What is being protected here is the right to be the person I happen to be, whether or not I display integrity in my acts. It is this deeper sense of psychological integrity or coherence which is protected by the right to integrity.

If this analysis is correct, then the fact that other people obtain personal information about me cannot be a transgression of my personal integrity. These others now know what kind of person I am, and this may of course harm me, but it does not interfere with my right to be this sort of person. My right to be a rabid racist[4] is not violated by other people knowing that I am a racist. This knowledge will probably increase the probability of others confronting me and trying to change my views, but the right to integrity is not a right not to be confronted with opposing views. The right is only violated if I am brainwashed or *forced* to change my views.

We know that there are certain ways of life that are discriminated against in society. In the Western world, homosexual life is a good example.[5] If prejudice against homosexuals is widespread and strong in the population, or, even more important, if there are statutes prohibiting homosexual activity, then it could be argued that the mere disclosure of sexual preference would lead to such social pressure that it in itself could be an infringement of the integrity of the person in question. Or, more generally, there can be cases in which the disclosure of a piece of personal information will curtail the possibility of a person to be the person he or she wants to be to such a great extent that it will be an infringement of integrity. This is, however, not the usual case.

Rather, as our analysis of the context-dependency of 'sensitive' information suggests, such disclosure can cause other people to act

---

[3] Bernard Williams, *Moral Luck* (Cambridge: Cambridge University Press, 1981): 49 (emphasis in original).

[4] We do not, of course, intend to imply that such a right would be inalienable.

[5] Although prejudices in this area are changing for the better in most countries.

in ways that harm the person in question. The right to autonomy cannot be the basis for an extensive right to control personal information either. We agree with the analysis and definition of autonomy presented by Gerald Dworkin: Autonomy is a second-order capacity to reflect critically upon one's first-order preferences and desires, and the ability either to identify with these or to change them in light of higher-order preferences and values. . . . Liberty, power, and privacy are not equivalent to autonomy.[6]

According to this definition protection of the right of autonomy involves protection against undue interference with my deliberations and my acts. Using a similar argument as the one presented above in the section on integrity, disclosure of personal information about me cannot constitute undue interference with my deliberations or acts.

Let us assume that somebody installed a hidden video camera in my bedroom in order to tape the sexual activities of me and my wife. This would in no way violate my integrity or my autonomy. I could still be the person I want to be, and perform the deliberations and acts I want to perform, but nevertheless we would still like to say that the installation of such a camera in my bedroom is wrong. As long as I don't know of its existence it is difficult to say that it constitutes a direct harm to me, so a direct utility argument is not promising. The most natural way to argue is therefore through the right to privacy. We understand this right not only as a right to maintain a personal sphere from which other people can be excluded at will, but also to include a right not to be *scrutinized* by others, even in public places.

To illustrate the second aspect of this right, let us take a situation that is quite common during the summer in Denmark. On *public* beaches it is well in keeping with accepted norms of behaviour that men and women walk around, go swimming, and sunbathe both naked and in swimsuits. Spending my holidays on such a beach it sometimes happens, of course, that my eyes are caught by some attractive person, who, after bathing, leaves the water and walks towards her screen, and for a moment (or two) I allow myself to watch her progress. Let us now suppose that a peeping Tom has hidden himself and a video camera with a telescopic lens in the sandhills in order to tape her. Are there any morally relevant differences between the two situations that can explain the intuition that the peeping Tom's way of acting is morally wrong, but mine is morally acceptable?

---

[6] Gerald Dworkin, *The Theory and Practice of Autonomy* (Cambridge: Cambridge University Press, 1988): 108.

In the former case my eyes were just caught by the apparition, whereas the peeping Tom has hidden himself and his camera with the intention to record systematically what he sees. The difference between the two situations can also be seen from the fact that, when the woman is out of my focus, I do not follow her to make further observation, whereas the peeping Tom all the time will focus his camera on the woman and even try to get recordings of her sunbathing behind the screen.

There seems, in other words, to be a morally significant distinction between just casually observing another person and making 'the same observations' of the person in question with the intention of scrutinizing her. Furthermore, in the first situation it is hard to see that there could be any transgression of the woman's right to privacy. In the other situation, however, the peeping Tom violates such a right in the sense of a right not be scrutinized by others, even in public places.

If this analysis is to the point, it shows that the ways in which person-related data are gathered at public places must be taken into account in the moral evaluation of a research project, even though the person or group of persons is in no way harmed by the research. This is even true if the person or group of persons, by contrast to being harmed, actually derives some benefit from a study, as the notorious 'Tearoom Trade Study' exemplifies.[7] In the mid-1960s, the sociologist Laud Humphreys conducted his 'tearoom trade' study with the aim of describing homosexual practices in public restrooms and of learning about the lifestyles and motives of the men who participated in them. ('Tearoom' was the term used by male homosexuals to describe places such as public restrooms where homosexuals engage in sexual activity.) He gained access to the 'tearooms' by masquerading as a 'watchqueen'. A 'watchqueen' is a person, who derives pleasure by observing homosexual activity and, in exchange for the right to do this, serves as a lookout with the responsibility to warn others in the 'tearoom' of approaching strangers who might be police or blackmailers. After observing the activities in the 'tearoom', he then followed some of the men to their automobiles and by recording the registration numbers of their cars he was able to determine their home addresses. A year later he once more changed his

---

[7] Laud Humphreys, *Tearoom Trade* (Chicago: Aldine Publishers, 1970); A. J. Kimmel, *Ethics and Values in Applied Social Research* (Newbury Park, Calif.: Sage Publications, 1988).

apparent identity and contacted the men in their homes claiming to be a health-service interviewer doing a 'Social health survey of men in the community'.

Among the findings of Humphreys' study were that many of the subjects were married and lived as accepted members of their communities. Only a small percentage were members of the gay community. By these findings the study was dispelling stereotypes, myths, and prejudices about homosexual activity and because of this it was praised by some members of the gay community. Nevertheless, it could be argued that the research methods employed in generating this information vitiated the otherwise laudable purpose. In American legal use, privacy has a much wider scope, almost coextensive with non-interference, but this seems to be a misuse of the term.[8]

What are then the limits of the (moral) right to privacy, and how should it be applied in the present context? On a basic level, privacy entails that I am not obliged to tell anything about myself to anybody. Nobody possesses an unrestricted right to information about me, a justification must be produced every time somebody wants information. In society, the right to privacy is often set aside in the pursuit of more important societal goals, but it should enter the calculations as a prima-facie right. In the research context, the balance shifts more towards recognizing privacy. Research is (we believe) an important societal activity, but it is not essential to the immediate function of a society in the same way as taxation, social security, or defence. It is therefore reasonable to require explicit informed consent when information is gathered for research purposes.

It is, however, not obvious what a recognition of a right to privacy as an important consideration entails for the use of information which is already stored in registers. It could be argued that privacy has already been relinquished, and that this legitimates further use of such information for research purposes. On the other hand, why should consent to one use of a specific item of information constitute or imply consent to a distinct and different use of the same information?

The three rights above seem to fall into the following hierarchy of importance: (i) Integrity (i.e. my right to be the person I want to be); (ii) autonomy (i.e. my right to do the things I want to do); and (iii)

---

[8] See Dworkin, *Theory and Practice of Autonomy.*

privacy (i.e. my right to protect a secret private sphere). The hierarchy is not absolute and lexical. A minimal infringement of my autonomy may be less morally important than a major infringement of my privacy, but we believe that the ordering nevertheless captures an important rule of thumb. If this is granted, then it follows from the argument above that an extensive right to control personal information can only be based on the weakest of these three rights, i.e. the right to privacy.

It could be argued that one important right is missing from the analysis, i.e. the right not to be harmed by others. We have deliberately postponed the discussion of this right, because it differs from the three rights analysed above in several ways. Unless one is wedded to a strong reading of the thesis that 'rights and duties are correlated', it is doubtful whether it is sensible to posit a right not to be harmed by others. It seems to us much more sensible instead to analyse the duty not to harm others. This duty is clearly and decisively attributable to persons and its scope can be fairly precisely delimited. In the present context, this duty falls on the researcher wanting to use personal information. He or she must ask the question: 'Can this research project conceivably harm someone?'

In answering this question, the researcher has to take into account both the purpose of the study and its likely results. If he, for instance, lives in a society with strong racist prejudices, then it might just be the case that he shouldn't even study whether or not there are any connections between race and intelligence.[9]

Where Should the Use of Information be Controlled?

The use of the information in public and private registers must be controlled to prevent infringements of privacy and possible harm to persons. Retrieval and linkage of such information can create significant harm to individuals and groups, but it is not immediately obvious how such regulations should be designed.

There are two main options:

1. Control of the types of information that a given register owner is allowed to store.

[9] N. J. Block and G. Dworkin (eds.), *The IQ Controversy* (New York: Pantheon Books, 1976); H. J. Eysenck and L. Kamin, *The Intelligence Controversy: H.J. Eysenck vs. Leon Kamin* (New York: Wiley, 1981).

2. Control of the use of information which is stored in given registers.

In the health care context, control of storage of information runs into problems because of our general lack of predictive powers. We are not always (read 'seldom') able to predict which items of information could become useful, and which could become harmful. This problem occurs both in clinical practice and in research. Who would, for instance, have predicted that the labour union membership files from the 1930s and 1940s from asbestos factories would become essential in establishing the link between asbestos and cancer as well as in securing financial compensation for the workers so affected? Because of this lack of prediction, it will be difficult to operate a sensible system of control on the storage side.

Control on the use of registers will also suffer from this lack of predictive powers, but to a lesser degree because such control can take account of both the present state of society (including prevalent prejudices) and of the present knowledge about the subject matter. One way of use is the linking of information already stored but hitherto kept separate, for example in two different registers. The paradigmatic problem here is that while the information in both registers at the time of storage was totally innocuous, and would probably remain so if kept separate, the linking of information might pose a threat to the privacy and/or be harmful for specific persons as well as groups of persons. This problem cannot be solved by regulating storage of information, but only by regulating use.

In Denmark, we have a central national register where every citizen is registered under a specific code number. The register contains information about name, address, and occupation, among other things—by itself, quite innocuous. There is another register containing information about people (their names and personal code numbers) who have sought treatment by chiropractors. By itself, this information is also quite innocuous, and is used when the social security services reimburse the chiropractors. But let us further suppose that a young physician in the process of doing some research linked those two registers and this revealed that a number of consultant doctors at departments of physical therapy (physiotherapists) had been treated by chiropractors. This finding might pose a threat to the privacy of some of the physiotherapists insofar as *the researcher* got an insight into some of his colleagues' private lives. This finding was, however, not foreseen when the information was stored in the two separate registers, and it was only created through linkage. Both registers have fully legitimate purposes, and there is no reason why the storage of this information in person-identifiable form should not be allowed. The problem is the use and linkage.

Another important consideration concerns the way in which such findings are accessible to others, for example through publication. It is commonly accepted that such information should only be accessible in an anonymous version, by deleting names and personal code numbers. But, even so, the publication of the proportion of physiotherapists who have sought treatment by chiropractors could be harmful to each individual physiotherapist as well as to the group as a whole, even though none of them was identifiable.

It should also be remembered that making information about persons accessible in an anonymous version might not be sufficient to protect their privacy. Anonymity does not ensure non-identification. Let us imagine a person living in a relatively small community, where she has an account in the local bank. On the statements of the account one can see where she draws on the account. The statements show a regular pattern with money being used in the local supermarket during weekends as well as in a city 100 miles away during the working week. It also appears that sometimes, while away from home, she frequents some of the more sleazy places. Because of this pattern of expenses, she would be easily identifiable by people in the community, even if the information was only made accessible in an anonymous form: she is the only one in the community who happens often to be away from home.

This again points to a control of the use of stored data, and not a control of storage. Even if the data of expenditure had been stored in an anonymous form in this example, it would not be a sufficient protection if use was left uncontrolled.

New Information from Old Samples

A specific problem in medical research is the constant development of new diagnostic techniques which can be applied to already existing biological samples stored in hospitals and laboratories. The problem is not new, but the development of new genetic technology has made it more prominent. From blood and tissue samples stored for many decades or centuries, new and important genetic information can be extracted.[10] The original donors of the material could not, for obvious reasons, have consented to this use of the material, since nobody could have predicted that such a use would become possible, and we cannot simply imply consent to any and all uses of the material. Does this then mean that new and explicit consent is necessary for all new uses of stored biological samples? Not necessarily!

The main purpose of this chapter has been to show that the establishment of hard and fast rules about the storage and use of personal information within health care is a suboptimal approach to information control. In this case the question of whether or not we can imply consent, and thereby avoid seeking new consent, is intrinsically connected with the effect of producing this new information, with the purpose of producing it, and with the type of information produced. There can be no general rules, but each new experiment must be assessed on its own merits, and the main question must be whether the new information can harm the original donors of the material, their descendants, or the group to which they belong.[11]

The researchers themselves, or various expert committees, may not be the best people to perform such a balancing exercise, but maybe one could use a 'proxy group' of people having the condition in question, or people representing the group or population from which the biological samples were originally drawn.[12]

It is sometimes claimed that genetic information is special because it is predictive of the future of the person in question. The concept of genetic information is difficult to define in a precise manner since knowledge about the genes of a person can be obtained in many ways, only some of which involve the science of genetics. The colour of my eyes is, for instance, genetically determined, so everyone with the relevant theoretical knowledge can immediately get information about some of my genes.

It is probably true that the generation and use of predictive information raises problems different from the ones raised by the

[10] Genetic diagnosis has been performed on Egyptian mummies.

[11] Genetic studies on Egyptian mummies may uncover all kinds of incestuous kinship relationships, and this may reflect *badly* on the rulers of the dynasty in question, but it is difficult to see how this can be a real harm to them, and even more difficult to see of whom one should seek consent.

[12] N. Fost, 'A Surrogate System for Informed Consent', *Journal of the American Medical Association* **233** (1975): 800–3.

generation and use of information which is exclusively 'present-state related', but there are many other forms of information which are also predictive in this sense without being genetic, and there are many non-predictive pieces of genetic information (for example the present use of gene-tests in forensic science which is not predictive but rather 'confirmatory'). If somebody got hold of my teenage diaries, these would contain a lot of predictive information, which I would not like to see publicized, but they would also contain a lot of non-predictive information which could be of interest to researchers, and which I would gladly let them analyse (for example the language used by teenagers in the 1970s).

The emphasis should therefore not be laid upon prediction or genetics *per se*, but upon what is predicted. Some predictions are trivial, and others are very important, and the evaluation of a specific research project using old biological samples must therefore be based upon a thorough analysis of the exact purpose of the project and not just on whether or not it can be put under the label of 'genetic' or 'predictive'.

14

AIDS and Insurance

TOM SORELL AND HEATHER DRAPER

In commercial markets for life insurance in the West, individuals apply for policies that pay very large sums of money in the event of premature death, and successful applicants are charged premiums according to the insurers' calculations of the risks: the greater the risk, the higher the charge or premium. Certain medical conditions, leisure pursuits, and jobs are known to carry a higher risk of death than others, and policies are weighted accordingly. Thus, people with high blood pressure are charged more than people with normal blood pressure, smokers are charged more than non-smokers, and mountain climbers and skydivers are charged more than chess players. Insurance companies routinely elicit information about risky medical conditions, leisure pursuits, and jobs in deciding whether to accept applications for life insurance and in deciding how to fix levels of premiums. If it is morally permissible for them to do so, and to charge more to those whom they classify as the higher risks; if it is morally permissible for insurers even to refuse to take on some risks, is it morally permissible for them to do these things in the case of people who are at relatively high risk of contracting HIV disease?

The same questions arise for commercial health insurance. Firms enter the health insurance market to make a return on their premium income, the income from sales of other financial services, or the income from investors. They do not enter the market to reduce the amount of illness or suffering. If certain medical conditions, occupations, or 'lifestyles' carry a high risk of expensive hospitalization or other medical treatment, aren't insurance companies within their rights to ask searching questions and charge high premiums before taking on these risks? Aren't they within their rights to refuse appli-

The authors would like to thank Peter Roth, Ivan Massow, and the insurance brokers Howell Shone for assisting them with the research for this chapter.

cations or 'proposals', to adopt insurers' jargon, if the risks are judged to be too high?

Morality and the Size of the Commercial Insurance Sector

Different answers to these general questions can be given according to the size of the commercial sector for health insurance in a given country. In countries where health insurance is funded out of high rates of taxation and is used to pay for virtually all medical treatment dispensed through a comprehensive network of public hospitals and primary care practices, commercially provided health insurance is not one's only protection against the cost of hospitalization, nursing care, or medicines. Indeed, commercially provided health insurance may not typically be intended to protect people on limited incomes from overwhelming medical costs. It may cater instead to those people (some with big incomes) who want very quick access to medical treatment and expertise, sometimes to quite exclusive sources of medical treatment and expertise. When this is the niche filled by private health insurers, refusals of policies do not deprive applicants of health insurance, even quite good health insurance, and so the moral case for restricting insurers' latitude to refuse may not be very strong either. Again, if a commercial health insurance industry operates alongside a successful and compulsory state health insurance regime, it may be in a difficult market, since it has to appeal to people who have already paid for health insurance through their taxes, to pay a second time for what may turn out to be the same treatment dispensed by doctors who are also employed in public hospitals. Perhaps the difficult market justifies their being more careful about the risks they take on.

Things stand differently where the commercial health insurance market is dominant and there is a relatively small state health insurance scheme. Here there are more opportunities for commercial insurers, more after-tax income for individuals to invest in insurance, and far less of a safety net for anyone who is refused insurance. The consequences of refusal are far more serious for individuals, while the costs to firms of accepting risky applicants can in principle be offset by the proceeds of a far greater number of low-risk policies from those in the population at large. For all of these reasons morality tells in favour of commercial firms taking on risks that it would not be reasonable for them to take where the public sector was dominant.

Morality also tells in favour of fixing premiums for those at higher risk at levels that reflect the profits generated by the extremely low-risk proposers who are forced to take out policies in the absence of a state health service. The strength of the case against refusal and against fixing high premiums varies, of course, with the actual costs of claims; the costs of hospitalization, diagnosis, medical equipment, and drugs may make any claim, and not just the exceptional claim, extremely costly for the insurer. In that case, the force of the argument against the insurer refusing proposals has to be felt also by the mechanisms determining the costs of the claims, i.e. the mechanisms determining the prices of drugs, medical equipment and hospital rooms, the fees of doctors, and the wages of other medical staff. It is hard to insulate the ethics of health insurance from the ethics of dealings in the health industry at large.

Morality and Private Insurance in Welfare States: HIV in the UK

If the moral importance of refusals of commercial insurance increases with the relative size of the private sector in health services, what are we to say of the moral importance of refusals of insurance, or of setting commercial premiums high, in countries with big public-sector health insurance regimes? Is it morally important to have wide access to the commercial insurance market even in countries like these? As regards the UK, the answer is 'Yes', because commercial insurance is normally used to secure loans to buy housing, to provide income during a period of illness if one is self-employed, and to provide for loss of income when an income-earner or the income-earner in a household dies. If it is morally important for there to be a wide access to those forms of insurance, then, other things being equal, it is unfair for access to this market to be barred to anyone or made particularly difficult for anyone. But there is evidence that access is difficult for those who are taken by insurers to be at significant risk of contracting HIV disease. Access to life insurance may be difficult for homosexual men or men who are thought to be homosexuals, and it may be difficult for those with other, supposedly risky, 'lifestyles'.

According to figures compiled by the World Health Organization up to February 1990, the incidence of reported cases of AIDS in the

UK is lower than that in many other Western countries: fifty cases per million of the population, compared to 491 cases per million in the USA, 181 in Switzerland, 160 in France, and 132 in Canada. Indeed, the incidence in the UK is lower than that of Spain, Denmark, Italy, the Netherlands, West Germany, and Belgium.[1] Of AIDS-related deaths in the UK, only about 40 per cent were estimated to be deaths of people with life insurance.[2] Again, since 1987, the actuarial profession in the UK has been active in making projections of the growth of the disease, and in making recommendations about underwriting policy. This means that UK insurers are in a relatively good position to estimate risks in their current underwriting, and are placed in a market in which there is some reason to think that HIV disease is not running out of control. On the other hand, they are obliged to honour AIDS-related claims on life policies taken out before 1987, claims which may cost the insurers a great deal of money. In view of these commitments, the absence of any prospect of a cure, and the likely increase in AIDS-related deaths over the next two decades, UK insurers have for some time declined all proposals of life insurance from those who are known to have tested HIV positive,[3] and they have made acceptance of proposals from other people depend on answers to lifestyle questionnaires or, less often, on the results of HIV tests. The lifestyle questionnaires are triggered by applications for insurance of more than £10,000 from single males and more than £75,000 from married males. They may also be triggered by applications by two men for a joint mortgage linked to a life insurance policy. HIV tests are required where the life cover applied for by a single male exceeds £150,000 and where the cover applied for by married males or by females is more than £250,000.[4]

Lifestyle Questionnaires and HIV Tests

Are questionnaires and HIV tests morally permissible prerequisites for obtaining insurance? Insurers are entitled to base their decisions

[1] C. D. Daykin, 'The epidemiology of HIV infection and AIDS', *Journal of the Institute of Actuaries* **117** (1990): 51–95, cited in Peter G. Moore, 'Some ethical issues in British insurance', *Business Ethics: A European Review* **2** (1993): 134.

[2] *AIDS Bulletin* no. 5 (London: Institute of Actuaries, 1991): 25.

[3] Some HIV-positive people in the UK do have cover under private group insurance. Others have access to financial products, such as Personal Equity Plans and pensions, which function like life policies in guaranteeing the repayment of mortgages.

[4] *AIDS Bulletin* no. 5: 20.

about policies and premiums on estimates of risk, and to the extent that the answers to the questionnaires and the results of HIV tests are necessary for estimating risk, that is a reason for obtaining them.[5] Unfortunately, it is doubtful that questionnaires have always elicited answers that are good guides to risk. On the contrary, in the past they have sometimes appeared to classify every taker of an HIV test and every homosexual as a member of a high-risk group. In the case of homosexual men, the impression of high risk has sometimes been reinforced by doctors asked by insurers to comment on the health of their patients.[6] Some doctors mistakenly regard homosexuality itself as a health risk. The fact is, however, that celibate homosexual men and HIV-negative homosexual men in stable partnerships who practise safer sex are not at great risk of contracting HIV disease. As for the significance of HIV tests, these can be taken by particularly cautious members of low-risk groups, such as heterosexual women, and by travellers meeting immigration requirements.

A proposer's disclosure of a past HIV test is no longer regarded by insurers as evidence of belonging to a high-risk group. For instance, of more than 4000 men aged between 20 and 55 HIV-tested for work with British Aerospace in Saudi Arabia, none is known to have been refused insurance as a result of testing, and the Preston Public Health Laboratory that conducted the tests has received only around twenty requests for verification that the testing was routine. But insurers are still clumsy in their wording of questionnaires, and answers are open to unfair interpretation. It is unclear that even the form of question now recommended by the Association of British Insurers is satisfactory. The preferred wording of question for insurance proposals is currently:

---

[5] It is true that the questionnaires may be intrusive, in that sexual behaviour has a bearing on the risk of contracting HIV disease, and in that one's own sexual behaviour is normally a private matter; but other private matters, such as one's income and level of indebtedness, are sometimes required to be disclosed on questionnaires, apparently without generating much controversy; so either there is something specially private about one's sexual activity, or it cannot be privacy alone that makes the completion of lifestyle questionnaires morally dubious.

[6] A question that we have no space to deal with is that of the morality of insurers using GPs as sources of secondary screening information, such as information concerning the HIV status or sexuality of patients. The practice may give doctors who have no scruples about revealing this information too much power over patients, and it may burden those who wish not to harm their patients' chances of obtaining insurance, and who may feel a strong temptation to lie in the interest of protecting these changes.

Have you ever

(*a*) been personally counselled or medically advised in connection with HIV (AIDS) or any sexually transmitted disease?
Please give dates and circumstances*
or

(*b*) had an HIV (AIDS) test? (Please give dates, circumstances* and results)

*To enable the company to process this application as quickly as possible and to reduce the need for further investigation, please indicate if the counselling or test was for routine screening (e.g. for blood donation, antenatal, employment, occupational health) or other reasons.

Despite the asterisked clause, question (*b*) suggests that if someone has had a 'non-routine' HIV test, e.g. the extra-cautious heterosexual woman, then that is evidence of belonging to a high-risk group. This is by itself a reason for rewording the question. And there are objections to insurers asking about HIV tests—as opposed to positive results—at all. A study jointly commissioned by the Association of British Insurers and the UK Department of Health in 1991 showed that fears about the uses which insurers make of an admission of having an HIV test has put off as many as tens of thousands of people in the UK from having a test.[7]

Question (*a*) also turns out to be objectionable. For example, it might be answered affirmatively by anyone getting health advice in connection with travel to the Third World. Since the consequence of 'wrong' answers to (*a*) or (*b*) is not just refusal by one insurance company in the UK—refused applicants' names can be entered on an Impaired Lives Register that will be available to all insurers—these objections are not unimportant. Straight questions about intravenous drug use, frequent change of sexual partner, and sexual contracts in countries with a high incidence of HIV disease would at least be directly relevant to the estimation of risk, would not stigmatize celibate or non-promiscuous homosexuals, and might be no more

[7] Sharon Kingman, 'Insurers inconsistent over HIV: Britain', *British Medical Journal* **306** (1993): 1496. Perhaps the moral importance of more testing justifies removing obstacles to testing, such as insurance company questioning about HIV tests. Or perhaps it justifies a system of private insurance in which the risks of taking bad risks by not asking questions are shared by more than a few willing firms. Under the current 'lots-of-questions-asked' arrangements, people are not only put off taking tests, but proposers who risk being classified unfairly as high risks are put off making applications for insurance in straightforward ways. Instead of applying for policies with one insurance firm at a time for one financial product at a time—mortgage protection or life insurance, say—they apply simultaneously to many firms, hoping that one insurer's refusal will not worsen the chances of another's accepting.

intrusive than less direct questions routinely asked already. Moreover, while they might not be answered truthfully (a problem to which we shall return), these questions might be answered no less truthfully than the questions now being asked.

Carrying out an HIV test on a proposer of insurance is a check on misrepresentation in the lifestyle questionnaire, but it can create anxiety, and if the test result is positive and made known to anyone other than the proposer, it can mean ostracism, the loss or curtailment of employment, the break-up of a relationship and family life, and possibly even homelessness. These things add to the considerable misfortune of having the disease, and so the character of the testing regime is not morally neutral. In the UK the Terrence Higgins Trust has been trying to persuade insurers to pay not only for HIV tests but for pre- and post-test counselling. In view of the dread attached to HIV disease there is a good moral argument for the proposal, and, as those who test negative will presumably need little if any time with a counsellor, the proposal may not be impractical or hugely expensive. Moreover, whatever the counselling adds to the costs of testing, it is presumably justified commercially by the savings made when bad risks are disclosed. Spending a little more on the testing process may not only save insurers' money that would have been spent subsequently on claims; it may also be—if the counselling is impartial enough—a good image-building measure for an industry that is sometimes thought to be impersonal and unsympathetic.

Money may not be the only thing that has to be spent on testing: sufficient time for reliable testing must also be found by insurers. Two recent cases in the UK of false-positive tests for HIV disease have caused scientists at the Public Health Laboratory Service to speak out to the national press about the pressure for quick results on private testing laboratories by insurers.[8] This pressure, and the financial costs of running checks when there is a positive test result, may increase the number of unchecked results released by private laboratories. People with false-positive results will be caused huge distress unnecessarily, and perhaps people will begin to wonder whether even negative results are reliable.

---

[8] *Independent on Sunday*, London, 19 Sept. 1993, p. 9.

Levels of Premium

One safeguard against insurance losses on HIV disease is the testing of proposers; another is the loading of premiums, i.e. charging differentially high prices for life cover to some groups, prices inflated to compensate for previously undetected risk, or to reflect possibly unfounded anxiety about the size of risks already taken on. In 1988 many British insurers reacted to reports of an AIDS epidemic by increasing, sometimes by as much as threefold, premiums for life insurance charged to young single men. One London-based specialist in financial services who deals with the problems of HIV-positive clients has told us that 'following the AIDS scare of the eighties, life assurance premiums were loaded across the board by approximately £5 per £1000 insured per year.'[9] This is morally objectionable for the same reason that some of the assumptions of the lifestyle questionnaires are morally objectionable: it is indiscriminate about who is a risk, and so it unfairly charges too much to many who are low risks. Worse, it violates the principle supposedly respected elsewhere in insurance practice: that it is unfair to make low-risk proposers subsidize high-risk proposers.[10] Some companies escape some of these objections by offering lower premiums for policies that exclude AIDS as a cause of death, but they do not seem to be typical. Worse, the moral wrongs of premium loading have been compounded since the 1980s. In April 1993, the UK government concluded that heterosexuals ran very small risks of contracting HIV disease: insurers who had raised premium levels in 1988 announced no lowering of

[9] Personal communication, Ivan Massow Association.

[10] In public insurance schemes some low-risk subscribers pay the same as some high-risk subscribers who are themselves to blame for being high risks. Thus non-smokers in the general population of the UK subsidize the costs to the health service incurred by the treatment of heavy smokers. It is sometimes suggested that a principle of solidarity justifies this way of spreading the costs of risk among members of a population (*cf.* Per Sandberg, 'Costs and ethics of not asking about HIV in life insurance', 1993, unpublished). There is something to be said for this thought where the condition generating the cost is the result of misfortune; but a principle of solidarity might also require people who have the opportunity to cut risks to their health, and potential costs to a public health system, to do so. In a public health system heavy smokers and drinkers are not only harming themselves but also making calls on resources that are more justifiably directed to those who can't help having their health problems. A principle of solidarity justifies helping others through an insurance pool; but it also justifies a policy of not drawing upon the pool unduly.

premiums and some were reported in the national press to have no plans to reduce them.[11]

A means of offsetting some of the risk of insurance companies while allowing for low life premiums is a term insurance policy with one premium level that the proposer contracts to pay, and another lower, typically much lower, premium, which the proposer is actually charged. One twenty-five-year term policy for £100,000 offered by Equitable Life in May 1993 to a 25-year-old male requires the proposer to contract to pay premiums of £42.17 per month, though the actual charge at the time would only be £12.17 per month. There are still moral objections to the premium level set by the contract if the proposer belongs to a low-risk group, but the actual premium charged was in fact lower than that for a term policy for the same sum assured with an AIDS exclusion.

Pay-outs

Figures reported in the UK press and confirmed by the Association of British Insurers as coming from one of its internal reports, indicate that pay-outs in 1992 on life insurance policies for AIDS deaths had amounted to £40 million in a six-month period, compared to £31 million in a slightly earlier six-month period.[12] These figures may in fact be an underestimate, since the cause of death of some policyholders may not always have been suspected to be AIDS. The figures were considered newsworthy because of the rate of increase between half-yearly periods that they indicated: 30 per cent. No one knows exactly how much will have to be paid out in the future, but if the sums increase into the hundreds of millions annually, insurance firms in the UK may be inclined to challenge or delay paying claims. There is precedent for this in other areas of insurance where individual claims can be extremely high, e.g. the insurance of residential buildings against subsidence in the UK in the 1980s. And where AIDS deaths are concerned, there may be scope for insurers to resist claims by saying that factors material to risk on life policies failed to be disclosed or were lied about when the policies were first proposed or offered. Companies faced with claims in the next century may allege that false answers were given to lifestyle questionnaires in the 1990s. Even if

---

[11] *Independent on Sunday*, London, 9 May 1993, p. 19.
[12] *Independent on Sunday*, London, 7 Feb. 1993, p. 1.

they do not and only launch investigations to assure themselves that there is no fraud, the effects on innocent, potential beneficiaries of life policies could be very damaging. Not only might the survivors of the policyholder be impoverished while waiting for a pay-out that they could legitimately have expected to have received promptly, but they might also have to suffer insinuations about the sexuality and fidelity of marriage partners and parents, not to mention worries about their own health, and ostracism or prejudice from third parties drawn into an investigation of a claim.

Since the chances of causing distress to innocent people in investigating an insurance claim on an AIDS-related death are likely to be much higher than the costs of investigating an ordinary life claim or a claim for burglary or car crime; since the precautions taken at the underwriting stage are much higher; and since premium levels for life insurance have been adjusted upwards very sharply, there is a strong moral argument for a no-fuss claims settlement regime, and, short of this, for an infrastructure able to conduct sensitive, not just impartial, loss-adjusting investigations.

Early Realization of the Value of Life Policies

People with AIDS or who are diagnosed as HIV positive may have a greater need for money at the end of their lives than the would-be beneficiaries have after the deaths of the policyholders. In cases like these it is sometimes possible for HIV-positive holders of valid life insurance policies who have a prognosis of short life-expectancy (two years or less) to sell the policies for a high proportion of their full value. In the UK there is, to our knowledge, only one organization—Life Benefit Resources—that arranges the sale on these terms of life policies, and the safeguards they offer potential participants in their scheme seem to offer a possible model of good practice. The organization advises applicants to get independent financial advice, operates a cooling-off period during which sellers of life policies can return the sum they are paid and get the policies back, makes no judgements about how people want to use their money, and does not penalize anyone financially if they live beyond the two-year period.

Health Care Workers

We have been concentrating on problems for those at risk of contracting HIV disease of getting fair treatment from providers of personal life insurance. Other forms of insurance carry their own moral
dangers. We shall now be focusing on some kinds of insurance that
apply in the health care field. We shall consider the moral risks associated with income-protection policies and so-called 'dread disease'
policies for health care workers.

Income-protection policies are taken out in the UK by, among
other people, doctors who haven't yet got permanent contracts with
a Health Authority and who could be without an income if they contracted HIV disease before they were given such a contract. The protection may also be needed by doctors who would not be able to
continue practising in a certain branch of medicine or medicine at all
if they became HIV positive. As in the case of 'dread disease' policies,
income-protection policies can carry exclusions for HIV disease not
contracted in the course of one's normal duties as a health care
worker. Clauses like these are an invitation to the 'with-fuss' settlement regime for AIDS-related claims that was condemned in the last
section. If claims are contested, it will be natural for insurance firms
or loss adjustors to try to invoke evidence of a lifestyle outside work
that could as easily have accounted for HIV disease as a needlestick
injury or mucous membrane exposure to blood. Patients might come
under pressure to be tested to verify claims. The danger of damage or
distress to these third parties, to legitimate claimants, and to innocent dependants of these claimants justifies either having a negative
HIV test as a condition of getting income-protection cover, or else
not offering the policy.

Different moral objections are attracted by certain 'dread disease'
policies. Scottish Amicable offers a 'Critical Protection' policy in its
range of 'Provider' policies. The policy pays out a lump sum up to a
maximum of £500,000 upon the diagnosis of a major illness, such as
cancer, kidney failure, or coronary artery disease. Insurance against
HIV disease is offered only to 'medical and hospital personnel', by
which is meant not only doctors, nurses, and midwives but also hospital cleaners and caterers, hospital porters, and hospital laundry
workers. The explicit targeting of these ancillary workers seems to
trade on discredited beliefs and fears about the ways the disease can

be contracted. Worse, were ancillary workers to contract to make regular payments, they would be protecting themselves against a very small risk out of wages that are notoriously low to begin with. The same is true of some grades of nurses. In other words, there are moral objections to the marketing of this policy. In addition, the policy has the same sort of 'with-fuss' settlement risk as has been discussed in relation to the income-protection scheme: it, too, disclaims liability for HIV disease that the insurer is not satisfied is contracted in the course of the policyholder's duties as a medical or hospital worker.

Conclusion

Current practice in the UK insurance industry is either plainly unfair, or risks being unfair, to single male proposers of life insurance in particular. Lifestyle questionnaires may not be a good guide to risk, and yet they are only justified as an aid to calculating risk. The HIV-testing regime is not always sensitive enough. Premium loading is sometimes unreasonable. There are moral risks associated with the investigation and payment of claims on life policies, risks that may not be justified by the probability of fraud, and cover for HIV disease for health care workers can carry dubious exclusion clauses and can be objectionably marketed. There have been improvements in the use of answers to questions about HIV tests, but the recommended form of question is still flawed.

15

Should We Routinely Test Pregnant Women for HIV?

REBECCA BENNETT

Suppose I were to suggest that all identifiable homosexual men[1] should be routinely tested for HIV.[2] I might try to justify this suggestion as an attempt, not only to give these men more information about their own health, but also in the hope that those who are aware of their HIV positivity may be more likely, in the light of this knowledge, to take action to protect others from possible HIV infection. If I were to concede that routine testing for HIV, even where it allows an 'opt out' option, is both practically challenging and ethically questionable (being at best manipulative and at worst strongly authoritarian), I could, in my defence, point to the established public health precedent of imposing comparable measures in times of crisis, for instance mandatory vaccinations and quarantine.[3]

Although it is generally accepted that public health policy should seek to encourage individuals who believe they may be infected with

---

This chapter addresses the situation as it exists in countries where antenatal care, the 'risk-reducing' methods described below, and abortion are accessible.

[1] I am aware that because of lack of space it is not possible in this chapter to go into the complexities of the wider issues that surround homosexuality and HIV testing. What is represented here is, clearly, an unsophisticated and highly simplistic argument regarding male homosexuality and HIV testing, adopted as a literary device with the aim of clarifying the issues under consideration.

[2] The actual logistics of a policy of routine testing of known homosexual men are relatively unimportant to this discussion, especially as it is my belief that such a policy would probably prove to be extremely unhelpful as well as offensive. However, for the sake of this discussion, such a policy could entail the suggestion that homosexual men be routinely tested for HIV, at the same time as other routine tests (e.g. for syphilis) are performed, without explicit consent when attending STD clinics or in other medical settings where blood is taken.

[3] *Cf.* J. Harris and S. Holm, 'If only AIDS was different!', *Hastings Center Report*, **23**/6 (1993): 6–12.

HIV to come forward and receive advice and, where appropriate, be tested for HIV, we would likely consider any calls to single out a specific group in society—such as homosexual men—and subject them to routine HIV testing as an unacceptable infringement of civil rights, and reject them. Such authoritarian measures as the *routine* testing of individuals for HIV can, in view of the history of public health interventions, only be adequately justified when implemented on grounds of overriding effectiveness. There are probably many people who would support a move to routinely test all known homosexual men for HIV, but unless it could be shown, with some certainty, that great harm could be avoided as a result of such a policy there would seem to be no grounds on which a policy of routine testing should be given serious consideration. Without persuasive evidence to suggest such a policy's overwhelming effectiveness, those who call for routine testing of homosexual men lay themselves open to accusations of scapegoating and discrimination. The persuasive evidence is *not* forthcoming.

A policy of routine testing of known homosexual men is likely to increase the number of individuals who are aware of their HIV-positive status. These individuals may, as a result of this information, be more likely to protect others from infection. However, they may not. Routine testing for HIV necessarily involves testing without the explicit consent of the patient and, even though there might be an option to refuse testing, there is a danger that a policy of routine testing would create an atmosphere of coercion which, in all likelihood, will not facilitate information dissemination and counselling. It would be difficult to develop a strongly persuasive argument that the benefits that come of an increase in the numbers of homosexual men who are aware of their HIV status clearly outweigh the possible drawbacks. It is not difficult, however, to envisage that routine testing of homosexual men could prove counter-productive in the fight against AIDS, leading to an erosion of the relationship of trust between patient and doctor, and creating a feeling of persecution among this group of people, this in addition to the obvious infringements of the right to privacy which such a policy entails.

It seems that, until convincing evidence can be produced for the overriding effectiveness of a policy of routine testing of identifiable homosexual men, respect for personal autonomy dictates that attempts to introduce such a policy should be rejected. And it follows from this that if calls for routinely testing other groups in society are to be afforded serious consideration, it is because this kind of evidence, of overriding effectiveness, is available.

Although calls for the routine testing of specific groups for HIV are usually dismissed as unjustifiable on grounds of efficacy alone, there has been a great deal of support for calls for routine testing of pregnant women for HIV.[4] Routine antenatal HIV testing shares many of the 'advantages' and drawbacks that might be envisaged for the routine testing of homosexual men. On the one hand, it may be that a policy of routinely testing pregnant women for HIV would be likely to increase the number of women aware of their HIV status and, perhaps, even encourage them to protect themselves and others from infection. On the other hand, routine antenatal testing will not only entail women dealing with unsolicited information of a deeply distressing nature and a bleak prospect, but may lead, all too easily, to those women feeling pressurized into courses of action they would not have sanctioned had their autonomy not been vitiated. The duress this implies does not facilitate a free choice.

It has been proposed[5] that the HIV-antibody test be included within the standard battery of tests performed as part of antenatal care unless specific objections are expressed. Pregnant women are routinely tested for a number of conditions including syphilis, hepatitis, and rubella. No explicit consent is sought for these tests and many women are likely to be unaware of what exactly they have been tested for. The patient is informed of any positive results and offered advice and treatment where available.[6]

Routine HIV testing of pregnant women with an option to 'opt out' is very different from a policy of routinely *offering* HIV testing to pregnant women on an 'opt-in' basis. This distinction is borne out by the fact that 'opt-in' HIV testing is unlikely to result in as great an uptake as 'opt-out' testing. Routine testing clearly involves a certain amount of coercion: the aim seems to be to secure the testing of not

---

[4] See 'Doctors call for more HIV tests in pregnancy', *Sunday Times*, 16 Oct. 1994; D. J. Goldberg and F. D. Johnstone, 'Universal named testing of pregnant women for HIV', *British Medical Journal* **306** (May 1993): 1144–5; C. Ulanowsky and B. Almond, 'HIV and Pregnancy', in B. Almond (ed.), *AIDS: A Moral Issue* (London: Macmillan, 1990): 41–55; J. Beder and N. Beckerman, 'Mandatory HIV screening in newborns: the issues and a programmatic response', *XI International Conference on AIDS, Vancouver, 1996*, Abstract ThC 4613.

[5] By Richard Smith, a consultant gynaecologist at the Chelsea and Westminster Hospital, London, cited in 'Doctors call for more HIV tests in pregnancy' and Ulanowsky and Almond, 'HIV and Pregnancy'.

[6] *Cf.* Ulanowsky and Almond, 'HIV and Pregnancy'.

only those women who would have elected to be tested under an 'opt-in' policy, but also those women who would not have chosen to seek information about their HIV status.

Are we justified in singling out pregnant women to be subjected to an HIV-testing regime which is necessarily paternalistic in nature? What are the likely benefits of such a policy, and are they such that they make pregnant women a 'special case' in terms of routine testing for HIV? In order to evaluate whether the benefits of routine testing are likely to be so great as to justify routine antenatal HIV testing, it is necessary to determine why, and in what circumstances, it may be considered useful to test pregnant women for HIV. It is my intuition that, as may be the case with calls for the routine HIV testing of all known homosexual men, of the various hypotheses which might be put forward in support of the routine testing of pregnant women for HIV, few warrant serious consideration. My task in this chapter will be to analyse some of the more forceful motives which may be adduced to support calls for routine antenatal HIV testing. It is hoped that, by examining these possible grounds for routine antenatal HIV testing, those that do not stand up to serious examination may be discarded and others which do call for serious consideration can be identified, allowing analysis of these more persuasive motives without distraction.

What Justification is there for Routinely Testing Pregnant Women for HIV?

1. *To allow women to make fully informed decisions about their futures*
Policy which encourages individuals to come forward and be tested for HIV is generally considered to be central to any public health initiative relating to HIV/AIDS. Although there is no cure for AIDS, if an individual is aware of her HIV-positive status she may be able to make more informed decisions about the future. They may choose to undergo prophylactic treatment, or to take steps aimed at the protection of others. It may be that antenatal care is seen as providing an intervention point at which it is convenient to test for HIV. In this way, the number of individuals who are aware of their HIV status could be easily increased.

However, if the reason that it is deemed to be a good thing for pregnant women to be routinely tested for HIV is the hope that the number of HIV-positive individuals who are aware of their infection, and are thus able to make more informed decisions about their futures, is increased, then surely this justification would be equally applicable to the routine testing of *all* individuals (receiving medical care). While it is likely that information about the HIV status of a pregnant women may have significant influence over the decisions she makes about her future, it is not clear that information about the HIV status of any other individual is likely to have any less of a significance in decision-making. Yet routine HIV testing of all individuals seeking medical care would appear to be ethically problematic.

It is normally assumed that explicit consent is essential if an individual is to be tested for HIV. Not only is HIV likely to bring about disease and premature death, but it is also likely to put a strain on personal relationships and may lead to social discrimination and stigmatization. Before being tested for HIV, it is important that the individual understands the likely consequences of proceeding with the test and accepts these. Tests carried out routinely and without explicit consent, such as tests for syphilis performed at STD and antenatal clinics, may be justified in terms of efficacy. As syphilis is easily cured, it may be considered acceptable to prevent disease and premature death by acting without a patient's explicit consent. However, does it follow that it is acceptable to act without a patient's consent in order that the patient may be aware that he or she has a life-threatening disease for which there is, as yet, no cure?

2. *To give health care professionals the information they need to protect themselves from possible infection*

In most other areas of medical care, it is felt that it is not necessary for health care professionals to know the HIV status of a patient in order to be able to protect themselves from possible infection. As a general rule, medical professionals are advised to act as if all patients are HIV positive and to take appropriate precautions against infection with every patient. Is the care of pregnant women a special case, as some kinds of orthopaedic surgery may be, where it might be argued that health care professionals are entitled to know the HIV status of their patients? For example, are the risks of infection higher than in other medical treatments? Might it be, perhaps, that the precautions necessary to reduce the risk of infection perhaps hinder the work of the medical professional, and are thus impractical to maintain for patients?

Even if we were to conclude that pregnancy is a special case in which routinely testing patients for HIV is justifiable in order to protect medical staff from possible infection, it would not actually be possible to determine accurately, in every case, which women were, in fact, infected. The time lag between infection and the detectability of antibodies indicates that even with periodical testing throughout pregnancy there would still be women whose HIV positivity would be missed. In view of this, it seems that medical professionals suggesting the routine testing of pregnant women as a way of minimizing the risk of transmission to themselves or colleagues would not only have to take every precaution with those women who proved to be HIV positive but would be prudent to treat women whose tests were negative *as if they were* HIV positive, making routine testing on these grounds superfluous.

3. *To produce epidemiological data*
Epidemiological data allow us to predict and plan for future infection rates and transmission modes of HIV. Pregnant women represent a useful and convenient section of society from which to gain epidemiological data. They have blood taken for other tests, they are sexually active, and they represent a fair cross-section of society since all socio-economic, ethnic, and cultural groups are represented.

However, the above reasons are reasons why pregnant women might be included in *unlinked screening programmes* specifically to gain epidemiological data; they are not arguments in favour of *routine named HIV testing* of pregnant women. Epidemiological information can be collected without anyone else, including the woman herself, knowing the HIV status of the particular person. With unlinked screening of surplus blood taken for other reasons it should not be possible for the result to be traced back to a particular individual.

4. *To allow women to protect their own health*
It is unclear what effect pregnancy has on the health of an HIV-positive woman but there is the chance that it may have a negative effect[7] and, as a result, it may be important for women to be encouraged to obtain information that will allow them to decide whether to risk their own health by continuing a pregnancy. However, until

---

[7] E. E. Schoenbaum, K. Davenny, and P. A. Selwyn, 'The impact of pregnancy on HIV-related disease', *Royal College of Obstetrics and Gynecology* (1988): 65–75.

there is convincing evidence that pregnancy actually *does* have a significant detrimental effect on the woman's health in terms of HIV infection, this cannot be taken as an adequate justification for routine testing of pregnant women.

5. *To benefit the resulting child*

Vertical transmission of HIV is the transmission of the virus from an HIV-positive mother to her child, either during pregnancy, birth, or breast-feeding. In Europe there is thought to be a 15 to 20 per cent chance of infection for a child born to an HIV-infected woman—the figure is slightly higher in Africa.[8] About 15 per cent of infected children die in their first year of life,[9] while others may live into their early teens. There is some evidence that by employing certain 'risk-reducing' measures during pregnancy and birth the vertical transmission rate of HIV can be reduced. However, anonymous unlinked screening programmes in inner London, for example, have shown that while up to 1 in 200 women booked at antenatal clinics are HIV positive, it is thought that less that one-fifth of these women are being recognized as HIV positive during their antenatal care.[10] It is statistical evidence of this kind that has been cited as the prompt for many calls for a policy of routinely testing pregnant women for HIV. The hope is that, if women are aware of their HIV positivity early on in pregnancy, this will enable more women to take full advantage of measures available which may minimize the risk of vertical transmission.[11]

Results from an American–French trial which involved the use of Zidovudine during pregnancy, labour, and in the neonatal period showed a two-thirds reduction (from 25.5 to 8.3 per cent) in the risk of infection for the infant.[12] Evidence exists that, in a woman with established HIV infection, breast-feeding approximately doubles the

---

[8] M. L. Newell and C. S. Peckham, 'Risk factors for vertical transmission and early markers of HIV-1 infection in children', *AIDS* **7** (1993): S591–7.

[9] European Collaborative Study, 'Natural History of vertically acquired HIV-1 infection', *Paediatrics* **94**/6 (1994): 815–19.

[10] F. J. Holland, A. E. Ades, C. F. Davison, S. Parker, T. Berry, M. Hjelm, *et al.*, 'Use of anonymous newborn serosurveys to evaluate antenatal HIV screening programmes', *Journal of Medical Screening* **1** (1994): 176–9.

[11] See 'Doctors call for more HIV tests in pregnancy'; D. J. Goldberg and F. D. Johnstone, 'Universal named testing of pregnant women'; Ulanowsky and Almond, 'HIV and Pregnancy'.

[12] Centres for Disease Control, 'Zidovudine for the prevention of HIV transmission from mother to infant', *Morbidity and Mortality Weekly Report* **43** (1994): 285–7.

risk of transmission.[13] It has also been suggested that delivery by caesarean section may reduce the rate of vertical transmission, but the results from individual studies have not been able to confirm this.[14]

It is generally assumed that we have a moral right to act in a way of our choosing unless this action is likely to harm or wrong another. Thus, although we may recognize a right to remain in ignorance of one's HIV status, it seems reasonable that the right to remain in ignorance should be overridden by other individuals' right not to be harmed. Although we may believe that knowledge of our HIV positivity may make us more likely to protect sexual partners or those with whom we share needles, knowledge of HIV status is not necessary or sufficient to protect these third parties from harm. It is possible to protect others from infection while remaining ignorant of one's HIV status by avoiding activities that expose others to risk of infection. However, unlike HIV associated with sexual contact or drug use, it may not be possible for a pregnant woman to protect her future child from HIV infection without knowing that she is HIV positive.

It is possible for a homosexual man, for instance, to make a strong argument against taking a routine test on the grounds that he intends to protect others from infection by *assuming* that he is HIV positive and acting accordingly. This option does not appear to be open to the pregnant woman. Assumption of HIV positivity in this case may result in the termination of a pregnancy where there is no risk of vertical transmission or in continuation with a pregnancy and the taking of possibly unnecessary risks for both the pregnant woman and her future baby's health by taking Zidovudine, having a caesarean section, and not breast-feeding. It may also be the case that hospitals will be reluctant to give expensive and potentially dangerous treatment without any evidence that the potential harm these treatments may cause are outweighed by the potential benefits involved in reducing the risk of passing on HIV infection.

Routine testing for HIV as discussed here necessarily puts pressure on pregnant women to be tested. In addition, whatever safeguards are put in place there are likely to be instances where routine testing of pregnant women puts pressure on those who test positive to accept

[13] Newell and Peckham, 'Risk factors for vertical transmission'.
[14] European Collaborative Study, 'Risk factors for mother-to-child transmission of HIV-1', *Lancet* **339** (1992): 1007–12.

certain 'treatments' even in some cases including abortion.[15] Other groups in society may justifiably argue that their right to remain in ignorance be respected as it is clearly possible to remain in ignorance of one's HIV status without causing harm to others. But, if it can be shown that routine testing of pregnant women for HIV is likely to prevent great harm to resulting children, then this would appear to be a compelling argument in favour of routine HIV testing for pregnant women.

At present, evidence regarding the effects on vertical transmission rates of Zidovudine use and delivery by caesarean section is not only inconclusive, but also incomplete. In addition the long-term effects of Zidovudine use during pregnancy and after birth on the woman and any resulting child are yet to be discovered. At best, the evidence suggests that women could reduce the risk of vertical transmission from around a 25 per cent chance to an 8 per cent chance, but the possibility is not yet ruled out that these 'risk-reducing' measures may not be effective and may prove detrimental to the health of both mother and child.

It is also difficult to make a strong case that great harm is likely to be avoided if HIV-positive women opt for a termination. A child born to an HIV-positive mother is more likely to be born uninfected than infected. Statistics suggest that the likelihood (at least in Europe) is that for each five children born to HIV-positive mothers, four will be uninfected and the fifth would be likely to live for a number of years without illness. Even in the light of these relatively optimistic statistics, there will be some who still conclude the harm likely to be caused by an HIV-positive woman giving birth to a child is such that even termination of pregnancy is a preferable option. However, evidence suggests that a positive HIV-test result has little effect on the decision-making of pregnant women with a majority of women who are aware of their HIV-positive status continuing with their pregnancy.[16] Studies show fewer than 10 per cent of HIV-positive

---

[15] There is a great deal of evidence of pressure put on pregnant women who have received a positive HIV-test result as a result of voluntary testing for HIV to terminate their pregnancy. See e.g. Marge Berer, *Women and HIV/AIDS: An International Resource Book* (London: Pandora Press, 1993) in which she cites personal accounts and the 1987 recommendations of the American College of Obstetrics and Gynecology that 'infected women should be encouraged not to become pregnant and should be provided with appropriate family planning assistance, sometimes including the option of abortion.'

[16] F. D. Johnstone, R. P. Brettle, L. R. MacCallum, J. Mok, J. F. Peutherer, and S. Burns, 'Women's knowledge of their HIV antibody state: its effect on their decision

women choose to terminate their pregnancy. Even where women decide to terminate their pregnancy as a consequence of a positive HIV test they more often than not go on to have a subsequent pregnancy within a year that they do not terminate.[17]

Conclusions

We have seen that most of the hypotheses which can be adduced for routine testing of pregnant women, however plausible they may at first appear, do not stand up to close scrutiny. While it is possible that routine testing may enable some individuals to make more informed decisions about their futures, and it is also feasible that an increase in information about transmission routes and numbers infected with HIV would be useful to epidemiologists, public health departments, and health care providers, what is not clear is why these hypotheses should favour the routine testing of pregnant women specifically, rather than other, or all groups in society. If increasing the information available to individuals and other concerned bodies is deemed such a positive advantage in the fight against HIV/AIDS that it is thought to compensate for the infringements of autonomy involved, surely this justification, if accepted, would not only support the routine testing of pregnant women but also the routine testing of all members of society. Thus, unless we are prepared to advocate the routine testing of *all* individuals, then justifications on these grounds cannot be used as reasons for introducing a policy of routine HIV testing of pregnant women. The only possible justification for the routine testing of pregnant women for HIV which remains is that which focuses on the benefits of such testing to the children born of these women. But is routine HIV testing really likely to benefit these children?

Routine testing of homosexual men and other groups is normally rejected on the grounds that the evidence available does not suggest

whether to continue the pregnancy', *British Medical Journal* **300**/6 (1990): 23–4; P. A. Selwyn, R. J. Carter, E. E. Schoenbaum, *et al.*, 'Knowledge of HIV antibody status and decision to continue or terminate pregnancy among intravenous drug users', *Journal of the American Medical Association* **261** (1989): 3567–71.

[17] P. Selwyn *et al.*, 'Knowledge of HIV antibody status'; A. Sunderland, H. Minkoff, J. Handte, G. Moroso, and S. Landesman, 'The impact of HIV serostatus on reproductive decisions of women', *Obstetrics and Gynecology* **79**/6 (June 1992): 1027–31.

that the benefits of such a policy are likely to be such that they justify compromising autonomy in this way. While routine testing may increase the numbers of those who are aware of their HIV positivity, such a policy is likely to prove unhelpful for individuals, and perhaps counter-productive for the future of HIV prevention. However, suppose a cure, or a very effective treatment was made available. It is only then that routine testing of identifiable homosexual men would not seem to be so abhorrent.

Similarly, if it could be shown that antenatal treatments existed that would be likely to prevent great harm to the resulting child if the status of the mother had been known, then it might be that a policy of routine antenatal HIV testing could be justified on these grounds. Yet, at the present time, with treatments, and knowledge about the effects of these treatments limited, it would appear that, even if routine testing identified all HIV-positive pregnant women, there is no compelling evidence to suggest that this would prevent great harm to the resulting child. HIV-positive women are likely to go ahead and have children, even when aware of their own HIV-positive status, and the possible harms and benefits of the 'risk-reducing' treatments currently available have not yet been clarified.

A policy of routine testing of groups for HIV involves the testing of individuals without their explicit consent. The routine testing of any group is likely to entail a number of undesirable consequences, including serious infringements of autonomy. If we accept that it is not justifiable to routinely test homosexual men without strong evidence that such a policy would be clearly beneficial, and if we agree that no clear evidence exists that routine testing of a pregnant woman is likely to be of overriding benefit to either the woman or her future child, then just as we would reject routine testing for other groups, we should likewise reject the routine testing of pregnant women.

I am not suggesting that antenatal HIV testing should be rejected altogether. What I am suggesting is that a policy of routinely *offering* HIV testing as part of antenatal care would be a preferable option to the routine HIV testing of pregnant women. Routinely *offering* an HIV test to pregnant women may not produce as large an increase in the numbers of women aware of their HIV status as routine testing might, but it would, nevertheless, enable the identification of a good number of HIV-positive women, and without infringing their autonomy.

If conclusive evidence existed that the testing of pregnant women for HIV leads, necessarily, to genuine and significant benefits for these women and their future children, then, but only then, might we say that we have a strong case for supporting a policy of routine testing of pregnant women. But we can hardly justify this inherently coercive policy in the absence of such evidence. Such evidence remains elusive. And even if such evidence were discovered, I would still counsel extreme caution.

16

Who Should Know about My HIV Positivity and Why?

HETA HÄYRY

Suppose that I am HIV positive, in other words, that my blood contains traceable antibodies to the human immunodeficiency virus, which in its turn is the causative agent of the acquired immune deficiency syndrome, AIDS. Suppose, further, that so far I am unaware of the fact, and so is everybody else. The questions that I propose to answer in this chapter are: 'Who should know about my HIV positivity?', and 'Why?'

Who Has an Interest in the Knowledge?

There are five groups of people who may want, or need, to know about my HIV positivity. First, it can be reasonably argued that I myself have an interest in the knowledge. Individuals often want to be aware of all the important aspects of their health status, and it is undoubtedly an important aspect of my condition that I have contracted the virus which is the causative agent of the fatal immune deficiency syndrome.

Second, people with whom I come in close physical contact may wish to know about my HIV positivity. These people include, primarily, my sex partners, those with whom I share syringes and needles as an intravenous drug user, and individuals to whom I donate or sell my organs, cells, or other body tissues. This category can also be extended to my team-mates and opponents in sports which may involve bleeding, the nurse's aides, nurses, doctors, surgeons and

My thanks are due to Felicity Kjisik, Lecturer in English, University of Helsinki, for revising the language of the chapter.

dentists who cater for my health care needs, members of my family, my friends, and my professional colleagues, fellow workers, and clientele.

Third, the knowledge concerning my HIV positivity can be of use to individuals and groups with whom I have made contracts, agreements, or economic arrangements which entail legal rights or obligations. This category accommodates at least my employers, employees, insurance companies, and business associates. At a more general level, other employers and the insurance trade at large may have an interest in knowing about my HIV positivity, since statistical data concerning the prevalence of the virus among various social, ethnic, and genetic subgroups can provide good grounds for economic calculations.

Fourth, statistical information regarding the prevalence of the virus, as well as individualized data identifying its carriers including myself, can be of interest to those who have undertaken to prevent citizens from inflicting harm on themselves or on others. The public health authorities, who all over the world have assumed the responsibility for preventing diseases in the population, can argue that they should normally be allowed to know about my HIV positivity. Furthermore, there are exceptional circumstances in which the public authorities in the fields of education, law enforcement, and legal corrections can claim that the knowledge concerning my positive HIV status would further the goals set for their work.

Fifth, and finally, some people seem to think that they should be allowed to know about my HIV positivity even if none of the foregoing criteria is fulfilled, simply because they or someone they feel responsible for could encounter me in their daily lives, for instance, in the street, in a restaurant, or in a crowded bus.

Since the interest that individuals and groups have in my health status is based on different motives in each category, the cases which can be made for and against disclosing the information vary considerably in strength.

On What Grounds?

As regards the justification of the disclosure, there are three types of argument which ought to be considered. First, prudential arguments are based on the long-term self-interest of the individuals themselves.

If the disclosure of my HIV status is likely to promote my own future well-being, prudence dictates that I should accept it. Similarly, if precise knowledge concerning my medical condition would be genuinely profitable to some other people, for instance, my business associates, then they would have prudential reasons for trying to acquire the information.

Second, moral arguments demand that we do what is right and avoid what is wrong. There are, of course, a variety of ethical theories which all define the right and the wrong in their own particular ways. But it is quite sufficient for my present purpose to focus on three traditional moral views, namely negative utilitarianism, pure deontology, and virtue ethics. According to negative utilitarianism, it is always undesirable and prima-facie morally impermissible to inflict suffering on sentient beings. The overall rightness and wrongness of actions depends on the total net balance of suffering produced by the various action alternatives. Pure deontology, in its turn, states that it is always right to perform one's duty, and wrong deliberately to neglect one's obligations. Virtue ethicists challenge both these action-oriented views by emphasizing the significance of personal integrity and character traits which tend to contribute to the goodness of the individual's life as a whole.

The third type of argument which can be applied to the disclosure of my HIV status concerns legality and socio-political expediency. It is held in most liberal societies that the actions of individuals should not be restricted by the public authorities unless the actions in question are liable to cause injury or severe offence to other people. In more traditional countries, legal regulations are often founded on ancient laws, prevailing customs, and religious ideas. Due to these differences, the outcome of legal arguments varies strongly from one jurisdiction to another.

Should I Know?

My prudential obligation to know that I am HIV positive has been defended by appeals to medical expertise, but it has also been undermined on medical and psychological grounds.[1] Some physicians

[1] In all the factual matters concerning HIV and AIDS, the reader is referred to the following articles and their bibliographies: M. Häyry and H. Häyry, 'AIDS and a small North European country—A study in applied ethics', *International Journal of*

have argued that individuals who are HIV positive should find out about their condition as quickly as possible, because those who are aware of their infection can protect themselves better than those who are unaware of the fact. During the symptomless incubation period of HIV infection, the length of which can apparently extend from years to decades, the only way to slow down the progress of the disease is to avoid other, more minor, infections. According to some medical authorities, exposure to such minor infections can make the carrier of the virus more prone to develop full-blown AIDS.

The medical objection against this line of argument is that since there is no actual cure to full-blown AIDS, nor to the early stages of the condition, the benefits of knowing about one's HIV positivity remain marginal. Even granting that I could postpone my death for a while by avoiding additional viruses and infections, the knowledge would not offer much consolation, as it would not help me to rid myself of the impending illness. On the contrary, experts have maintained that the psychological effects of the disclosure can be quite devastating. The knowledge about one's own HIV infection, so it has been said, causes anguish and suicidal thoughts in the individuals in question, diminishes the value of the individual's life, and is likely to destroy all human relationships between the carriers of the virus and their families, relatives, and friends. Many people have committed suicide when they have learned that 'their prospect is continuing infectivity to others, as well as a chance of progression to death or presenile dementia.'[2] The case for my prudential duty to know about my own HIV positivity seems to be, then, less than conclusive.

Seen from the moral point of view, however, the situation is drastically different. It can be argued that those who know about their HIV positivity are less prone to pass on the virus to others through sex and through donating blood or other body tissues. If this argument is valid, negative utilitarians can recommend the disclosure on the ground that it is likely to prevent suffering, and deontological moralists because it is presumably our duty not to inflict harm on others. Virtue ethicists, in their turn, can hold that persons of

---

Applied Philosophy 3/3 (1987): 51–61; H. Häyry and M. Häyry, 'AIDS now', *Bioethics* 1/4 (1987): 339–56; M. Häyry and H. Häyry, 'AIDS, society, and morality—A philosophical survey', *Philosophia* 19/4 (1989): 331–61; H. Häyry, 'HIV and the alleged right to remain in ignorance', in C. Peden and J. K. Roth (eds.), *Rights, Justice, and Community* (Lewiston, New York: Edwin Mellen Press, 1992): 165–75.

[2] E. S. Searle, 'Knowledge, attitudes, and behaviour of health professionals in relation to AIDS', *Lancet* (3 Jan. 1987): 28.

integrity should not be involved in any kind of self-deception, and should not, therefore, deliberately overlook facts regarding their own health status. All major ethical theories seem to assert that I have at least a prima-facie moral obligation to know about my HIV status.

The prima-facie duty to know does not, however, necessarily justify the enforcement of the obligation by legal sanctions. Fear, suspicion, and discrimination make it, in most parts of the world, imprudent for HIV-positive persons to reveal their condition, and this undermines their initial duty—and even ability—to protect others by sharing the information. Since legal coercion would, in the prevailing circumstances, probably cause more suffering than it would prevent, there are no compelling negative-utilitarian reasons for the regulation of the actions of HIV-infected persons. Deontologically speaking, the right of individuals to defend themselves against prejudice and discrimination reduces their responsibility for others to the point where the prima-facie duty to know becomes almost completely inapplicable. And as personal integrity cannot be imposed upon agents by external force, there are no virtue-ethical grounds for coercive legal sanctions. The prima-facie moral obligation to know about one's HIV infection does not, according to these ethical theories, seem to imply a corresponding legal duty.

Threats of Contagion

People with whom I come in intimate physical contact, and individuals who receive blood or organs donated by me, most often have every prudential reason to believe that they should know about my HIV positivity. The AIDS virus can be transmitted by sexual intercourse, by shared syringes and needles, and by donated body tissues, and it is obvious that at least my HIV-negative sex partners, fellow drug users, and receivers of my blood and organs would reasonably like to be aware of my condition. Similar observations can be extended to all those groups who are in some way exposed to my blood or other body fluids. These groups include, for instance, nurses' aides, nurses, physicians, surgeons, dentists, as well as family members and friends with whom I share household utensils, toilet equipment, and sanitary ware. The strength of the prudential case to know about my HIV positivity varies, of course, according to the degree of intimacy between myself and those who claim that they should be informed.

Medical professionals have sometimes argued that they should be allowed to know about the positive HIV status of their patients, because lack of knowledge prevents them from performing their moral duty, which is to see to it that people with various ailments are provided with the best treatment available for their condition. This argument is supported by the fact that the Hippocratic tradition requires physicians to benefit their patients and to contribute to their medical welfare.[3] On the other hand, however, the demand of beneficence has been undermined during the last decades by the introduction of the principle of autonomy to health care ethics. The principle of autonomy states that medical professionals ought to respect the self-determined, self-regarding choices of their informed and competent patients even if the choices in question are potentially harmful.[4] According to this principle, I am entitled to remain in ignorance concerning my own HIV positivity, whereas physicians are prohibited to seek the information on paternalistic grounds.[5]

Other-regarding moral considerations seem to suggest, however, that my condition should be disclosed to individuals who are exposed to the AIDS virus by my behaviour or by their personal or professional relationship to me. To contract the virus is a grave harm, and according to negative utilitarian precepts people should be allowed to decide for themselves whether they want to run the risk of contagion or not. Deontological theories, in their turn, usually condemn acts of lying as immoral, and thereby make it my duty to answer truthfully questions which concern my health status, including questions which concern my HIV positivity. The prima-facie duty to tell the truth presumably also binds other people who know about my condition, and myself even in situations where nobody has actually asked the crucial question but a failure to disclose the information could, nonetheless, be interpreted as an instance of dishonesty.

---

[3] On the physician's duty to benefit patients see e.g., T. L. Beauchamp and J. F. Childress, *Principles of Biomedical Ethics*, 2nd edn. (New York: OUP, 1983): ch. 5.

[4] Ibid.: ch. 3; H. Häyry, *The Limits of Medical Paternalism* (London: Routledge, 1991): ch. 7.

[5] Ibid. 154–5. *Cf.*, however, Häyry, 'HIV and the alleged right to remain in ignorance', and J. Harris, *The Value of Life: An Introduction to Medical Ethics* (London: Routledge & Kegan Paul, 1985): 208–9.

My utilitarian and deontological obligation to tell others about my HIV positivity is not significantly weakened by the fact that some of the people I have the duty to inform may be engaged in immoral or illegal activities at the time of the exposure to the virus. Although the intravenous use of certain drugs without medical authorization is against the law in many countries, the illegality does not annul my moral obligation to protect my fellow drug addicts. And although extramarital sexual practices may be considered immoral, this does not liberate the adulterers from their duty to protect their casual partners. In an impartial assessment of the strength of the obligation, the only relevant factors are the probability of contagion and the degree to which other people can be expected to protect themselves from it.

The prima-facie moral duty to inform others does not, however, automatically generate a civic obligation which could be justifiably enforced by legal sanctions. The case against coercive threats in this context is analogous with the defence of my right to remain in ignorance concerning my own HIV positivity. Although there are both utilitarian and deontological reasons for the disclosure, there are also, in the majority of cases, good grounds not to force people into telling about their health status. If those who are found HIV positive are discriminated against in everyday life, as they are in most Western countries today, their duty to inform others is considerably diminished. The law can only be brought to bear on the few cases where the risk of contagion is serious and those exposed to it cannot be expected to protect themselves. A family doctor, for instance, can be legitimately required to disclose my HIV positivity to my husband if she knows that our sex life is active and that I intend to conceal the risk from him. Similar legal requirements cannot, however, be extended to casual extramarital affairs, within which everybody can be expected to protect her or himself.[6]

Economic Harm

Economic considerations can make it desirable for employers, employees, business associates, and insurance companies to find out about my HIV positivity. Since the infection is a potential cause of

---

[6] For a more detailed discussion of this distinction, see Häyry and Häyry, 'AIDS, society, and morality': 349–51.

disabling illness and premature death, contracts and agreements which are made with me without knowing about my condition can be highly unprofitable. The economic harm that I could inflict on other people provides them with prudential reasons to claim that they should be informed. Furthermore, appeals to the threat of harm can be employed in negative utilitarian arguments against holding back information. According to negative utilitarian thinking, there is a prima-facie moral duty not to conceal facts which, if known, could prevent other people from involuntarily inflicting harm on themselves or on third parties.

The obligation to protect others against economic loss is, however, considerably less binding than the duty to safeguard innocent individuals against physical harm. All economic decision-making is based on risk calculation, and from the viewpoint of my employers, employees, and business associates my possible HIV positivity is only an unknown factor among other unknown factors in the cost-benefit analysis. Many people would, of course, like to ascertain my HIV status, but if their interest in the matter is based only on a desire to maximize their own economic profit, then my fear of discrimination alone provides, both morally and legally speaking, a sufficiently good reason not to satisfy their idle curiosity.

There are, to be sure, cases where the employer's interest in my health status is not purely economic, and cannot therefore be easily dismissed on account of my needs. Hospital administrators, for instance, can argue that they have no right, let alone a duty, to hire HIV-infected surgeons, physicians, or nurses, who could pose a fatal and unnecessary threat to the health of the patients. Similar arguments can be presented by all those employers who can show that the HIV positivity of their workers could endanger their clients. But in these cases the duty to abstain from inflicting harm, and the subsequent duty to reveal the result of the test, is owed directly to the patients or clients, not to the employers or the stockholders, although the latter groups may stand to lose from the concealment.

As regards insurance companies, their representatives can argue that if I do not report my HIV positivity when I apply for a life or health policy, other policyholders will be unjustly burdened by the unforeseen cost of my medical treatment and premature death. This argument can be interpreted as an appeal to the precepts of negative utilitarianism, in which case the economic harm possibly inflicted on others is outweighed by my own fear of discrimination. But the reference to injustice is also open to a deontological reading. Many deontological theories hold, in one form or another, the principle that I should not do unto others what I do not want to be done unto me. According to this interpretation, the crux of the argument could be that since I do not want other people to profit unfairly at my expense, I should not try to profit unfairly at their expense, either.

It is not normally considered unfair, however, to collect on an insurance when the terms of the policy are met. Insurance companies define the payments of life and health policies on the basis of epidemiological data, and the expenses caused by AIDS-related ailments and deaths should already have been accounted for, at a general level, in the fees. The only way to benefit unfairly at the expense of other policyholders would be to conceal deliberately one's HIV positivity from the underwriter. This type of deception could be partly counteracted by the insurers by asking the applicants whether they have been tested for HIV or not, and if they have, by denying them insurance unless they disclose the result of the test. But this solution, in its turn, would be problematic on negative utilitarian grounds. Individuals who are aware of their own HIV positivity can protect themselves and others better than those who are not, while the insurer's questions would provide individuals with an economic incentive to remain in ignorance. Despite the apparent unfairness of concealing the information, then, the wisdom and utility of forced disclosure can well be questioned.

Public Harm

Public health authorities can claim that they should know about my HIV positivity, because they are responsible for protecting the society at large from an HIV pandemic, and because the success of their efforts depends on the availability of epidemiological data, including the knowledge concerning my HIV status. In the framework of negative utilitarianism, this argument can be seen as an appeal to the harm indirectly inflicted on other people by my denial to reveal my HIV positivity. A deontological reading of the argument could state that since I would not like other people to undermine public health programmes by concealing personal medical information, I should probably not engage myself in such reprehensible behaviour, either.

The indirect harm referred to in the negative utilitarian thesis is in the majority of cases relatively remote but, in spite of that, morally significant. If there is a chance that the knowledge concerning my HIV positivity could help the public authorities to restrain the spread of AIDS, then it is, inescapably, my prima-facie moral duty to disclose the information. When it comes to overall moral duties and legally enforced obligations, however, the situation is different. The harm directly inflicted on HIV-positive persons by discrimination is, as a rule, more considerable than the injury that can be indirectly caused to HIV-negative individuals by medical secrecy.

Similar observations can be applied to the deontological argument which is based on the reciprocity of obligations. In an ideal world I would, no doubt, want individuals to do their best to help the public authorities in their attempt to prevent the spread of deadly diseases. But in an ideal world I would not have to consider the possibility of discrimination against individuals who are known to carry the AIDS virus. In the real world people do have a prima-facie moral duty to disclose their HIV positivity to the health authorities, but the obligation can be easily overturned by their legitimate desire to protect themselves and others from the ill effects of popular prejudice and unfair treatment.

A different line of argument which is, nonetheless, based on a concept of public harm has been supported by righteous citizens who believe that persons infected by HIV are morally dangerous sinners, liable to corrupt other people by their mere presence. These guardians of public morality have, from time to time, insisted on isolating all known carriers of the virus from the rest of society, either by physical constraints or by devices which reveal the infection even to their casual acquaintances. The moralistic attitudes have, especially during the early years of the AIDS epidemic, been prevalent among medical professionals and lay persons alike.[7] The Chief Medical Doctor of the Infectious Disease Section, Department of Health Services in Sacramento, for instance, has been reported to announce in one case that unless the directives regarding sexual contact given by the department are carefully followed, the authorities will quarantine the patient's home 'by posting a placard at his residence which indicates that a person with a communicable disease which can be transmitted by intimate contact resides in this

---

[7] By the early years of the AIDS epidemic, I mean the first half of the 1980s. See ibid. 331–3.

household'.[8] This official statement, which was made nearly a decade ago, would probably be condemned by today's public authorities in the West, but it would still be favoured by many persons in the street.

The moralists who want my HIV positivity to be publicly displayed seem to hold the mistaken belief that only certain groups of people, presumably homosexual males and intravenous drug addicts, can be infected by the virus. It would not make much sense, from their viewpoint, to quarantine newborn babies or celibate persons who have contracted the virus through HIV-positive blood products, as these individuals can hardly be considered a threat to public morality or the common good. It seems, in fact, that the moralistic zeal is founded on irrational fears and aversions rather than on any genuine regard for the good of society.

Who Should Know?

Who, then, should know about my supposed HIV positivity, and why? The answer can be divided into three parts.

Prudentially speaking, all those who can be harmed by my condition, either physically or financially, should try to obtain the information. I myself am an exception to this rule, since the knowledge does not necessarily improve my life-quality.

Seen from the ethical viewpoint, I should probably find out about my infection, since I have a prima-facie moral duty to protect others from harm, and the awareness is known to make people take this duty seriously. In addition, morality also dictates that I have a prima-facie obligation to reveal my HIV positivity to individuals I might infect, to economic associates I might otherwise wrong, and to public authorities who can use the information to prevent the spread of the disease.

But these prima-facie moral duties usually fail to generate overall obligations which could be justifiably enforced by legal sanctions. Due to the constant threat of discrimination, I am in most cases entitled to protect myself by concealing my positive HIV status from others. The only conceivable legal duty that I can have in this context is the duty to inform individuals whom I could infect but who cannot be expected to protect themselves unless they know about my infection.

---

[8] M. A. Somerville, 'Structuring the legal and ethical issues raised by AIDS', in A. Lloyd (ed.), *Proceedings of the Conference AIDS: Social Policy, Ethics and the Law* (Monash: Centre of Human Bioethics, 1986): 31; 45 n. 31.

17

Is There a Right to Remain in Ignorance of HIV Status?

CHARLES A. ERIN

> The ground for taking ignorance to be restrictive of freedom is
> that it causes people to make choices which they would not have
> made if they had seen what the realization of their choices
> involved.

A. J. Ayer

A recurring question—philosophically speaking, one of the most interesting—in the discussion of issues related to testing and screening for HIV is 'do people have a right to remain in ignorance of their HIV status?'[1] Those who assume (often without question) the existence of a right to remain in ignorance seem to think along something like the following lines: non-voluntary testing for HIV is unethical—it is morally wrong to test an individual against her will, without her prior fully informed consent; this being so, we may deduce that individuals hold a right not to be tested; the right not to be tested is equivalent to a right to remain in ignorance of HIV status. Such a line of reasoning is intuitively attractive and, at this superficial level, sounds plausible, but, as I will show, the argument proceeds far too swiftly.

---

[1] See e.g. Heta Häyry, 'HIV and the alleged right to remain in ignorance', in Creighton Peden and John K. Roth (eds.), *Rights, Justice, and Community* (Lewiston: Edwin Mellen Press, 1992): 165–75; Heta Häyry, *The Limits of Medical Paternalism* (London: Routledge, 1991): 149–55; Brenda Almond, 'Introduction: war of the world', in Brenda Almond (ed.), *AIDS: A Moral Issue—The Ethical, Legal and Social Aspects* (Basingstoke: Macmillan, 1990): 12–14; Roger Crisp, 'Autonomy, welfare and the treatment of AIDS', in B. Almond, *AIDS: A Moral Issue*, 70, 76–7. See also e.g. Rebecca Bennett, 'Should We Routinely Test Pregnant Women for HIV?' and Heta Häyry, 'Who Should Know about My HIV Positivity and Why?', Chs. 15 and 16 in this volume.

The Right to Know

One can approach the question of the right to remain in ignorance from a number of directions. It is my intuition that one of the most productive ways of addressing the question is from the basis of the right to know. If we allow, as I think most would, that I have a right to know my HIV status where it is known by another, can I simultaneously hold a *right* to remain in ignorance of my HIV status? Or can I simultaneously be under a *duty* to know my HIV status?

Surely, the right to remain in ignorance and the duty to know are mutually exclusive: if a person is under a duty to know, it would seem illogical to attribute to him also a right to remain in ignorance. Thus, if I can show that, in certain circumstances, a person *is* under a duty to know his HIV status,[2] I will have shown that, *in these circumstances*, this person cannot hold a right to remain in ignorance. I will have shown, at least, that if the right to remain in ignorance does exist, it cannot exist as a 'general' right,[3] possessed by all those who can possess rights; rather, it must be a 'special' right, a right which relies heavily on circumstances for its grounding.[4]

Let me start with some basic observations. Rights are generally taken to be grounds for the imposition of duties upon others.[5] This implies that, whatever else a right may involve, it will involve a Hohfeldian[6] claim on the part of the right-holder. If, for the moment,

---

[2] If the individual's HIV status is not known, this will imply he is under a duty to discover his HIV status, i.e. to undergo an HIV test.

[3] Which is how the right is normally viewed by those who accept its existence.

[4] By which I mean that, if this right exists, it must be a right which depends on context for its ascription—to this extent, it is quasi-contractual in nature, and is not, therefore, a 'natural', or 'human' right. Here, I am drawing on the distinction (between 'general' and 'special' rights) developed by H. L. A. Hart in 'Are there any natural rights?', *Philosophical Review* **64** (1955): 175–91.

[5] See e.g. Joseph Raz, 'On the nature of rights', *Mind* **93** (1984): 199; or Alan Gewirth, *Reason and Morality* (Chicago: University of Chicago Press, 1978): 104.

[6] W. N. Hohfeld, *Fundamental Legal Conceptions as Applied in Judicial Reasoning*, edited by W. W. Cook (New Haven: Yale University Press, 1919; repr. 1966). I do not have the space here to give a review, let alone an analysis of Hohfeld's acclaimed classification of fundamental legal conceptions. However, I will endeavour to ensure that, for readers unfamiliar with Hohfeldian nomenclature, the contexts within which I place those of the eight terms that I use will provide sufficient sense for the purposes of this chapter. There is an abundant literature dealing with Hohfeld, but those interested could do little better than look to L. W. Sumner's most lucid exposition in his *The Moral Foundation of Rights* (Oxford: Clarendon Press, 1987): ch. 2.

we work with this simple[7] view of rights—as claims which impose correlative duties on another or others—we seem to obtain the following picture, and let us confine ourselves to consideration of two-party relations (which represent the paradigm in any case). Say Blue knows Red's HIV status. If Red holds the right to know against Blue, Blue is under a duty to apprise Red of his (Red's) HIV status.

'Mandatory rights'

Joel Feinberg points to the special case of 'mandatory rights',[8] where the right to do x coincides with the duty to do x. It is the possibility of just such a coincidence between the content of a right and the content of a duty which I wish to explore, the possibility that a person might simultaneously hold a right to know and be under a duty to know. In normal usage, a person who holds a right is thereby put in a normatively advantageous position, and to be under a duty is usually thought of as (morally) burdensome. Generally, when we encounter examples of mandatory rights, we are able to counter our misgivings as to their analytical rigidity—the term 'mandatory right' itself has the air of an oxymoron—by observing that the duty concerned in some way places the duty bearer in a position of advantage, or, put more plainly, the duty is in the duty bearer's own good. In Feinberg's own words:

[W]hen we use the language of rights in this way to refer to duties, we do so because we think that some of our duties are so beneficial that we can make *claim* against others to provide the opportunity for, and to abstain from interference with, our performance of them.[9]

We see this in, for example, a child's right to attend school. Here we do not have to work too hard to portray the coincident duty to attend school as of advantage to the child. However, reverting to the previous example, if Red not only holds a right to know his HIV status, but is simultaneously under a duty to know his HIV status, it is more difficult to envisage this duty as normatively advantageous for Red.

---

[7] And, as it turns out, rather simplistic.
[8] Joel Feinberg, *Rights, Justice and the Bounds of Liberty: Essays in Social Philosophy* (Princeton: Princeton University Press, 1980): 157–8.
[9] Ibid. 157.

'Half-liberties'

Looking at this situation from Blue's viewpoint, and taking it for granted that a rule system will not demand and simultaneously prohibit the performance of some act,[10] we can say that if Blue is under a duty (correlative to Red's right against her to know his HIV status) to apprise Red of his HIV status, then Blue must be free to fulfil this duty. Borrowing again from Feinberg,[11] we can say that Blue has a resultant 'half-liberty' to inform Red. This notion of half-liberties is worth dwelling on a while. As L. W. Sumner recognizes, a Hohfeldian liberty constitutes, simply, a deontic permission.[12] There is thus a 'departure from ordinary usage [which] lies in the fact that the Hohfeldian liberty does not guarantee any choice among alternative options, since having the liberty to do something is compatible with lacking the liberty not to do it.'[13]

Now, consider the four statements P, Q, R, and S below, where Green and Yellow are two persons and x is a given act:

P: Green has no duty to Yellow to x.
Q: Green has no duty to Yellow not to x.
R: Green has a liberty with respect to Yellow to x.
S: Green has a liberty with respect to Yellow not to x.

If statements P and Q are true, then Green has the two logically distinct liberties itemized in statements R and S respectively. Following Feinberg, we may say that R and S each represent a *'half*-liberty', and where P and Q are true simultaneously, that R + S (where '+' indicates the conjunction of the two statements) constitutes a *'full* liberty'. This full liberty, supporting as it does a choice among available options with no normative restrictions, captures more nearly the intuitive notion of a liberty.

To summarize, an agent must be at liberty to do that which she has a duty to do; the agent cannot, of course, be at liberty not to do what she has a duty to do. In terms of half-liberties, if I have a duty to do something, I must have the half-liberty to do it; but if I do have a duty to do it, I cannot be free not to do it; and, if I do not have the half-liberty not to do it, I cannot have the full liberty to do it or not to do it as I choose. As we shall see, under one theory of rights, this has great significance.

[10] A fair demand of any rule system.
[11] Feinberg, *Rights, Justice and the Bounds of Liberty*.
[12] Sumner, *Moral Foundation of Rights*: 26.   [13] Ibid.

A 'bare' duty to know?

Can a person be under a duty to know that which she has no right to know? It would be a particularly mystifying, and likely unfair state of affairs which allowed Red to be under a duty to know his HIV status but did not permit Blue, the person who holds this information, the freedom to tell him—indeed, common sense suggests that Blue should be not only at liberty to tell Red, but should be under a duty to do so. However, we do not hold duties *against* other persons.[14] In normal usage, both everyday and technical, we hold *rights* against others, and are under duties *to* others. Our duties do not, in any readily intelligible sense, obligate others. It is therefore difficult to see how Red's duty to know can muster, of its own resources, a claim to know which will entail Blue being under a duty to tell.

By strong implication, it begins to look as though Red's duty to know may not exist in isolation of Red's right to know, as strange as this may sound. At the very least, Red's fulfilment of his duty to know is heavily reliant on a *claim* to know against Blue—which Red's right to know must incorporate for it to be a right. Assuming Blue has a *full* liberty in regard of supplying the information to Red, Red's successful discharge of his duty to know is jeopardized if Blue is not under a duty to inform Red of his HIV status; in the absence of this duty on Blue, Red leans necessarily, but perilously, upon Blue's beneficence or whim.

As we have seen, an agent's duties are grounded in the claims of *others*. A duty which relies so crucially on *a right of the duty bearer* seems to go against the grain of rights talk, and the analytical credentials of the duty to know are, to this extent at least, thrown into question. However, I will now attempt to show that I have not been barking up the wrong tree to this point.

---

[14] Except, *perhaps*, in a sense again attributable to Feinberg. When discussing mandatory rights, Feinberg writes:

> [T]he rights in question are best understood as ordinary duties with associated half-liberties rather than ordinary claim-rights with associated full liberties, but . . . the performance of the duty is presumed to be so beneficial to the person whose duty it is that he can *claim* the necessary means from the state and noninterference from others as *his* due. Its character as claim is precisely what his half-liberty shares with the more usual (dictionary) rights and what warrants his use of the word 'right' in demanding it [emphasis in the original]. (*Rights, Justice and the Bounds of Liberty*)

The choice theory of rights

On one particular view of rights, that of the choice theory,[15] an essential element in the holding of a right is the element of control afforded the right-holder. That is to say, the right-holder should be free to maintain a claim or to waive it (thereby abrogating the correlative duty borne by the object of the right)—this element of control being provided by Hohfeldian powers. It is thus tempting to view the right to know and the right to remain in ignorance as two aspects of the same right. If I have the right to know an item of information, *x*, then some other person or persons must be under a correlative duty to apprise me of *x*. If, however, I have the (half-) *powers*[16] necessary to afford me control over that right, then it seems to follow that I may voluntarily waive the claim to know, so abrogating the correlative duty. And in so doing, effectively I am empowered to remain in ignorance of *x*. And this is an important distinction, for it suggests that the so-called 'right' to remain in ignorance may not exist as a *right*: it is more plausible to suppose that there might exist a *power* or, more accurately, a *half*-power to remain in ignorance which constitutes an integral element of the right to know.

Core and periphery

It is now common to distinguish between 'liberty-rights' and 'claim-rights', the former often being taken as intimately related to the choice conception of rights under discussion, and the latter similarly linked to the interest conception (see below). A helpful way of illuminating the difference between these two kinds of rights is to consider the useful distinction drawn by Carl Wellman between the core of a right and its periphery.[17] The core defines the content of the right and its 'scope', that is its subject and object. A liberty-right is a right to perform some act or not as one chooses and thus has as its core a full liberty. A claim-right is a right that some other performs some act and so has at its core a claim. The periphery of a right contains any additional elements necessary for the protection of its core.

[15] Propounded by H. L. A. Hart in his 'Are there any natural rights?'.

[16] As with liberties, powers can be half- or full. Holding a half-power to affect a given normative relation is compatible with not having a power not to affect it. An agent has a full power when she can either affect or not affect a given relation.

[17] Carl Wellman, *A Theory of Rights: Persons under Laws, Institutions, and Morals* (Totowa, NJ: Rowman & Allanhead, 1985): 81 ff.

Thus the periphery of a liberty-right includes a 'protective perimeter' of claims, powers, immunities, etc., and that of a claim-right may include liberties, powers, immunities, etc.

A full liberty imposes no constraints on others and so a liberty-right must have a periphery and is complex by nature. Whilst a claim-right (according to the interest conception) need not have a periphery (since a claim imposes constraints on others), the majority of claim-rights will also be complexes of Hohfeldian elements. It is the core that unifies the right as any additional elements within the periphery will be associated with the core:

The picture . . . is of two different kinds of rights consisting of two different bundles of Hohfeldian elements. Both the distinction between the two kinds and the unity of each bundle is given by the core elements. A right of either kind is not a random assortment of Hohfeldian positions. Instead, it consists of nested layers of components, each added in order to enhance the integrity or efficacy of its predecessors.[18]

It is not difficult to see why liberty-rights may be confused with the choice conception of rights (and, as will become apparent in due course, why claim-rights are predominantly associated with the interest conception of rights). However, as Sumner demonstrates, while the choice conception is 'most at home with' liberty-rights, thanks to the choice guaranteed by the full liberty at their core, it can accommodate either variety of right (as can the interest conception).[19] For the choice conception to recognize claim-rights as standard cases of rights, says Sumner, 'the right-holder (in one way or another) [must have] powers over the duties entailed by the core claim plus the (full) liberty to exercise these powers. . . . Thus while the choice conception requires every right to contain a full liberty it need not insist that the liberty be located in the core . . . In effect, the choice conception treats claim-rights as assuring higher-order choices'.[20]

So far so good, or so it would seem. Wellman's distinction between the core and the periphery of a right facilitates an understanding of my proposal that the purported 'right' to remain in ignorance is not actually a right, but an element of a right, a half-power to remain in ignorance located within the periphery of the right to know. All this

---

[18] Sumner, *Moral Foundation of Rights*: 48–9. [19] Ibid.: ch. 2.
[20] Ibid. 49. (Similarly, the interest conception will recognize liberty-rights as long as claims are included in the periphery which protect the liberty at the core.)

according to the conception of rights afforded by the choice theory of rights, which is, after all, the correct way to view rights! However, I have not yet said what is the point of rights on the choice theory, and it is here where, I think, this approach runs into trouble. On the choice conception of rights, the *raison d'être* of rights is the protection and promotion of personal autonomy, and this gives us a picture of the right-holder as, in Sumner's words, 'the active manager of a network of normative relations connecting her to others'.[21] I would argue, though the constraints of space do not permit me to do so with any rigour here, that the possession, and thus the acquisition of relevant information is crucial to the maximal autonomy of any particular choice. This is key to the protection and development of the managerial abilities which the choice theory of rights demands of right-holders. And it is therefore difficult to see how a theory of rights which is so critically geared to the protection and promotion of autonomy—in turn, according to my view, crucially reliant on the possession of information—can, by its very constitution, permit the right to know to incorporate the half-power to remain in ignorance.[22]

Despite the result of analysis on the choice theory of rights (on the face of it, a paradoxical result), whether or not there exists a right or a half-power to remain in ignorance may be academic. Whilst all genuine rights impose correlative duties, it is possible for moral obligations to stand alone, in absence of a right to which they are correlative.[23] This being the case, if we can produce a compelling argument for the existence of an obligation to know such information as one's HIV status, and if it can be shown that the basis of such an obligation is, in some relevant sense, 'stronger' than the grounding of a right or power to remain in ignorance,[24] then we may have

[21] Sumner, *Moral Foundation of Rights*: 47.

[22] There is an analogy here with voluntary self-enslavement. See e.g. Joel Feinberg, *Harm to Self* (New York: OUP, 1986): 71–9; Robert Young, *Personal Autonomy: Beyond Negative and Positive Liberty* (London: Croom Helm, 1986): 72–4; and my *Persons and Bodies: Autonomy, Rights and Property*, in preparation.

[23] In this context, the asynonymy of the terms *duty* and *obligation* is significant. I reserve use of *duty* to describe those obligations which are correlative to rights, while *obligation* I take to refer to a wider moral concept. This is something I take up in my *Persons and Bodies: Autonomy, Rights and Property*, in preparation.

[24] This sounds like the language of utilitarianism, but the kind of moral analysis I have in mind merely requires that we admit that rights talk does not exhaust moral discourse. It might be that the existence of an obligation to know will fall out of a utilitarian calculus, but attaching precedence to such an obligation will likely rely on a deontological approach.

the basis for the introduction of something like a theory of 'obligations as trumps'.

With this in mind, let us explore the reasons why a person might wish to hold a right to remain in ignorance of his HIV status—inasmuch as rights are generally thought of as normatively advantageous, we may, with an appeal to common sense, expect that rights are devices which people wish to hold.[25]

The interest theory of rights

There are good reasons why a person may wish to know his HIV status. There are also, it can be said, good reasons why someone may wish to remain in ignorance of his HIV status. We can say, then, that people may *have an interest* in knowing their HIV status and that they may also *have an interest* in remaining in ignorance of their HIV status. This notion of having an interest is central to one particular and, it must be said, popular theory of rights. Put simply, on the interest theory of rights, if an individual's interest in x is a sufficient reason to hold others to be under a duty to protect that interest, that individual holds a right to x.

Psychological burden and discrimination

Reasons for not wishing to be apprised of one's HIV status would, it may be presumed, fall into two categories. First, there is a definite psychological *cost* attached to undergoing an HIV antibody test and psychological pressures associated with knowing one is HIV positive.[26] Second, those who are HIV positive or have AIDS are, even now, liable to be subjected to unfair discrimination—which will, of course, have a strong psychological element—ranging from interpersonal discrimination, for example the manifestation of prejudice in

---

[25] I will ignore here the implications of my contention that with rights come responsibilities, that rights are not simply positions of advantage, but have also a morally burdensome character. This is an idea which I work out fully in my *Persons and Bodies: Autonomy, Rights and Property,* in preparation.

[26] See e.g. British Psychological Society Special Interest Group on AIDS, *Counselling, HIV Testing and Behaviour Change*, consultative document prepared by the Special Interest Group on AIDS of the British Psychological Society (not paginated).

physical violence,[27] to societal discrimination in, for example, the provision of insurance.[28]

It has been accepted for some time that discrimination against those who are HIV positive or have AIDS is a major obstacle to the success of health policies aimed at the control of HIV transmission.[29] Indeed, in 1988 in the USA, a Presidential Commission came to the conclusion that discrimination was 'impairing this nation's ability to limit the spread of the epidemic'.[30] Theories of justice aside, then, we have strong, practical grounds for ensuring equal protection, concern, and respect for HIV-positive individuals and those with AIDS.[31] However, until such time as we achieve this, the threat of unfair discrimination remains a valid reason for a person's HIV status being private and a plausible reason for an individual wishing to remain in ignorance of his status. On the interest theory of rights, this might be taken as sufficient to establish the right.

Motivation for seeking a test

In a British study, McCann and Wadsworth report similar motivations for seeking an HIV antibody test as found in the USA:

(i) in order to get medical treatment for HIV; (ii) to make needed changes in lifestyle; (iii) to clarify an ambiguous medical condition; (iv) to inform sexual decision making; and (v) to relieve the psychological distress of not knowing one's HIV status.[32]

[27] See e.g. J. Mann, D. J. M. Tarantola, and T. W. Netter (eds.), *AIDS in the World* (Cambridge, Mass.: Harvard University Press, 1992): 769 ff.

[28] See Tom Sorrel and Heather Draper, 'AIDS and insurance', Ch. 14 in this volume. For a comprehensive investigation of anti-discrimination legal instruments (or the lack thereof) in Europe, see Council of Europe, Steering Committee for Human Rights, *Comparative Study on Discrimination against Persons with HIV or AIDS* (Strasbourg: Council of Europe, 1993), a study by the Swiss Institute of Comparative Law, Lausanne, Switzerland.

[29] Charles A. Erin and John Harris, 'AIDS: Ethics, justice and social policy', *Journal of Applied Philosophy* 10 (1993): 165; see also Ferdinand Schoeman, 'AIDS and privacy', in F. G. Reamer (ed.), *AIDS and Ethics* (New York: Columbia University Press, 1991): 241–2.

[30] *Report of the Presidential Commission on the Human Immunodeficiency Virus Epidemic* (Washington, DC: US Government Printing Office, 1988): 119.

[31] *Cf.* Erin and Harris, 'AIDS: Ethics, justice and social policy', *passim.*

[32] K. McCann and E. Wadsworth, 'The experience of having a positive HIV antibody test', *AIDS Care* 3 (1991): 45. The American reports to which McCann and Wadsworth refer are D. Ostrow *et al.*, 'Disclosure of HIV antibody status: behaviour and mental health correlates', *AIDS Education and Prevention* 1 (1989): 1–11, and K. Siegal, M. Levine, C. Brooks, and R. Kern, 'The motivations of gay men for taking or not taking the HIV antibody test', *Social Problems* 36 (1989): 307–11.

It is the last reason identified here which is of particular interest in the present discussion. There are psychological burdens involved both in knowing one is HIV positive (taken here to be a possible reason for wishing to remain in ignorance of HIV status) and in not knowing whether one is HIV positive (a motive for finding out one's HIV status). And the interest in finding out HIV status—the relief of this psychological distress—is an interest equally of those who are HIV positive but do not know it and of the 'worried well'.

A Consequentialist Approach

If a person is HIV positive, but does not know it, we may feel that the confirmation of his HIV status is academic: we could say that it would be 'better' for that person to enjoy life to the full while he has no symptoms and let the onset of symptoms signal confirmation of his HIV positivity. However, this is to ignore the serious consequences of a known HIV status for that person's interactions with others, and it is this factor in particular which validates adopting a consequentialist approach to the proposed right to remain in ignorance.

If we look to the potential consequences of respecting the right to remain in ignorance of HIV status, what result will the performance of a cost-benefit analysis (in the spirit of an utilitarian calculus) yield? Before attempting this, we should note two points. First, we are talking about *potential* costs and benefits, and will be dealing with predictions, and any result so yielded will likely suffer from wide margins of error, even when our predictions are informed. Second, I would contend that the utilitarian calculus is inimical to the concept of rights.[33] However, whilst such a calculation might lead us to draw conclusions about the existence or not of a right to remain in ignorance, what the calculation is more likely to reveal is whether or not a person—in a certain set of circumstances—is under a moral obligation to discover his HIV status, and since obligations may exist which are not duties correlative to rights, the calculation may have little or nothing to say in terms of *rights* talk.

[33] *Cf.* e.g. Leslie A. Mulholland, 'Rights, utilitarianism, and the conflation of persons', *Journal of Philosophy* **83** (1986): 323–40. But see also R. B. Brandt, 'Utilitarianism and moral rights', *Canadian Journal of Philosophy* **14**/1 (March 1984): 1–19; and Jeremy Waldron, 'Rights in conflict', *Ethics* **99**/3 (April 1989): 503–19.

Ignorance is bliss?[34]

With this in mind, let us nevertheless attempt to predict some possible real implications of fulfilment of the right. It could be said that the HIV-positive person who remains in ignorance has, on the one hand, obviated the psychological burden of knowing he is HIV positive until such time as the onset of symptoms reveals this information. During this intervening, asymptomatic period, the person carries on his life in his preferred manner and his choices and preferences are not affected by what some might term his 'death sentence'.[35]

However, this 'ignorance-is-bliss' approach falls down for some particularly cogent reasons. First, it could be countered that there may be an equal, perhaps greater, psychological burden associated with not knowing one's HIV status depending, for one thing, on one's perception of one's so-called 'at-risk' status. Second, assuming this person is complacent, or convinced, perhaps through denial, that he is not HIV positive, he is in a position to put the lives of others at risk. It is somewhat of a tragic irony that, because of the nature of some HIV-transmission modes, it is often those who one cares for most that one puts at (greatest) risk. Whilst it may be argued that, in principle, the (intrinsic) value of the life of a loved one should not be viewed as any greater or less than that of any other person, the concept of solidarity can be used to justify our showing a greater concern for those we love than for others, and considering how we would feel about endangering the very lives of *those we love* does push this general consideration into high relief.

Autonomy of the ignorant?

I have claimed above that to make genuinely autonomous choices one must first ensure one is fully in possession of the pertinent facts.[36] Even if we were prepared to accept a choice to remain in ignorance as an autonomous choice, I think we are forced to admit that this

---

[34] From Thomas Gray's *Ode on a Distant Prospect of Eton College*:
Where ignorance is bliss,
'Tis folly to be wise.

[35] It is generally accepted that this is a destructive way to view the effects on one's life of a positive test for HIV antibody, and the more enlightened would favour a positive approach as encapsulated in the phrase 'living with HIV'.

[36] This is the thinking behind informed consent doctrine in medical practice.

choice can be 'autonomous' only to the extent encompassed by the occurrent sense of autonomy, and that this choice actually undermines the moral agent's dispositional autonomy.[37] But it is this latter sense which gives such force to the protection and promotion of autonomy as a moral imperative.

If we are genuinely concerned to protect and promote personal autonomy, then we should ensure that, as far as is possible, we are apprised of any information which could influence our life decisions, that is any information which may have a significant bearing on our life plans. Thus, the doctor should inform the patient of a diagnosis of terminal cancer, and this disclosure should not be influenced by the opinion of relatives that, for example, 'the news will kill her'. Nobody, not even the patient herself, can know with certainty what the reaction to such news will be. What can be said is that such news may have far-reaching effects on the patient's plans for the future.[38] Thus, if I am told that it is unlikely I will live out this year, I may wish to attempt to accomplish in the short term many of my life goals which I had previously scheduled for the long term, there now not being a long term: I may wish to put my affairs in order and ensure to the best of my ability that, following my demise, my family will be protected from the legal trauma which often ensues from a person's death; I may wish to take the luxury holiday I had always promised myself; I may wish to spend my remaining days wallowing in self-pity; or I may wish to devote myself single-mindedly to the completion of my pet project in political philosophy which I had previously envisaged as the crowning achievement of a long career in academe.

There are two distinct aspects to remaining in ignorance of information germane to my decision-making. First, if, as I maintain, my choices cannot reasonably be termed autonomous if such information has not been taken into account in coming to them, then I am deluding myself if I believe such choices to be 'genuine' or 'authentic'. Whether an individual can be said to have behaved unethically by wronging himself (and no other) and whether, indeed, one *can* wrong oneself, are questions I will not address here.

---

[37] I follow here the distinction drawn by Robert Young. According to Young, the *occurrent* sense of autonomy refers to 'autonomy of the moment', while the focus of the *dispositional* sense is on the 'person's life as a whole'—Young, *Personal Autonomy*: 5.

[38] If one does not ignore or repress it, one can say, with some certainty, that this information *will* have such effects.

However, the second aspect is one which we cannot ignore and this involves the wronging and, possibly, harming of others.

Full disclosure facilitates autonomous choice, but, in at least many situations, full disclosure is an ideal. Indeed, the very notion of the autonomous management of one's life is itself idealistic. In reality, there will be many practical constraints on personal autonomy, and we may also identify certain theoretical limits to the autonomous choices which a person should be free to make. There is a sense in which the chief among these is an analogue of the principle of non-maleficence: we should be free to make autonomous choices so long as these choices do not wrong or harm others by, for example, undermining or vitiating *their* capacity for autonomous choice.[39]

The information which we share with others in our dealings with them is crucially important in deciding whether our autonomous choices will lead to their being wronged, and are thus unethical. Furthermore, in the current context, remaining in ignorance of our HIV status could lead us to acts which will put others at risk of harm. Manifestly, we cannot share information which we do not ourselves possess. If we are serious about not wronging others, and if we are serious about not causing harm to others, then it might seem that not only does there exist an obligation to know one's HIV status where it is known, but also there exists a moral obligation to discover one's HIV status where it is not known.[40] But we must be careful here not to ascribe this obligation *generally*. The common belief that we may act as we wish subject to the proviso that we do not harm or wrong others[41] admits of a more lenient interpretation in this context. If discovering one's HIV status was the only way of protecting others from harm or wrong at our hands in these circumstances, i.e. the only way of meeting the requirements of the proviso, then, yes, we would have justified the existence of a general obligation to know and denied the existence of the right to remain in ignorance. But it is not. One could behave ethically in ignorance of one's HIV status by behaving *as if one were* HIV positive and adopting all practices which

---

[39] It can be seen that the principle of respect for autonomy, usually viewed as purely advantageous to the individual, actually implies significant responsibilities.

[40] The coincidental implication of such a contention seems to be that in order not to wrong others we must not wrong ourselves (assuming that we can wrong ourselves and that undermining our own autonomy constitutes wronging ourselves).

[41] If what I have said about a causal link between information and autonomy is correct, *acting as we wish* in the absence of knowledge of our HIV status cannot, necessarily, be equated with *acting autonomously*.

are associated with responsible behaviour in this context.[42] Or we could abstain from all known 'risky' acts.[43] In reality, such behaviour in ignorance of HIV status would likely prove very difficult, and demanding of a high level of self-discipline. But perhaps it would be not much more difficult than if one actually did know one was HIV positive.

Conclusions

If my overarching moral consideration is the avoidance of wrong or harm to others which may result from my choices and consequent actions, in cases where I can reasonably ensure that no wrong or harm to others will come of my ignorance of my HIV status, then there seems to be no reason why I should be under a moral obligation to discover my HIV status. Clearly I *can*[44] remain in ignorance, but this does not necessarily entail that I have a right to do so, any more than it entails, of itself, that I act morally by doing so. On the basis of the consideration offered here, however, we may say that, in such circumstances, a person is morally at liberty to remain in ignorance of his HIV status.[45] However, where I am not prepared to act

---

[42] I am grateful to Rebecca Bennett for useful discussion of this point.

[43] There is yet another sense in which the obligation to know or find out my HIV status *might* be abnegated. Suppose that White is in a stable, monogamous relationship with Violet, and that White does not have sex with anybody other than Violet. White and Violet know that Violet is one of the rare individuals who is homozygous for the defective CKR-5 gene (having inherited two copies of the defective gene, one from each of her parents) and that she is thus protected from the sexual transmission of HIV 1—see R. Liu, W. A. Paxton, S. Choe, D. Ceradini, S. R. Martin, R. Horuk, M. E. MacDonald, H. Stuhlmann, R. A. Koup, and N. R. Landau, 'Homozygous defect in HIV-1 coreceptor accounts for resistance of some multiply-exposed individuals to HIV-1 infection', *Cell* **86** (Aug. 1996): 367–77. In such a case, the moral justification for White's obligation to discover his HIV status, even if he is not behaving as if he was HIV positive, appears, to a large degree at least, to be undermined. However, from my understanding of Liu *et al.*, the defect in CKR-5 may not provide protection against infection with HIV 1 via T-cell mediated routes, and nor does it necessarily provide protection against infection with HIV 2. It therefore seems that the obligation to know should be reinstated. I am grateful to Sally John for useful discussion of this point.

[44] 'Can' in an alethic sense.

[45] *Cf.* H. L. A. Hart, *Essays on Bentham: Jurisprudence and Political Theory* (Oxford: Clarendon Press, 1982): 173–4:

> Bentham . . . occasionally speaks as if a unilateral liberty were sufficient to constitute a liberty-right. On this footing a liberty-right to do an act would be compatible with, and indeed entailed by, an obligation to do it. The right-holder would not, as

as if I were HIV positive and cannot reasonably predict that I will not, by my actions, undermine another's autonomy or put her at a real risk of harm, I am under a moral obligation to discover my HIV status, and thus cannot claim a 'right' to remain in ignorance. The strong context sensitivity of the purported 'right' to remain in ignorance—if and where it exists—entails that it cannot be a general right which I possess by virtue of my qualification as a right-holder.

Postscript

I have deduced, more than argued, here that in circumstances where a person does not put others at risk of his harming or wronging them, this person may be morally at liberty to remain in ignorance of his HIV status. I must admit to some unease with this result, unease which, I suppose, follows from the problem I have identified with analysis on the choice theory of rights. If, as I maintain, there is a causal link between knowledge—especially knowledge about myself—and my autonomy, how can a theory of rights which has as its very basis the idea that rights exist to protect and promote autonomy allow me a right to remain in ignorance of information as crucially important to my self-development as my HIV status.

The deductive reasoning employed above does seem to suggest the existence of a 'special' right to remain in ignorance under certain, specific conditions. Nevertheless, as a choice theorist, I find this very difficult to accept, and the paradox, which a right to remain in ignorance implies, hard to tolerate.

in the case of a bilateral liberty, be free to choose whether to do an act or not; he would be at liberty to do an act only in the sense that he was not under an obligation not to do it. Bentham does not discuss the appropriateness or otherwise of extending the notion of rights to include unilateral liberty; *but it seems clear that a general extension to include all unilateral liberties would neither accord with usage nor be useful* [emphasis added].

Annexe

European Commission
Directorate General XII
Biomedicine and Health Research Programme (BIOMED 1)
and
Cooperation in Science and Technology with Central and
Eastern European Countries (PECO)

'AIDS: Ethics, Justice, and European Policy'

The Centre for Social Ethics and Policy
University of Manchester
United Kingdom

Summary of Conclusions and Recommendations

Conclusions

1. *The reciprocal relationship: an ethical framework for HIV/AIDS social policy*

1.1 There is a strong moral obligation to protect others from HIV infection.

1.2 If there is to be adherence to the principle of equal protection for all citizens then the State should take all reasonable steps to protect individuals with HIV and AIDS from discrimination and stigmatization.

1.3 There is a strong moral obligation to protect those with HIV and AIDS from discrimination.

1.4 When activities that pose a *significant* risk of infection cannot be or are not avoided there is a moral obligation on people who are or believe they may be HIV seropositive to warn anyone who is likely to be harmed by the omission of information which might enable them to protect themselves.

1.5   There is an obligation to protect oneself against infection, not least because of the relationship between self-protection and protection of others.

1.6   There is no general moral obligation to be tested in order to determine one's HIV serostatus.

2.   *Reciprocity of obligations: a legal framework?*

2.1   The European Community has adopted a policy in relation to HIV/AIDS which emphasizes the importance of respect for the rights of those who are, or may be, HIV seropositive.

2.2   Such a policy has also been endorsed by the Council of Europe, the body responsible for monitoring the European Convention on Human Rights.

2.3   Implementation of that policy has largely been left to the discretion of individual States.

2.4   States, and those institutions directly responsible for supply, have an obligation to act to ensure that supplies of blood and other body products are free of blood-borne diseases.

2.5   Failure to discharge such responsibilities entitles infected persons to compensation and, if there is evidence of flagrant disregard of the welfare of potential patients, criminal proceedings may be appropriate.

2.6   States have an obligation to safeguard the fundamental rights of persons who are or may be HIV seropositive. This necessarily involves protection of key positive rights such as rights to employment, housing, health care, and access to public facilities, as much as negative rights to autonomy, liberty, privacy, and confidentiality.

2.7   In general, negative rights are protected in most European States. Exceptionally, in all jurisdictions, either by virtue of legislation on communicable diseases or general principles of law, the risk to others is held to justify some modification of the rights of the individual.

2.8   Positive rights are less well protected. Legislation, on the French or British model, limiting discrimination on grounds of disability or health status looks to be the most promising means of giving substance to the rights of those who are or may be HIV seropositive.

2.9   The duty of care owed by one citizen to another in all European jurisdictions necessarily imposes a reciprocal obligation to safe-guard others from the risk of contracting HIV.

2.10 The health care professions have played and should continue to play a key role in setting standards for the exercise of that duty on the part of professionals.

2.11 It would be undesirable and impracticable to define that duty in relation to sexual conduct as a general duty to disclose actual or potential positivity.

2.12 The criminal law has been invoked to punish gross disregard of the legal duty to protect others.

3. *Recommendations*

3.1 To maximize the effectiveness of any social policy relating to HIV/AIDS the Council of Europe and the European Union must continue to develop a common, coordinated approach to the problem, and individual countries should be urged to coop-erate in this endeavour.

3.2 Anti-discrimination programmes, including legislation, should be implemented or where they are implemented maintained, in order to protect HIV seropositive individuals' access to employment, housing, health care, and education.

3.3 Education and the dissemination of information about HIV is an essential part of social policy on HIV/AIDS. An anti-discrimination component should be an integral part of any information and education programme.

3.4 In order to ensure that the conditions exist in Society to give due respect to the rights of HIV seropositive persons, consider-ation must be given to reviewing and repealing any existing legislation criminalizing, and thus stigmatizing, homosexual relationships.

3.5 The State's responsibility for public health requires that all fea-sible measures are implemented to ensure the safety of supplies of blood and other body products. Criminal and civil sanctions are appropriate where public officials or others responsible for such body products fail to discharge their responsibilities.

3.6 Condoms, needles, syringes, bleach, care, treatment, trials, and support should be readily accessible including to those in prison or in the armed services.

3.7 Legislation to criminalize the transmission of HIV or possibly transmissive acts is inappropriate and impractical. Therefore, the moral obligation to protect others from HIV infection should not generally be enforced through the criminal law.

3.8   New and specific legal sanctions should *not* be introduced in order to punish those who pass on HIV infection to others or those who do not disclose their HIV positivity to others who are likely to be at risk of infection.

3.9   Mandatory testing of individuals and groups is unlikely to be an effective way of limiting the HIV epidemic and may be counterproductive. Any existing legislation promoting mandatory testing should be repealed.

3.10   Confidential, voluntary testing with adequate counselling should be free and available to all.

3.11   Confidentiality is not an absolute in health care practice. There may be situations in which the risk of serious harm is so great and in which the persons at risk can be forewarned and so protected that disclosure is justified.

3.12   If breaches of confidentiality are sanctioned, then this fact and the circumstances in which breaches may occur should be publicized in advance.

3.13   Safeguards should be put in place to ensure as far as possible that confidences are broken only in extreme circumstances.

3.14   A moral obligation to disclose the HIV status of patients in order to protect another individual from infection should not be translated into a legal duty to disclose HIV status.

Bibliography

Aggleton, P., Homans, H., Mojsa, J., Watson, S., and Watney, S., *AIDS: Scientific and Social Issues—A Resource for Health Educators* (Edinburgh: Churchill Livingstone, 1989).

Almond, B. (ed.), *AIDS: A Moral Issue—The Ethical, Legal and Social Aspects* (Basingstoke and London: Macmillan, 1990).

Barre-Sinoussi, F., Cherman, J. C., Rey, F., Nugeyre, M. T., Chamaret, S., Gruest, J., *et al.*, 'Isolation of a T-lymphocyte retrovirus from a patient at risk for acquired immune deficiency syndrome (AIDS)', *Science* **220** (1983): 868–71.

Bartlett, J. G., 'Zidovudine Now or Later?', *New England Journal of Medicine* (1993): 329, 351–2.

Bayer, R., 'Screening and AIDS: The limits of coercive intervention', *Annals of the New York Academy of Sciences* **530** (1988): 159–62.

—— 'The Dual Epidemics of Tuberculosis and AIDS: Ethical and Policy Issues in Screening and Treatment', *American Journal of Public Health* **83** (1993): 649–54.

Beauchamp, T. L., and Childress, J. E. (eds.), *Principles of Biomedical Ethics*, 2nd edn. (New York and Oxford: OUP, 1983).

Beecher, H. K., 'Consent to clinical experimentation—myth and reality', *Journal of the American Medical Association* **195** (1966): 39.

Bennett, R., Erin, C.A., and Harris, J., *AIDS: Ethics, Justice and European Policy. Final Report to the European Commission* (Luxembourg: Office of Official Publications for the European Communities, 1998).

Berer, M., *Women and HIV/AIDS: An International Resource Book* (London: Pandora Press, 1993).

Bor, R., Millar, R., and Johnson, M., 'A testing time for doctors counselling patients before an HIV test', *British Medical Journal* **303** (1991): 905–6.

Boyd, K. M., 'HIV infection and AIDS: The ethics of medical confidentiality', *Journal of Medical Ethics* **18** (1992): 173–9.

Brandt, A. M., 'AIDS in Historical Perspective: Four Lessons from the History of Sexually Transmitted Diseases', *American journal of Public Health* **78**/4 (1988): 367–71.

Brazier, M., 'Patient autonomy and consent to treatment: the role of the law', *Legal Studies* **7** (1987): 169.

—— and Lobjoit, M. (eds.), *Protecting the Vulnerable: Autonomy and Consent in Health Care* (London: Routledge, 1991).

—— *Medicine, Patients and the Law*, 2nd edn. (London: Penguin, 1992).

Brazier, M., 'Rights and Health Care', in R. Blackburn Mansell (ed.), *Rights of Citizenship* (1993).

British Medical Association, 'HIV antibody testing: summary of BMA guidance', *British Medical Journal* **295** (1987): 940.

Brudney, K., and Dobkin, J., 'Resurgent Tuberculosis in New York City', *American Review of Respirational Diseases* **144** (1991): 745–9.

Centres for Disease Control, 'Zidovudine for the prevention of HIV transmission from mother to infant', *Morbidity and Mortality Weekly Report* **43** (1994): 285–7.

Di Clemente, R., 'The Emergence of Adolescents as a Risk Group for Human Immunodeficiency Virus Infection', *Journal of Adolescent Research* **5**/1 (Jan. 1990): 7–17.

Clavel, F., Guetard, D., Brun-Vezient, F., Chamaret, S., Rey, M., Santos-Ferreira, M. O., *et al.*, 'Isolation of a new human retrovirus from West African patients with AIDS', *Science* **233** (1986): 343–6.

Cohen, J., 'The HIV Vaccine Paradox', *Science* **264** (May 1994): 1072–4.

—— 'Clinical Trial Monitoring: Hit or Miss?', *Science* **264** (June 1994): 1534–7.

Concorde Co-ordinating Committee, 'Concorde: MRC/ANRS randomised double-blind controlled trial of immediate and deferred zidovudine in symptom-free HIV infection', *Lancet* **343** (1994): 871–81.

Connor, E., Sperlling, R., Gelber, R., *et al.*, 'Reduction of maternal infant transmission of HIV type 1 with Zidovudine treatment', *New England Journal of Medicine* **331** (1994): 1173–80.

Cooper, D. A., Gatell, J. M., Kroon, S., Clumeck, N., Millard, J., Goebel, F. D., *et al.*, 'Zidovudine in persons with asymptomatic HIV infection and CD4+ cell counts greater than 400 per cubic millimeter', *New England Journal of Medicine* **329** (1993): 297–303.

Corbitt, G., 'Early confirmation of HIV p24 antigenaemia in infants born of HIV-positive mothers', *Journal of Infection* **26** (1993): 367–70.

Corbitt, G., *et al.*, 'Effect of switching from first- to second-generation enzyme-linked immunosorbent assays on screening for human immunodeficiency virus antibody', *Serodiagnosis and Immunotherapy in Infectious Disease* **4** (1990): 217–20.

—— with D. J. Morris and E. Crosdale, 'Same-day testing for human immunodeficiency virus antibodies', *Journal of Virological Methods* **49** (1994): 367–70.

Corey, L. (ed.), *AIDS: Problems and Prospects* (New York: Norton Medical Books, 1993).

Daniels, N., *Seeking Fair Treatment: From the AIDS Epidemic to National Health Care Reform* (New York: OUP, 1995).

Daykin, C. D., 'The epidemiology of HIV infection and AIDS', *Journal of the Institute of Actuaries* **117** (1990): 51–95.

DeVita Jr, V. T., Hellman, S., and Rosenberg, S. A. (eds.), Curren, J., Essex, M., and Fauci, A. S. (associate eds.), *AIDS: Etiology, Diagnosis and Prevention*, 3rd edn. (Philadelphia: J. B. Lippincott, 1995).

Dunbar, S., and Rehm, S., 'On visibility: AIDS, deception by patients, and the responsibility of the doctor', *Journal of Medical Ethics* **18** (1992): 180–5.

Dworkin, G., *The Theory and Practice of Autonomy* (Cambridge: Cambridge University Press, 1988).

Dyson, A., 'The body of Christ has AIDS: Resurrection and Pastoral Theology', in G. Stanton and S. Barton (eds.), *Resurrection. Essays in Honour of Leslie Houlden* (London: SPCK, 1994): 165–76.

Edgar, H. and Sandomire, H., 'Medical privacy issues in the age of AIDS: legislative options', *American Journal of Law and Medicine* **16** (1990): 155.

Ehrnst, A., Lindgren, S., Dictor, M., Johansson, B., Sonnerborg, A., Czajkowski, J., *et al.*, 'HIV in pregnant women and their offspring: evidence for late transmission', *Lancet* **338** (1991): 1007–12.

Engelhardt Jr., T., *The Foundations of Bioethics* (Oxford: OUP, 1986).

Erin, C. A., and Harris, J., 'AIDS: Ethics, justice and social policy', *Journal of Applied Philosophy* **10** (Sept. 1993): 165–73.

European Collaborative Study, 'Risk factors for mother-to-child transmission of HIV-1', *Lancet* **339** (1992): 1007–12.

—— 'Natural History of vertically acquired HIV-1 infection', *Paediatrics* **94**/6 (1994): 815–19.

Farber, L., 'Unblinded mandatory HIV screening of newborns: Care or coercion?', *Cardozo Law Review* **16** (1994): 169.

Feinberg, J., *Social Philosophy* (Englewood Cliffs, NJ: Prentice-Hall,1973).

—— *Rights, Justice and the Bounds of Liberty: Essays in Social Philosophy* (Princeton: Princeton University Press, 1980).

—— *Harm to Self* (New York: OUP, 1986).

Fitch, K. M., Perez Alvarez, L., *et al.*, 'Occupational transmission of HIV in health care workers. A Review', *European Journal of Public Health* **5** (1995): 175–86.

Gewirth, A., *Reason and Morality* (Chicago: University of Chicago Press, 1978).

Giesen, D., 'From Paternalism to Self-Determination to Shared Decision Making', *Acta Juridica* (Cape Town, 1988): 101–27.

—— *International Medical Malpractice Law* (Kluwer, 1988).

—— 'Medical Malpractice and the Judicial Function in Comparative Perspective', *Medical Law International* **1** (1993): 1–16.

—— 'Vindicating the Patient's Rights. A Comparative Perspective', *Journal of Contemporary Health Law and Policy* **9** (1993): 273–309.

—— 'Liability for Transfusion of HIV-infected Blood in Comparative Perspective', *Professional Negligence* **10** (1994): 1.

Giesen, D., and Hayes, J., 'The Patient's Right to Know—A Comparative View', *Anglo–American Law Review* **21** (1992): 101–2.

Gillett, G., 'AIDS and confidentiality', *Journal of Applied Philosophy* **4**/1 (1987): 15–20.

Goldberg, D. J., and Johnstone, F. D., 'Universal named testing of pregnant women for HIV', *British Medical Journal* **306** (May 1993): 1144–5.

Goudsmit, J., Paul, D. A., Lange, J., Speelman, H., Noordaa, J., Van der Helm, H., *et al.*, 'Expression of human immunodeficiency virus antigen (HIV-Ag) in serum and cerebrospinal fluid during acute and chronic infection', *Lancet* **ii** (1986): 177–80.

Grmek, M. D., *History of AIDS: Emergence and Origin of a Modern Pandemic* (Princeton: Princeton University Press, 1990).

Gurtler, L. G., Hauser, P. H., Eberle, J., von Brunne, A., Knapp, S., and Zekeng, L., 'A new subtype of human immunodeficiency virus type 1 (MVP-5180) from Cameroon', *Journal of Virology* **68** (1994): 1581–5.

Harris, D., and Haigh, R. (eds.), *AIDS: A Guide to the Law* (London: Tavistock/Routledge, 1990).

Harris, J., *The Value of Life* (Routledge & Kegan Paul, 1985).

—— *Wonderwoman and Superman* (Oxford: OUP, 1992).

—— 'Ethics and HIV', in *Science in Parliament* **51**/5 (1994): 9–14.

—— and Holm, S., 'If Only AIDS Were Different', *Hastings Centre Report* **23**/6 (1993): 6.

—— —— 'Is there a moral obligation not to infect others?', *British Medical Journal* **311** (1995): 1215–17.

Hart, H. L. A., 'Are there any natural rights?', *Philosophical Review* **64** (1955): 175–91.

Häyry, H., 'Who should know about my HIV positivity and why?' (abstract). *European Philosophy of Medicine and Health Care* **2**/2: 123–4.

—— 'HIV and the alleged right to remain in ignorance', in C. Peden and J. K. Roth (eds.), *Rights, Justice, and Community* (Lewiston, New York: Edwin Mellen Press, 1992): 165–75.

—— 'Voluntary Euthanasia and Medical Paternalism', in Timo Airaksinen and Wojciech W. Gasparski (eds.), *Practical Philosophy and Action Theory*. Praxiology: International Annual of Practical Philosophy and Methodology (New Brunswick and London: Transaction Publishers, 1993).

—— and Häyry, M., 'AIDS now', *Bioethics* **1**/4 (987): 339–56.

Häyry, M., 'Do I have a right to know the HIV status of others?' (abstract), *European Philosophy of Medicine and Health Care* **2**/2: 124–5.

—— and Häyry, H., 'AIDS and a small North European country—A study in applied ethics', *International Journal of Applied Philosophy* **3**/3 (1987): 51–61.

—— —— 'AIDS, society, and morality—A philosophical survey', *Philosophia* **19**/4 (1989): 331–61.

Higgins, D., Galavotti, C., O'Reilly, K. R., Schnell, D. J., Moore, M., Rugg, D. L., and Johnson, R., 'Evidence for the effects of HIV antibody counselling and testing on risk behaviors', *Journal of the American Medical Association* **266** (1991): 2419–29.

Hobbes, T., *Leviathan* (London: Penguin Books, 1987).

Hohfeld, W. N., *Fundamental Legal Conceptions as Applied in Judicial Reasoning*, edited by W. W. Cook (New Haven: Yale University Press, 1919; repr. 1966).

Illingworth, P., *AIDS and the Good Society* (London and New York: Routledge, 1990).

Jonsen, A. R., and Stryker, J. (eds.), *The Social Impact of AIDS in the United States* (Washington, DC: National Academy Press, 1993).

Katz Miller, S., 'Too early for vaccine trial says AIDS experts', *New Scientist* **25** (1994): 6–7.

Kennet, W. (ed.), *Parliaments and Screening for HIV* (Montrouge, France: John Libbey Europe, 1995).

Kingman, S., 'Insurers inconsistent over HIV: Britain', *British Medical Journal* **306** (1993): 1496.

Laurence, J., 'Zidovudine in pregnancy—More questions than answers', *The AIDS Reader* **4** (1994): 74–6.

Lelie, P. N., van der Poel, C. L., Reesink, H. W., Huisman, H. G., Boucher, C. A. B., and Goudsmit, J., 'Efficacy of the latest generation of antibody assays for (early) detection of HIV 1 and HIV 2 infection', *Vox Sanguinis* **56** (1989): 59–61.

Letvin, N. L., 'Vaccines against Human Immunodeficiency Virus—Progress and Prospects', *New England Journal of Medicine* **32**/19 (1993): 1400–5.

Levine, C., 'Has AIDS changed the ethics of human individuals research?', *Law, Medicine and Health Care* **16** (1988): 167–73.

—— and Bayer, R., 'The ethics of screening for early intervention in HIV disease', *American Journal of Public Health* **79** (1989): 1661–7.

Lurie, P., *et al.*, 'Ethical, Behavioral, and Social Aspects of HIV Vaccine Trials in Developing Countries', *Journal of the American Medical Association* **271**/4 (1994): 295–301.

MacCallum, R., Mok, L., Peutherer, J., and Burns, S., 'Women's knowledge of their HIV antibody state its effect on their decision whether to continue pregnancy', *British Medical Journal* **300** (1990): 23–34.

Mann, J., Tarantola, D. J. M., and Netter, T. W. (eds.), *AIDS in the World: A Global Report* (Cambridge, Mass. and London: Harvard University Press, 1992).

Manning, W. G., *et al.*, 'The taxes of sin', *Journal of the American Medical Association* **261**/11 (1989): 1604–9.

Manuel, C., 'Ethique—Formation: douze questions pour susciter la reflexion', *Journal du Sida* **77** (1995): 22–3.

Manuel, C., *et al.*, 'AIDS: the rights and duties of health care providers', *AIDS and Public Policy Journal* **6** (1991): 37–40.

—— *et al.*, 'Elements de Reflexion sur le Dépistage VIH. Une Approche Ethique', *Médecine et Hygiène* **52** (1994): 904–9.

—— and San Marco, J. L., *SIDA—Les Enjeux Ethiques* (Editions Doin, June 1994).

—— *et al.*, 'Vertical transmission of HIV—a rediscussion of testing', *AIDS Care* **7**/5 (1995): 657–62.

McCann, K., and Wadsworth, E., 'The experience of having a positive HIV antibody test', *AIDS Care* **3**/1 (1991): 43–53.

McCusker, J., *et al.*, 'Effects of HIV antibody test knowledge on subsequent sexual behaviours in a cohort of sexually active homosexual men', *American Journal of Public Health* **78** (1988): 462–7.

McKeganey, N., and Barnard, M., *AIDS, Drugs and Sexual Risk—Lives in the Balance* (Buckingham: Open University Press, 1992).

Moore, P. G., 'Some ethical issues in British insurance', *Business Ethics: A European Review* **2** (1993): 134.

Morris, D. J., Corbitt, G., and Crosdale, E., 'Effect of switching from first-to second-generation enzyme-linked immunosorbent assays on screening for human immunodeficiency virus antibody', *Serodiagnosis and Immunotherapy in Infectious Diseases* **4** (1990): 217–20.

—— —— —— 'Same-day testing for human immunodeficiency virus antibodies', *Journal of Virological Methods* **49** (1994): 367–70.

Mortimer, P., 'ABC of AIDS: The virus and the tests', *British Medical Journal* **294** (1987): 1602–5.

Mortimer, P. P., and Parry, J. V., 'Non-invasive virological diagnosis: Are saliva and urine samples adequate substitute for blood?', *Reviews in Medical Virology* **1** (1991): 73–8.

Murphy, J. S., *The Constructed Body: AIDS, Reproductive Technology and Ethics* (Albany: State University of New York Press, 1995).

Newell, M. L., and Peckham, C. S., 'Risk factors for vertical transmission and early markers of HIV-1 infection in children', *AIDS* **7** (1993): S591–7.

Nozick, R., *Anarchy, State, and Utopia* (Oxford: Blackwell, 1974).

Ostrow, D. G., *et al.*, 'Disclosure of HIV antibody status: behavioural and mental health correlates', *AIDS Education and Prevention* **1** (1989): 1–11.

—— *Behavioural Aspects of AIDS* (New York: Plenum Press, 1990).

O'Sullivan, S., and Thomson, K. (eds.), *Positively Women. Living with AIDS* (London: Sheba Feminist Press, 1992).

Patton, C., *Inventing AIDS* (London: Routledge, 1990).

—— *Last Served?: Gendering the HIV Pandemic* (London: Taylor & Francis, 1994).

Peckham, C. S., Tedder, R. S., Briggs, M., Ades, A. E., *et al.*, 'Prevalence of

maternal HIV infection based on unlinked anonymous testing of newborn babies', *Lancet* **335** (1990): 516–19.
—— *et al.*, 'Why screen for HIV infection in pregnancy?', *Journal of Medical Screening* **1** (1994): 143.
—— —— 'Vertical transmission of HIV infection', *Acta Paediatr.* Suppl., **400** (1994): 43–5.
—— —— 'Risk of human immunodeficiency virus type 1—Transmission through breastfeeding', *Lancet* **430** (1992): 585–8.
—— —— 'Risk factors for vertical transmission of HIV-1 and early markers of HIV-1 infection in children', *AIDS* **7** (suppl. 1) (1993): S91–7.
—— —— 'Working towards a European strategy for intervention to reduce vertical transmission of HIV', *British Journal of Obstetrics and Gynecology* **101** (1994): 192–6.
—— —— 'Infant feeding policy and practice in the presence of HIV-1 infection', *AIDS* **9**/2 (1995): 107–19.
—— —— 'Caesarean section and risk of vertical transmission of HIV-1 infection', *Lancet* **343** [8911] (1994): 1464–7.
—— —— 'Natural History of Vertically Acquired Human Immunodeficiency Virus-1 Infection', *Paediatrics* **94**/6 (1994): 815–19.
—— —— 'Mode of Delivery and Vertical Transmission of HIV-1: A Review of Prospective Studies', *Journal of Acquired Immune Deficiency Syndromes* **7**/10 (1994): 1064–6.
Porter, R., 'History Says No to the Policeman's Response to AIDS', *British Medical Journal* **293** (1986): 1589.
Prusa, R., 'Some Aspects of Relation Between AIDS, Ethics and Children', *Czecho-Slovak Pediatrics* **50**/11 (1995): 323–4.
Rawls, John, *A Theory of Justice* (Oxford: OUP, 1992).
Raz, J., 'On the nature of rights', *Mind* **93** (1984): 199.
Reamer, F. G. (ed.), *AIDS and Ethics* (New York: Columbia University Press, 1991).
Roques, P. A., *et al.*, 'Clearance of HIV infection in 12 perinatally infected children: clinical, virological and immunological data', *AIDS* **9**/12 (1995): F19–26.
Schoenbaum, E. E., Davenny, K., and Selwyn, P. A., 'The impact of pregnancy on HIV related disease', *Royal College of Obstetrics and Gynecology* (1988): 65–75.
Schwartz, D. H., 'Potential pitfalls on the road to an effective HIV vaccine', *Immunology Today* **15**/2 (1994): 54–7.
Sharrard, M., and Gatt, I., 'Human Immune Deficiency Virus (HIV) antibody testing', *British Medical Journal* **295** (1987): 111.
Sherr, L., 'Pregnancy and paediatrics', *AIDS Care* **2**/4 (1990): 403–8.
—— 'Women and children', *AIDS Care* **3**/4 (1991): 423–32.

Sherr, L., *HIV and AIDS in Mothers and Babies: A Guide to Counselling* (Oxford: Blackwell Scientific Publications, 1991).
—— (ed.), *AIDS and the Heterosexual Population* (London: Harwood, 1993).
—— 'Obstetrics', in A. Broome and S. Llewelyn (eds.), *Health Psychology— Processes and Applications* (London: Chapman & Hall, 1994): 307–28.
—— 'Psychosocial Aspects of Providing Care for Women with HIV Infection', in H. Minkoff, J. A. DeHovitz and A. Duerr (eds.), *HIV Infection in Women* (New York: Raven Press, 1995): 107–23.
—— 'Suicide and AIDS—Lessons from a case audit in London', *AIDS Care* **7**/2 (1995): 109–16.
—— 'Coping with psychosexual problems in the context of HIV infection', *Sexual and Marital Therapy* **10**/3 (1995): 307–19.
—— (ed.), *Grief and AIDS* (London: Wiley, 1995).
—— 'Ante Natal HIV Testing—Which way forward?', *Psychology, Health and Medicine* **1**/1 (1996).
—— 'Pregnancy and childbirth', *AIDS Care* **9**/1 (1996): 69–77.
Siegal, K., Levine, M., Brooks, C., and Kern, R., 'The motivations of gay men for taking or not taking the HIV antibody test', *Social Problems* **36** (1989): 307–11.
Singer, P., *Rethinking Life and Death* (Oxford: OUP, 1995).
Sontag, S., *AIDS and Its Metaphors* (London: Penguin Books, 1990).
Squire, C. (ed.), *Women and AIDS* (Sage, 1993).
Stine, G. D., *Acquired Immune Deficiency Syndrome: Biological, Medical, Social and Legal Issues* (New Jersey: Prentice Hall, 1994).
Sunderland, A., Minkoff, H., Handte, J., Moroso, G., and Landesman, S., 'The impact of HIV serostatus on reproductive decisions of women', *Obstetrics and Gynecology* **79**/6 (1992): 1027–31.
Sumner, L. W., *The Moral Foundation of Rights* (Oxford: Clarendon Press, 1987).
Swiss Institute of Comparative Law, Lausanne, *Comparative Study on Discrimination against People with HIV or AIDS*, a study commissioned by the Council of Europe's Steering Committee for Human Rights (Strasbourg: Council of Europe, 1993).
Tovo, P. A., de Martino, M., Gabiano, C., Cappello, N., D'Elia, R., Loy, A., Plebani, A., Zuccotti, G. V., Dallacasa, P., and Ferraris, G., 'Prognostic Factors and Survival in Children with Perinatal HIV Infection', *Lancet* **339** (1992): 1249–53.
Van de Perre, P., Simonon, A., Msellati, P., Hitimana, D.-G., Vaira, D., Bazubagira, A., *et al.*, 'Postnatal transmission of human immunodeficiency virus type 1 from mother to infant', *New England Journal of Medicine* **325** (1991): 593–8.
Walker, A., 'Surgeons and HIV', *British Medical Journal* **302** (1991): 136.

WHO, 'Current and future dimensions of the HIV/AIDS pandemic: a capsule summary', WHO/GPA/RES/SF1/92.1 (1992).

Wikler, D., 'Who should be blamed for being sick?' *Health Education Quarterly* **14**/1 (1987): 11–25.

Williams, B., *Problems of the Self—Philosophical Papers 1956–1972* (Cambridge: Cambridge University Press, 1973).

—— *Moral Luck* (Cambridge: Cambridge University Press, 1981).

Winston, M. E., AIDS, 'Confidentiality and the right to know', *Public Affairs Quarterly* **2**/2 (1988): 91–104.

Woodhouse, D. E., Muth, J. B., Potterat, J. J., and Riffe, L. D., 'Restricting personal behavior: case studies on legal measures to prevent the spread of HIV', *International Journal of STD & AIDS* **4**/2 (1993): 114.

Working Group on HIV Testing of Pregnant Women and Newborns, 'HIV Infection: Pregnant Women and Newborns—A Policy Proposal for Information and Testing', *Journal of the American Medical Association* **264**/18 (1990): 2416–20.

Wormser, G. P., *AIDS and other Manifestations of HIV Infection*, 2nd edn. (New York: Raven Press, 1992).

Index